S0-CTU-870

SEX OFFENDER TREATMENT

Psychological and Medical Approaches

Sex Offender Treatment: Psychological and Medical Approaches has also been published as *Journal of Offender Rehabilitation*, Volume 18, Numbers 3/4 1992.

Paperback edition published in 1996.

The Haworth Press, Inc., 10 Alice Street, Binghamton, NY 13904-1580 USA

Library of Congress Cataloging-in-Publication Data

Sex offender treatment : psychological and medical approaches / Eli Coleman, S. Margretta Dwyer, Nathaniel J. Pallone, editors.

p. cm.

"Has also been published as Journal of offender rehabilitation, volume 18, numbers 3/4 1992"–T.p. verso.

Includes bibliographical references.

ISBN 0-7890-0069-5 (alk. paper)

1. Sex offenders–Rehabilitation. 2. Psychosexual disorders–Treatment. 3. Sex offenders–Psychology. I. Coleman, Eli. II. Dwyer, S. Margretta. III. Pallone, Nathaniel J.

[DNLM: 1. Drug Therapy. 2. Psychotherapy–methods. 3. Sex Offenses–psychology. W1 JO802U v. 18, no. 3/4 / 795 S5175]

RC560.S47S48 1992

616.85'83–dc20

DNLM/DLC 92-48795

for Library of Congress CIP

SEX OFFENDER TREATMENT

Psychological and Medical Approaches

Eli Coleman
S. Margretta Dwyer
Nathaniel J. Pallone
Editors

The Haworth Press, Inc.
New York London Norwood (Australia)

ABOUT THE EDITORS

Eli Coleman, Ph.D. Dr. Coleman is the Director and an Associate Professor of the Program in Human Sexuality, Department of Family Practice and Community Health, University of Minnesota Medical School, Minneapolis, Minnesota, USA. He has edited a number of other Haworth volumes, including *Psychotherapy for Homosexual Men and Women; Chemical Dependency and Family Intimacy,* and *John Money: A Tribute.* Dr. Coleman is also the Editor of the *Journal of Psychology and Human Sexuality.* He also coauthored "Standards for Treatment of Sex Offenders" (*Journal of Offender Rehabilitation*, Volume 16, Numbers 1/2) with Ms. Dwyer. Among many accomplishments and honors, Dr. Coleman is a past president of the Society for the Scientific Study of Sex. Well known for research and clinical work, Dr. Coleman is also an internationally recognized lecturer in human sexuality.

S. Margretta Dwyer, M.A., R.S.M. Margretta Dwyer is Coordinator of the Sex Offender Treatment Program at the Program in Human Sexuality, Department of Family Practice and Community Health, University of Minnesota, Medical School, Minneapolis, Minnesota, USA. She is the author of numerous articles on treatment and analysis of sex offenders. She has coauthored articles with Dr. Eli Coleman, including one in this volume regarding psychopharmological treatment of sex offenders. Ms. Dwyer also coauthored "Standards for Treatment of Sex Offenders" (*Journal of Offender Rehabilitation*, Volume 16, Numbers 1/2) with Dr. Coleman. She is recognized internationally for her work in the field, has studied sex offenders in the USA, Germany and Norway, and will engage in studies in Austria in 1993.

Nathaniel J. Pallone, Ph.D. Dr. Pallone is University Distinguished Professor, Psychology & Criminal Justice, at Rutgers — The State University of New Jersey, where he previously served as dean and as academic vice president. Among Dr. Pallone's most recent books are *Criminal Behavior: A Process Psychology Analysis* (1992), *Rehabilitating Criminal Sexual Psychopaths: Legislative Mandates, Clinical Quandaries* (1990), and *The Clinical Treatment of the Criminal Offender in Outpatient Mental Health Practice* (The Haworth Press, Inc., 1990). He is editor of the *Journal of Offender Rehabilitation,* published by The Haworth Press, Inc., and senior editor for North America of *Current Psychology.* Since 1976, he has chaired the Classification Review Board in New Jersey's Department of Corrections, a statutory "dangerousness review board" that assesses the readiness for release of sex felons incarcerated for treatment in the state.

The editors express their deep gratitude to Melva Dunn, Jenny Frantz, and Patricia Ohmans at the University of Minnesota, Jordan Leiter at Rutgers, and Naomi Fanning at the Haworth Press for their invaluable and intense work in the preparation of the manuscripts in this volume.

Contents

☐ INTRODUCTION

Sex Offender Treatment: Psychological and Medical Approaches 1

Eli Coleman
S. Margretta Dwyer

PSYCHODYNAMICS AND SEXUAL PATHOLOGY

☐ BEHAVIOR DYNAMICS

What Is In a Symptom? A Conservative Approach in the Therapy of Sex Offenders 5

Friedemann Pfafflin

The Psychodynamics of Sex Offenses and Implications for Treatment 19

Ingo C. Wiederholt, M.D.

☐ BEHAVIOR DYNAMICS & CLINICAL PROCESSES

The Role of Personality Disorders in the Treatment of Sex Offenders 25

Wolfgang Berner, M.D.
Peter Berger, M.D.
Karin Guitierrez, M.D.
Bettina Jordan, M.D.
Katharina Berger, M.D.

☐ ATTITUDINAL DETERMINANTS

Aggression against Women by Men: Sexual and Spousal Assault 39

Ann Marie Dewhurst
Robert J. Moore
Dennis P. Alfano

☐ PSYCHODYNAMICS

Dissociative Experiences of Sexual Offenders: A Comparison Between Two Outpatient Groups and Those Found to be Falsely Accused 49

S. Margretta Dwyer
B.R. Simon Rosser
Steven Sawyer

☐ MEASUREMENT & APPRAISAL

The Utility of the MMPI-2 with Pedophiles 59

Jim Mann
Walter Stenning
Christopher Borman

MEDICAL-PHARMACOLOGICAL APPROACHES

☐ CLINICAL PROCESSES: PHARMACOTHERAPY & PSYCHOTHERAPY

An Exploratory Study of the Role of Psychotropic Medications in the Treatment of Sex Offenders 75

Eli Coleman
John Cesnik, M.D.
Anne-Marie Moore
S. Margretta Dwyer

☐ BEHAVIOR DYNAMICS & PHARMACOTHERAPY

Buspirone and Paraphilic Sexual Behavior 89

J. Paul Fedoroff, M.D.
Ingrid C. Fedoroff

☐ CLINICAL PROCESSES: PHARMACOTHERAPY & GROUP THERAPY

Medroxy-Progesterone Acetate in the Treatment of Paraphilic Sexual Disorders 109

J. Paul Fedoroff, M.D.
Robert Wisner-Carlson, M.D.
Sharon Dean
Fred S. Berlin, M.D., Ph.D.

☐ TREATMENT VIA CHEMICAL IMPEDANCE

The Texas Experience with DepoProvera: 1980-1990 125

L.E. Emory, M.D.
C.M. Cole
W.J. Meyer, III, M.D.

PSYCHOLOGICAL APPROACHES

☐ DECISION PROCESS ANALOGUE

Perceptions of Child Sexual Assault 141

Jeffrey Edwin Drugge

☐ CLINICAL PROCESSES

The Remodeling Process: A Grounded Theory Study of Perceptions of Treatment among Adult Male Incest Offenders 167

Rochelle A. Scheela

☐ CLINICAL PROCESSES

Outpatient Treatment for Adolescents with Sexually Inappropriate Behavior 191

Tom Mazur
P.M. Michael

☐ CLINICAL PROCESSES

Developing Insight in Incestuous Fathers 205

Ronald E. Zuskin

CONCLUSIONS AND CAUTIONS

☐ CLINICAL PROCESSES

What Happens to Therapists Who Work with Sex Offenders? 217

Toni Farrenkopf

☐ SOCIAL POLICY & CLINICAL PRACTICE

False Accusations of Nosocomial Sexual Abuse 225

John Money

ALL HAWORTH BOOKS & JOURNALS ARE PRINTED ON CERTIFIED ACID-FREE PAPER

SEX OFFENDER TREATMENT: PSYCHOLOGICAL AND MEDICAL APPROACHES. Pp. 1-3.

☐ INTRODUCTION

Sex Offender Treatment: Psychological and Medical Approaches

Eli Coleman
University of Minnesota

S. Margretta Dwyer
University of Minnesota

Health professionals are eager to find new and effective modalities for sex offender treatment, whether in correctional institutions or in outpatient facilties. Increasingly, sex offenses are being reported to law enforcement agencies and offenders are being punished and/or remanded into treatment. Furthermore, communities have high expectations regarding the successful outcome of treatment. This volume presents some up-to-date research and theory on this topic.

We have co-chaired two international conferences on the treatment of sex offenders. The first conference was held in May of 1989; the second in September of 1991. We are planning a third international conference in September of 1993 in Minneapolis. By sponsoring these conferences, we hope to encourage professionals involved in research and clinical practice to share their expertise and to foster further research in this field.

At the first conference, we honored the lifetime scientific contributions of Gene Abel, M.D., and Kurt Freund, M.D. At the second conference, we recognized John Money, Ph.D., for his lifetime of scientific achievements regarding the nature and treatment of sex offenders and for his assistance in developing a more compassionate understanding of the sex offender. We also honored Fay Honey Knopp for widely disseminating knowledge in this field, through her role as Director of The Safer Society Program and Press. We are indebted to these pioneers in contemporary modes of sex offender treatment in non-correctional settings.

This volume comprises a selection of papers presented at the 1991 International Conference on the Treatment of Sex Offenders. By collecting these papers in a single source, we hope to further disseminate current "cutting edge" knowledge, thereby stimulating further research in this field.

The opening contribution, by Dr. Friedemann Pfafflin, a psychoanalyst at the Department of Sex Research at the University of Hamburg in Germany, some of the archaic and barbaric treatment once used for sex offenders, providing a historical perspective on research and treatment. Today, treatment of sex offenders involves interactive biomedical *plus* psychiatric *plus* psychological approaches based on sound perceptions of the sources of criminal sexual behavior. The first set of papers focuses on the psychodynamic and psychiatric disorders associated with the sex offender. Dr. Ingo Wiederholt from Germany discusses his theory of the psychodynamic forces which motivate a sex offense. Dr. Wolfgang Berner and his colleagues from Austria documents the types of personality disorders and discusses implications for more effective treatment. Using psychodynamic and feminist theory, Ann Marie Dewhurst and her colleagues from Canada test some hypotheses regarding sexual offenders and men who batter. They find that hostile attitudes towards women and depression correlate with interpersonal violence by men against women. Other authors in this section describe research which explores hypotheses of psychological disorders using psychometric tests. The results of these investigations suggest that researchers regard the reliability of some of these instruments with caution.

The next section presents findings on pharmacological interventions. Two papers describe the effectiveness of antiandrogen treatment, while two others review promising results of other pharmacotherapies, including the use of buspirone (Fedoroff and Fedoroff), lithium carbonate, and fluoxetine (Coleman, Cesnik, Moore and Dwyer). The results of these studies have implications for improved pharmacotherapeutic interventions and further understanding of the neuroendrocrinological and neuroanatomical abnormalities associated with some sex offenders. The paper by Drs. Emory, Cole and Meyer emphasizes that these pharmacotherapies cannot be used in a vacuum and that psychotherapeutic approaches must complement this type of treatment.

In the next section, five papers discuss treatment techniques and the public perception of sex offender treatment. Ronald Zuskin (USA) describes his techniques for developing insight in incest perpetrators. Also from the USA, Rochelle Scheela presents a study of the adult male incest offenders' perceptions of the treatment process. Tom Mazur (USA) describes the development and outcome of a unique adolescent treatment program using a family communication approach for individuals involved in sexually inappropriate behavior. All of these treatment programs are instituted under the scrutiny of the public and are affected by public perceptions of sex offenses. Another paper in this section (by Jeffrey Drugge, Canada) reports on some important findings in this regard.

This volume ends with two papers which offer a cautionary note to those who provide therapy for sex offenders. First is a paper by Toni Farrenkopf (USA) on the hazards of burnout, which outlines ways of coping and adaptation to avoid becoming cynical and dispassionate. Finally, John Money (USA) spells out the risk that practioners within the "sexual-abuse industry" take by making themselves vulnerable to accusations of sexually abusing their own clients or patients. In a fitting conclusion, Money proposes that as we develop more effective treatment modalities, we also promote prevention. Prevention involves saturating the media with explicit information about sexological health and pathology. Prevention involves public promotion of sexual health, early detection and early treatment of problems. Money admonishes legislators to restore or protect the right of doctor-patient confidentiality. Without these efforts, our ability to continue to develop new treatment modalities and to offer humane, compassionate treatment are threatened.

SEX OFFENDER TREATMENT: PSYCHOLOGICAL AND MEDICAL APPROACHES. Pp. 5-17.

☐ BEHAVIOR DYNAMICS

What Is In a Symptom?

A Conservative Approach in the Therapy of Sex Offenders

Friedemann Pfafflin

University of Hamburg

ABSTRACT This paper reviews more or less dreadful methods of treatment used with sex offenders, each based on the erroneous belief that sex offenders constitute a relatively homogeneous taxonomic class. Instead, sex offenders are people with a sad personal history, in which their deviant sexual behavior represents an effort to banish the pain they experienced during their developing years.

The first time I gave a paper on the "assessment and treatment of sex offenders" was at an International Congress on Law and Psychiatry in 1979 in Oxford; on that occasion my topic entailed discussing various more or less dreadful methods of treatment which had been traditionally used in my country and elsewhere. I mainly discussed three of these methods:

- *Imprisoning the patient to bring him to his senses*, specifically recommended in 20% of the reports written by psychiatrists on sex offenders submitted to the Hamburg law courts between 1964 and 1971. To quote one of them: "From a psychiatric and psychological point of view court-ordered punishment will constitute a healing shock, it will be a therapeutic thrust which will drive him out of his present lethargy and initiate the character development he needs to adjust to his place in society."

- *Surgical castration,* extensively carried out on sex offenders during the Nazi era in Germany and still employed, though only on volunteers, during the 'fifties and 'sixties. A law regulating the use of this procedure within a democracy was passed as late as 1969.
- *Stereotactical brain surgery,* which was carried out as an experiment on about seventy patients in Germany during the 'sixties and 'seventies.

There were two main alternatives to these methods:

- *Antiandrogen treatment,* which became available in the early 'sixties, initially only in pill form for oral application, with the disadvantage that regular consumption of the drug could not be controlled, making it impossible for physicians to guarantee its effectiveness in court. In 1977 an injectable drug was introduced, cyproterone acetate, which made treatment easier. The Food and Drug Administration has not given its permission for this drug to be sold in the U.S. Broadly speaking its effects are comparable with those of Depo-Provera, which is customarily used here.
- The other alternative was *psychotherapy.* In 1975 our department began a project offering psychotherapy to sex offenders who were not in prison. Between 1975 and 1979 a total of 160 men were examined and some sixty of them treated, using a combination of behaviorist and psychoanalytic techniques. It was the first project of its kind at a German university.

The question is: Has anything changed in the twelve years which have elapsed since then? Of course prison sentences are still meted out, but hardly anyone in the field dares to argue that they have any therapeutic value. Stereotactical brain surgery on sex offenders has been more or less banned, and, although surgical castration is still allowed, it is carried out very rarely. Hormone treatment is widely used. We dont have any exact figures but there can be no doubt that it is employed on a wide scale. The text books which recommend hormone treatment invariably stress that it is pointless unless combined with a talking cure. But it certainly more often is applied without than with a talking cure. Not much research has been done into its effectiveness. Apart from that all kinds of therapies have been tried out, and even criminal stories on television present sex offenders as people who are ill and not criminal.

Does this mean that everything has gotten much better? Is everything looking rosy when it comes to understanding perversions, deviations and paraphilic acts? I am afraid not. One can still hear loud calls for more punishment and attempts to clamp down on other areas such as pornography and harmless sexual behavior, so that, to give you just one example, a father hardly dares to share the bath with his two-year-old daughter for fear of being accused of sexually abusing her. But my interest doesn't lie in looking into such reactionary tendencies; what I should like to do is ask, what is in a symptom, and this I propose to do in three steps: *Firstly*, taking a look at the theories involved and explaining what I mean by a conservative approach; *secondly*, presenting three apparently similar cases to show how much and how little the theories help in explaining the patients behavior; and, *thirdly*, making some remarks about why it is so difficult to find therapists for these patients, despite the fact that we know a great deal about their symptoms.

TREATMENT OF SYMPTOMS

All kinds of therapies have been tried out in recent years, and studies presented from many different places. Eli Coleman has described some of them in his discussion of how to understand compulsive sexual behavior within the framework of the DSM. Most therapies aim exclusively at getting rid of the symptom, the deviant behavior, as fast and completely as possible, using techniques such as deconditioning, aversion, confronting the patient with his victims or simply administering drugs or hormones with or without combining this medication with a talking cure. As long as the one and only criterion for effective therapy is whether the symptom vanishes or not, therapists seem to be identified with the authorities and law givers, accept social norms unquestioned, gratify some of their patients craving to be punished and are content to remain on the superficial level that anything which society cannot tolerate should be gotten rid of. They do not take the symptom seriously, no matter what techiniques they apply or what diagnostic categories they use.

Other therapeutic approaches, all more or less rooted in psychoanalytic thinking, even when they wish to deny this, have attempted to understand the anxieties and problems which induce a person to put his deviant wishes into practice, or, to use John Money's picture, to wander along the paths of paraphilic love maps. We have learnt a great deal from such therapies: about the vital turning points in individual psychosexual development, about thresholds, about traumata, fears, conflicts, defence mechanisms, how erotic preferences occur and love maps are drawn, how, putting it in broad terms, coping mechanisms develop to enable the patients to tolerate the misery, indignity, pain and sorrow they suffered in the past.

If one reads some of the classic psychoanalytic explanations for these phenomena, they strike one nowadays as cumbersome and dogmatic, always referring to Oedipus complexes, castration fears and penis envy. At risk of trying your patience a little, here is one classic example from Fenichel's *Psychoanalytic Theory of Neurosis,* 1945. Explaining the anxieties behind exhibitionism, Fenichel lists three ways in which an exhibitionist has to defend himself against his fears of being castrated. First of all, he can conclude from the woman's reaction that he actually has a proper penis and has not been castrated; secondly he identifies with the aggressor by inducing a nervous reaction in his woman audience, or if she turns aside unimpressed can still imagine it and thereby he calms his own fears of falling prey to his mother's threat to castrate him because he longs to sleep with her; thirdly by showing off his penis he challenges the woman to show him hers, thus scoring a triumph over her castrated state.

To our minds, explanations like these seem highly unconvincing, since they merely describe stereotypes and seem to have no connection with the fears or traumata of an individual. They do however at least concede that there is a link between the anxiety and the symptom. In recent years psychotherapists have more carefully scrutinised the actual experiences their patients went through as children and have described them in words which seem to ring true in our ears, for instance Robert Stoller in his books *Perversion, the Erotic Form of Hatred* (1975) and *Sexual Excitement* (1979). One common factor in these studies is the assumption that, although paraphilic behavior is an inadequate response, it is at least an inventive and resourceful attempt on the part of the patient to cope with his problems and anxieties. John Money, whom one could certainly not accuse of being a devotee of psychoanalysis, puts it this way, "A shared principle of all paraphilic love maps is that they represent tragedy turned into triumph" (Money 1986, p. 36). For a brief moment the symptom transforms the trauma into a triumph. It is a creative act, an achievement which serves to stabilise the patient's identity and deserves to be respected as part of his structure and history. Just as one cannot remove a wart without risking further damage, it is asking for trouble to simply forbid or try to suppress paraphilic behavior. As opposed to a wart, however, it is not just something which gets in the way or is dysfunctional, even though it may upset the individual and surroundings; the symptom can always also be seen as a constructive and healthy reaction.

When I talk about a conservative approach in the therapy of sex offenders, I mean that the therapist should above all try to discover exactly how and to what extent the patient has managed to cope with the initial trauma, or, as is more likely, with the series of traumatic experiences which have led to and maintained the symptom, wrestling triumph from tragedy. The more deeply we can admire the patient for his resourcefulness in seeking a solution and at the same time understand the suffering he has undergone and is still undergoing, the greater is the chance that he himself will be able to dispense with the symptom of his own accord.

In this context, "conservative" means assuming that up till now the patient has had good reason to show his symptom and probably still needs it. As long as it is needed it should be conserved until it has been properly understood and can be put aside. Until this stage is reached my role as therapist is to work out in detail what induces the patient to behave in this way, to define what new insult it is which has probably opened old wounds and against which he is currently protecting himself. This is usually more easily said than done. To illustrate the problem here are three cases, officially all labelled exhibitionism. I shall return to the diagnostic impression underlying this category later.

THEORY MAY NOT HELP: THREE CASE STUDIES

The *first patient* is a twenty-five year old man who had been seen flitting around the neighborhood at night without any clothes on. Eventually he was arrested by the police, taken to court for exhibitionism and ordered to undergo therapy. He was more a flasher than an exhibitionist. He was a big strong man, very muscular, bearded, a carpenter by trade, an imposing physical presence, yet when he talked I had the impression that he was hardly there, his voice was so quiet and what he told me about himself seemed so unimportant. By and large, he said, he lead a quite normal life.

He was the youngest of four sons and still lived at home with his Iranian parents who rigidly maintained their national traditions despite having been living in Germany for more than twenty years. The family was run along strictly hierarchical lines. Each brother was under the thumb of the next elder one (with the eldest under the father's thumb), the mother ruled the roost, and when in doubt there was an uncle in Iran who had the last word. Everything was decided from above, what and how one should eat, where one sat at table, what clothes one wore, and what job one took, and even whether and how each member of the family was allowed to take part in conversations.

The patient told me all this without the slightest hint of complaint or a suggestion that it might be a problem. It all seemed absolutely normal to him, just as his regular nightly excursions without clothes seemed completely inexplicable. He had no idea why I was interested in finding out about his family; this in turn was hard for me to grasp, and we talked at cross-purposes, uneasily linked only by the courts instructions and my pledge to treat him. I felt irritated and helpless, and found it hard to concentrate on what he was saying during the sessions. I regretted having taken over the case. My mind tended to wander until I finally found myself imagining the patient slipping out into the night, year in, year out, summer and winter, and sliding naked through the streets and across the parks. I imagined him shivering, his feet freezing in the snow, or the warm summer wind stroking his skin, gently caressing him. Having mentioned his naked trips in our first conversation he never talked about them again, and simply recounted daily events in a factual tone. For me the sessions were a long, drawn-out misery which I only survived with the help of these fantasies.

In our setting, the situation at home was reversed; the patient tied me down with his repetitive, apparently inconsequential remarks. It felt like being smothered in rubbish, endless trivia and accounts of good behavior; the only way I could save my skin was by fleeing to join his nightly excursions naked under the stars, where I could breath freely, be myself and actually experience pain and pleasure. His special way of behaving became intelligible, feelable. In a sense he put me through what he had suffered at home for years and what he had again undergone at the hands of the court that sent him to me. It took some time before I could communicate this to him and before he could listen without feeling I wanted to rob him of his only refuge from his suffocating family.

The *second patient*, a thirty year old medical student who was in his twentieth semester and still had not passed his preliminary examinations, only came to the notice of the courts after spending years with a whole series of therapists. He was brought into court for exhibitionism on five occasions, always in the same shopping arcade and always in front of the same woman. I was asked to make an assessment of him.

This description of him — a medical student in the twentieth semester (wow, that's pretty impressive) who still hasn't passed his prelims (good heavens, what a disgrace) — captures something of the bewildering mixture of magnificence and disparagement which this patient experienced and conveyed. Both aspects coloured our first encounter: the patient, armed with a hat and a stick like a dandy, came forty minutes late, did not remove his coat or sit down, waved his stick about wildly and declared in a supercilious tone that he did not have the slightest inclination to talk to me. He had run through practically all the therapy programmes in Hamburg and used up all the therapists available. None of them wanted to have anything more to do with him, not even write a report on him. The way he entered into a new relationship was always the same: the patient introduced himself to the new therapist and assured him that he was the only person capable of helping him; at least he had found what he was looking for; all the other therapists were a dead loss and "assholes." Despite all the scorn he exuded there was something fascinating and charming about him; all the therapists must have fallen prey to this approach and he despised them all the more for accepting him. He was particularly damning about the women psychologists whom he had been able to charm into varying the therapy setting: prolonged sessions, meeting outside the practice, and so on.

He was equally biting about a doctor whose group therapy he had joined and who proved unable to prevent him from showing off his penis to the other members of the group. He had managed to provoke other therapists to react sadistically: they tried out shame aversion on him by instructing him to exhibit his genitals in front of women psychology students who had been instructed how to react. Nothing helped. His triumphant response to this degradation was to change therapists again and gleefully tell them what an "asshole" the therapist had been who had tried this out on him.

His story revealed that as a child he had often been a voyeur and that from early puberty onwards he had taken to showing off his penis. He experienced life as a series of sexualised encounters and seemed unable to conceive any way of behaving which was not exhibitionist. He recalled a scene in childhood when his grandmother fled screaming from the room when she saw his erect penis, it was so huge and beautiful. For the past fifteen years he had exposed himself five to ten times a day, always in different places and without being caught. Occasionally he had managed to attract a woman and have intercourse with her. He had dozens of sexual encounters but never saw the woman again.

He had gone into therapy not because he regarded showing off his penis as a problem but because he noticed that his sexual compulsions left him no time for an ordinary life. After all these therapies had failed he had finally landed with an experienced psychotherapist who refused to be taken in by him but equally felt no urge to punish him, the two reactions he knew all too well from his own family. Working with this therapist over a period of two years gave him the most reliable contact he had ever had, not too intimate, not too offhand, and this enabled him to turn his attention for the first time to matters other than his sexual obsessions. It also had an effect on his symptom: he no longer exhibited in front of any woman in any part of town but sought out women he liked in his neighbourhood and tried repeatedly to approach them; this was when he was arrested. Therapy had weakened his defence.

The *third patient* was a thirty-six year old man, also a carpenter, married, with a seven year old son. From time to time he was overcome by a deep urge to expose his penis; this was always accompanied by a profound feeling of guilt. These impulses seemed to suddenly overwhelm him, striking him quite out of the blue. One day he tried to stop two sixteen-year old girls who had twice ridden past him on their bicycles; he felt an irrestistible urge to rape them. The girls screamed, pulled themselves free and got away. The patient, whom the police had failed to catch, went to his general practitioner and was sent to me for treatment.

Apart from what I have just told you about him, he hardly managed to say anything about himself. Mostly he was completely silent, sat and stared at the floor or looked awkwardly past me. But he came regularly, once a week. I was extremely active and kept trying to find ways to get a conversation going. At the utmost we spent ten or fifteen of the fifty minute sessions actually talking to each other.

In the course of several years I gradually found out a little about his current situation, his unhappy marriage to a woman who was five years older and crippled, making any sexual activity painful and unpleasant to her. On the surface the patient could accept this but he could not work out any alternatives. He gave me the impression of seething with frustration, full of pent-up rage, although outwardly he seemed calm and under control. He also talked about how difficult he found it to relate to his son and his colleagues at work. The way we sat facing each other in silence, gazing at or past each other was often extremely tense and aggressive. My attempts to put this into words brought no change in the situation, and I was often very angry with the patient who could not let me approach him. This tension became intelligible only after I found out that he had grown up in crowded barracks where several families lived in extremely close quarters. He shared one room with his parents and his sister. There were quarrels and fights everywhere, not just in his family but, perfectly audible through the thin walls, in all the neighbouring families too, who assaulted one another verbally or physically, so that he felt utterly helpless and frightened for his own life and the lives of others. When he was as old as his son now was, his mother insisted on divorce and refused to let his father come back into the home.

He could only tell me all this in disconnected fragments, usually just after a bout of exhibitionism, luckily without being caught by the police. Sometimes his father used to come by on a motorcycle, apparently to get a glimpse of his children; he would stop at the opposite side of the road and look up at their window. The boys gaze met his, but there was no way of saying anything or waving, for his mother immediately noticed, marched over and intervened by pulling the blind down in front of his nose. The patient's comment on this loss of his father was "and that was the end of it." But of course it wasn't. On the contrary, he harbored an immense and overpowering hatred of his mother, whom he would have liked to "show it," but did not dare to because of her threatening behavior. Having told me this, the patient dreamed of splitting his mother's head open with an axe. He was appalled and extremely perturbed, and felt a strong urge to exhibit his penis again. Shocked by what he had experienced in the dream, he said he preferred to carry on being an exhibitionist.

These cases show it is rarely possible to name a single event to which the patient reacts in erotic triumph, and even if it is possible then it usually takes a long time to discover it. Money tells the story of a man who cruised compulsively:

> . . . whose addiction proved to be for large penises, the larger the better. He traced the origin of his addiction to the age of between four and five, when, through the open door, he saw his father showing his big penis to his older sister, and he felt excluded and jealous. The insatiable quality of his addiction could be attributed to the fact that, as an adult with an adult-sized penis, he could never find one proportionately as great as his fathers had been when his own had been that of a small boy (Money 1986, p. 37).

I assume that this strikingly precise description was not gleaned in a single interview with the patient. If one does obtain such information in the initial interview it means that the patient is perfectly aware of it, in which case it is hard to understand why the patient develops such behavior which can even become addictive. It seems likely that these are screen memories.

IDENTICAL BEHAVIOR FROM DIFFERENT SOURCES

I purposely chose three examples of one type of offence to make it clear how very different reasons may lie behind what seems at first glance to be the same kind of behavior. From the therapist's angle these three cases are very different: with the nocturnal wanderer, therapy had to concentrate almost exclusively on narcissistic aspects, whether and how he could literally feel and be aware of himself as an individual. With the second, the dandy, it was a matter of how to enter into and maintain relationships, and with the third how to cope with immense rage; his exhibitionist behavior protected him from doing anything worse, like raping or murdering a woman.

Obviously the terms I'm using here are very broad ones which do not more than set up a frame within which the details of the picture have to be fitted in one by one. I don't think it matters much whether one works along behavioral or psychoanalytic lines or a combination of both as my colleagues in Hamburg did, as reported in their book *Sex Offenders* (Schorsch et al., 1990), as long as one accepts that paraphilic behavior is a coping mechanism which once served a vital purpose and has since developed into an unspecific way of reacting to stress or disgrace of many kinds. Often the patient can give up his problematic behavior even if the original trauma is not discovered. There are all kinds of traumata, old ones and recent ones. If the patient discoveres in the course of therapy that his feelings are respected and his ideas taken seriously, the old wounds have a chance to scar over.

And this leads me to my last point: Why is it so difficult to find therapists for these patients, even though we by now know a great deal about how their symptoms develop and the mechanisms which maintain them. To answer this question I should like to use an image inspired by John Money's fine concept of a lovemap. Money described a wide range of paraphilic behavior and gave each one a tongue-twisting Greek name from acrotomo-philia via andromimeto-philia, apotemnophilia, auto-assassinophilia, biasto-philia, chrem-atisto-philia, hybristo-philia, klisma- philia, peodeikto-philia, scopto-philia to zoophilia. Let us imagine a map of these, a map of the Aegean Sea, with its lovely islands, stormy seas and Homeric heroes. If we gaze at this map, and read Homer and the Greek tragedies, we get some impression of the wonders and horrors of this far-flung corner of the world.

It is a quite different matter, however, to be washed up on one of these rocky shores, unable to speak a word of Greek, without any food or a proper boat, exposed to the bare rocks and the scorching sun, and be expected to travel round the country, especially when you meet Cyclops, Biastophilios, Autoassassinophilios and all the other inhabitants who have survived many a tragedy, are bursting with rage, or smitten with agony and gloom, and have not learned to welcome strangers with nicely turned phrases.

EACH PATIENT A NEW JOURNEY

This is the situation we face as therapists. Each therapy takes us off on a new journey, and we come across patients whose survival strategies are highly alarming and harmful to others. And if we want to understand them we have to be able to approach without frightening them.

When I told my colleagues at home about the three cases I have just presented to you their response was, "That's all very well; it's quite easy; they are harmless and don't do anything; it's no problem just to sit back and admire their symptom." It was like a trip to, say, Rhodos, which the crusaders civilized almost a thousand years ago.

So I tried out the other extreme and told them about treating a man who was tormented by his cannibalistic urges and tried four times to kill a boy in order to drink his blood and eat his testicles. During that therapy I had to "catch" his deeply hidden depression, and share it with him in order to reach him. "You're crazy," they replied, "you shouldn't get involved in things like that; it's much too dangerous."

In this case my colleagues proved right. During a difficult stage of the therapy the patient was ordered to appear in court; on his way there he again attacked a boy, though this time not seriously, and was ordered to go to a psychiatric institution four hundred miles away, which made it impossible to continue work together. There he finally managed to put his terrible phantasies into practice. Perhaps I had flattered myself, had hoped I could triumph over his tragedy, ignoring the fact that some therapies really cannot succeed if carried out on an outpatient basis, and perhaps also that one should not write papers on them before they are finished.

It is hard to bear when a therapy ends like this. It is perfectly understandable that therapists are often apprehensive and shun the risk of getting involved with these patients at all. Yet unless we can share something of the patient's deep-seated fears and his tragedy in the countertransference, there is little hope of really reaching him, which in turn means that he will not have a chance to change anything fundamental in his personality, to reshape his lovemap.

There is no such person as the exhibitionist, or the paedophile, the rapist or the sex offender, as the title of this paper seems to suggest. Group labels like these reduce the individuals involved to a single common factor which may be crucially important for their survival, perhaps even their healthiest side, but which always fails to describe their real trouble. Apart from a few with Greek ancestors they all have quite normal names, no tounge-twisters; they are called Meier, Dwyer, Money, Pfafflin or Coleman, and they all have a sad personal history in which their deviant sexual behavior represents a creative effort to banish the pain they experienced during their developing years. The damage done, the insults and traumata they could not avoid are all highly individual; all they have in common is a symptom, a constructive defence mechanism, a way of keeping themselves intact. This symptom should be treated with great care and respect until it becomes superfluous. This will only be possible if the fears which the patient experienced and tried to keep under control with the help of his symptom are experienced, borne and translated into words by the therapist.

REFERENCES

Money J (1986) Lovemaps. Clinical concepts of sexual/erotic health and pathology, paraphilia, and gender transposition in childhood, adolescence, and maturity. Irvington, New York

Schorsch E, Galedary G, Haag A, Hauch M, Lohse H (1990) Sex offender. Dynamics and psychotheraypeutic strategies. Springer, Berlin, New York

Stoller R (1975) Perversion. The erotic form of hatred. Pantheon Books, New York

Stoller R (1979) Sexual excitement. Dynamics of erotic life. Pantheon Books, New York

AUTHOR'S NOTE

Friedemann Pfafflin is at the Department of Sex Research, Psychiatric Clinic, Universitatskrankenhaus Eppendorf, Martinistr. 52, D- 2000, Hamburg 20 (Germany). This article was translated by Jane Wiebel, Hamburg.

Address correspondence to the author.

SEX OFFENDER TREATMENT: PSYCHOLOGICAL AND MEDICAL APPROACHES. Pp. 19-24.

□ BEHAVIOR DYNAMICS

The Psychodynamics of Sex Offenses and Implications for Treatment

Ingo C. Wiederholt, M.D.

Social Therapeutic Department of Sex Offenders, Munich

ABSTRACT This psychoanalytic view is based on the author's 21 years of experience as an expert witness for approximately 750 individuals who committed sex crimes. It is also based upon the author's clinical psychiatric experience in treating 170 sex offenders released from prison. These experiences form the theoretical basis for the treatment program described in this paper.

A sex crime is a defense against a threat of disintegration of the ego-identity "against a wrong person, at the wrong time, at the wrong place, with the wrong method, out of a wrong motivation, and with the wrong tools" (Wiederholt, 1980). It is a physically or psychologically brutal, aggressive act with the purpose of feeling superior and/or feeling protected by the victim. Rarely does it happen for the sake of sadistic torture.

Like everybody, the offender seeks proximity, self confidence and satisfaction of emotional needs in human interaction. He commits a sex crime when these needs are not fulfilled. The difficulty of handling emotion originates in the primary family, where gender identity develops according to the female and male prototype of mother or father.

RECOGNITION OF DYNAMICS

Prerequisite for recognition of the sex crime dynamics is the information one has to obtain from the offender. This is difficult, for the offender is mainly giving expected information to police or other juridical persons and institutions about external factors of his criminal act. This information is gathered to identify him as a perpetrator and to fulfill the required facts for sentencing. Rarely does one get information about psychic traumatization prior to the crime, about motivation to solve an intrapsychic chaos or derangement by a sex crime. Quite often the offender cannot answer these important questions because of life-long existing defense mechanisms (e.g., repression, denial, conversion, or escape into fugue-like states). Fearing punishment by the court or the loss of love and attention from relatives, he cannot break through these defense mechanisms.

Most information is gained from offenders when they want help, are ready to change their behavior in the future and suffer guilt towards the victim.

Empathy, reliable understanding and a clear cut definition of the role and goal of the examiner and/or future therapist, as well as stable setting of limitations facilitate dealing with the dynamic of a sex crime.

Motivation

Sex crimes are rarely sexually motivated (Groth, 1977, 1980; Schmidt, 1975; Stoller, 1979; Wiederholt, 1980, 1989).

The offender is, prior to his delinquent act, in a state of identity loss, in panic or in chaotic condition and seeks release from this intolerable derangement of his psychic equilibrium. Such a state is triggered by even minor doubts of interacting partners about the capabilities and integrity of the offender. It leads to a breakdown of defense mechanisms and into an emotional chaotic state which is similar to pre-suicidal states. Such states are averted by more or less intense aggressive acting out of criminal sexual behavior.

Criminal acting out in the form of sexual behavior can be derived from the fact that sexuality or its gratification is a replacement of emotionality which the person usually never sufficiently experienced during his interaction with parents. Extreme emotional deficits are replaced early in life by autoerotic gratification and later on by fantasized or real partner interaction including sexual acting out. For this reason a psychogenic hypersexuality exists with the partner more or less taken as a sex object, a lust-mediating mother surrogate, or a target of projected hate, revenge and/or aggression. The sex offender seeks immediate proximity in a state of isolation, loneliness and breakdown of familiar defense mechanisms. This state generally is felt as chaotic helplessness and leads to self contempt, loss of self-confidence. It triggers aggressive tendencies for the sake of immediate self-gratification. The intensity of aggressive or submissive impulses increases the possibility of planned or spontaneous sexual criminal behavior. The motives are domination, humiliation, or brutal physical or psychological acting out as expressions of superiority or submission, for security, protection and tenderness seeking, externally viewed as a stampede towards a false and pseudo-masculine identity or a regression into a pseudo-baby identity. The crime is a non-acceptable trial of separation or fusion, for it lacks concern for the needs of the victim, for the intense future damage to all people involved in the crime and does not respect the right of free will of the victim. At least the offender initiates in his chaotic psychic state the reaction of others capable of structuring and acting in a responsible form, which the offender cannot. The offender projects his own missing motivation upon others (police, court, family) and is secondarily motivated to structure his future life, either by planning new offenses without the chance to get caught or by making mistakes so that he gets caught and punished but is relieved of any responsibility for others around him.

Quite often the sex crime is an explosion with non-qualified methods at a point when the past life is subjectively perceived as miserable, worthless and no longer acceptable emotionally. The person delays a change, a planning and arranging of the future life because of lack of confidence in others and himself and because of fear of failure. Offenders can handle emotions and behavior of past learned strategies but are afraid of unconditioned trials of behavior change. They tend to stay to their past experience and want only not to commit a crime again. For them the crime is split off from their other entire personality structure.

A sex crime is most often a mirror image of former ego-identity threats and reactions, but in attacking his victim, the offender lacks the insight that it is an unconscious acting out against female or male representatives (parents) in the early personal development. The offender's goal is a repetitive trial to reach emotional separation or fusion or both from or with mother surrogates. A sexual assault can be taken as a minor copy of murder wishes towards mother or father without actual realization. Often one finds during exploration or treatment sessions that real or threatening incest situations play a role in the development of potential or real sex offender personalities. The crime is an aggressive and sexualized defense mechanism against extreme rejection or fusion wishes or anxieties of or with the mother or father. The victim is the realized fantasy partner, whereas the fantasy partner is the suppressed gender-identity representative.

DISCUSSION

Self confidence, the ability to handle distance and proximity and the creation of trust in others and himself are our goals in therapy. The incorporation of relatives, parents or spouses facilitates the process of maturation and often initiates a new interaction by dealing with former traumatizations without feelings of intense hate, revenge, grief and projection. These family sessions accentuate the feelings to distance from the past, allow participants to see the general dynamic of human interaction difficulties and the specific offender weaknesses which lead to a sex crime. Usually after months or even years of therapy, people replace hypersexual autoerotic behavior and fantasize emancipated non-sexual and sexual-partner oriented relationship.

Results of our therapy are difficult to document. We cannot measure luck, satisfaction and self confidence. We cannot predict the future of our treated and released patients. Returning to their professional and familial surroundings may trigger a relapse. We did document 8 years ago only the relapse of 58 patients 2 years after their release from prison. Rapists had a relapse of 9%, pedophiliacs of 51% and exhibitionists of 75%. The results of our new computation are yet not available.

SUMMARY

Referring to the excellent papers given by Pfafflin (1991) and Marshall (1991) elsewhere in this volume, therapy has its place in dealing with the threatening features of behavior of sex offenders so that future victimizers and victims are relieved of their anxieties.

Paraphilic sex offenders are treatable if they are minimally willing to treat themselves with the help of therapists. They should recognize their involvement in traumatizing relationships. Therapists should be motivated to help or treat mainly by being able to transfer humanistic views, attitudes and behavior, to build up reliable and trustful relationships with the offenders and not to have primarily narcisstic, academic or financial goals. Therapists must have the capacity to resist manipulation by the offenders. The method of therapy is less important than the necessity of dealing with the psycho-dynamic and problems of patients without new traumatization. Therapists themselves are quite often repetitive traumatizers by being identical parent surrogates with different methods of traumatization. Therapists should not make the patients symptom-free, but should let them find their own way to eliminate symptoms, replacing society-threatening behavior with acceptable human interactions. Positive mirror imagination in an unmanipulated way by important reference persons gives the victimizers the right and capability to live without destructive defense mechanisms.

Seven-year long experiences with the administration of anti-androgens (Cyproteron-acetate, Androcur) leads us to believe that externally administered chemicals may facilitate a calm and predictable functioning of sex offenders during treatment, but never will resolve the emotional deficits and emotional needs of individuals who commit a sex crime.

REFERENCES

Groth, N., Burgess, A.W., Holmstrom, L.L. (1977). Rape: Power, anger, and sexuality. *Am J. Psychiatry*, *134*(11), 1239-1243.

Groth, N., Burgess, A.W. (1980). Male rape: Offenders and victims. *Am J. Psychiatry*, *137*(7), 806-810.

Marshall, W. (1991, September 22-24). Effectiveness of treatment with sex offenders. Paper presented at the 2nd International Conference on the Treatment of Sex Offenders, Minneapolis, MN.

Pfafflin, F. (1991, September 22-24). What is in a symptom: A conservative perspective in the therapy of sex offenders. Paper presented at the 2nd International Conference on the Treatment of Sex Offenders, Minneapolis, MN.

Schmidt, G. (1975). Sexuelle Motivation und Kontrolle. In E. Schorsch & G. Schmidt (Eds.) *Ergebnisse zur Sexualforschung* (pp. 30-47). Koln, Wissenschafts-Verlag.

Stoller, R.J. 1979. *Perversion, die erotische Form von Hass.* Reinbek bei Hamburg, Rowohlt Verlag GmbH.

Wiederholt, I. (1980). Sexualitat: normale, deviante (perverse), kriminelle. In E. W. Stuttgart (Ed.). *Sexualmedizin in der Praxis* (pp. 342-387). New York: Gustav-Fisher-Verlag.

Wiederholt, I. (1989). Psychiatrisches Behandlungsprogramm fur Sexualtater in der Justizvollzugsanstalt Muchen. *Zeitschrift fur Strafvollzug und Straffalligenhilfe. Heft 4:* Edited by Gesellschaft fur Fortbildung der Strafvollzugsbediensteten e.V.: Wiesbaden.

AUTHOR'S NOTES

Ingo C. Wiederholt, MD, is a psychiatrist at the Social Therapeutic Department of Sex Offenders, Munich.

Address for correspondence: Ingo C. Wiederholt, MD, Social Therapeutic Department of Sex Offenders, Stadelheimer Strasse 12, 800 Munich 90, Germany.

SEX OFFENDER TREATMENT: PSYCHOLOGICAL AND MEDICAL APPROACHES. Pp. 25-37.

☐ BEHAVIOR DYNAMICS & CLINICAL PROCESSES

The Role of Personality Disorders in the Treatment of Sex Offenders

Wolfgang Berner, MD
Justizanstalt Mittersteig, Vienna

Peter Berger, MD
Justizanstalt Mittersteig, Vienna

Karin Guitierrez, MD
Justizanstalt Mittersteig, Vienna

Bettina Jordan, MD
Justizanstalt Mittersteig, Vienna

Katharina Berger, MD
Justizanstalt Mittersteig, Vienna

ABSTRACT In a sample of 30 consecutively admitted sex-offenders at Justizanstalt Mittersteig (a treatment facility inside the Austrian prison system, located in Vienna) we found 23 patients with a diagnosis of personality disorder (according to DSM-III-R). The distribution of diagnoses did not differ significantly from other samples found in a general outpatient clinic with the exception of a relatively high rate of "sadistic personality disorder" (9 patients). The meaning of this diagnosis is discussed and therapeutic strategies are delineated.

By definition, sex offenders have something in common: a sexual problem. However, sexuality cannot easily be isolated from all other desires and aspects of an individual's personality. Therefore, concentrating mainly on sexual stimuli as factors leading to a sexual offense may result in incorrect views about the problem.

In their article *Factors Related to Coercive Sexual Behavior in a Nonclinical Sample of Males*, Murphy, Coleman and Haynes (1986) mentioned numerous factors involved besides the arousal to sexual stimuli. These factors are grouped around rape-supportive attitudes about females such as acceptance of interpersonal violence; more general disregard for the rights of others; and the inability to separate seductive from friendly behavior or hostile from assertive behavior. A second group of factors is formed around personality traits represented for the authors by high MMPI scores on the Psychopathic (4) and Schizophrenic scales (8) or high rates in Eysenck's Personality Inventory on the Psychoticism and Neuroticism scales. They think that aggressive, hostile, emotionally labile individuals who are lacking empathy are likely to become sex offenders.

In our previous study (Berner, Karlick-Bolten, 1986), we found that the relapse rate in a five-year follow-up beginning with discharge from prison after a first sex-offense was significantly higher if a diagnosis of personality disorder was given (48% compared to 17% if only "Neurosis" was diagnosed). We concentrated our present research on that fact and looked for personality disorders in a group of 30 consecutively admitted and treated sex offenders in our institution "Justizanstalt Mittersteig." Our main question was whether the inaccurate clinical diagnosis of personality disorder could be better differentiated. This should be a basis for further follow-up studies. Therefore, we used a structured interview method for diagnosis. Distribution of diagnosis in these 30 consecutively admitted patients will be discussed as well as the consequences for therapeutic strategies.

METHOD

We used a structured interview (PDE-Loranger) which is more reliable than previously used instruments and which is under consideration by the World Health Organization as an officially recommended instrument (IPDE) for diagnosis of personality disorder (PD). This interview consists of questions for each item listed in the DSM-III and ICD-10 system for the diagnosis of personality disorders. Since there are overlappings of ICD-10 and DSM-III criteria,

157 questions have to be asked. In case the client admits that a certain long-lasting personality symptom (for instance procrastination) is given he is asked to produce convincing examples for the item in question. A manual helps to decide if the given example corresponds to the item criteria.

The admitted sex offenders were grouped in 3 segments according to the intensity of physical aggression used. The third group — sexual attacks on children — is the least directly physical aggressive and consists of child molesters who had not injured their victims physically or threatened them in a physical way. The following list shows these 3 groups. After their registration number the age when the offense happened is listed as well as the personality disorders diagnosed according to the interview. If the offense was carried out impulsively this is documented by a + sign. In only two cases a further diagnosis was to be stated, namely Case 9, who had the chromosomal aberration xyy and Case 4, who acquired a psychotic hallucination syndrome during his stay in the institution.

Diagnoses in parentheses mean that the threshold for a positive diagnosis was reached in a way that only the criterium "diagnosis probable" was fulfilled. It is evident from the above mentioned list that only 3 of our consecutively admitted patients were without the diagnosis of PD and another 4 were attributed only the diagnosis of a probable personality disorder. That means that only one-fourth of our patients have an exclusively sexual problem. The rest are in need of therapy concerning a variety of personal difficulties.

Taking the 23 patients with PD into consideration, it is again clear that patients with only one disorder are in the minority (3 patients, disregarding the "probable" diagnoses). We compared the distribution of diagnoses in our sample with a sample of 50 patients, screened for PD in an outpatient clinic under the same diagnostic procedure. This screening was part of a multicenter study by WHO/ADAMHA (Loranger et al., 1991) and the results of this study are not published yet. But there was no significant difference in the distribution of any diagnosis between these two groups (outpatient clinic, forensic institution) with exception of the diagnosis of sadistic personality disorder not found at all in the outpatient sample of the Vienna University Clinic and found in 9 cases of the sex offenders. If we take the just published preliminary results of the WHO/ADAMHA multicenter screening, it is interesting to note that in all centers together (which

Table 1. Thirty consecutively admitted sex offenders by type of offense, impulse characteristic, diagnosis

ID No.	Age	Impulse	Diagnosis
Type of offense			
Sexual killing (adult victims)			
1	25	+	paranoid/avoidant (borderline)
2	18	+	antisocial/narcissistic/sadistic
3	25	+	narcissistic
4	33	-	sadistic (antisocial/borderline)
5	17	+	—
Rape attacks (adult victims)			
6	26	+	paranoid/histrionic/avoidant/obsessive compulsive
7	31	+	paranoid/antisocial/borderline/avoidant
8	35	+	borderline (avoidant/sadistic)
9	29	+	borderline/avoidant
10	26	+	paranoid (sadistic)
11	22	+	antisocial
12	25	+	(antisocial/sadistic)
13	24	+	sadistic (antisocial)
14	24	-	paranoid/sadistic (antisocial)
15	38	-	antisocial/avoidant/sadistic
16	42	-	(antisocial/borderline/sadistic)
17	19	-	paranoid/borderline/narcissistic/histrionic/sadistic
18	36	+	—
19	29	+	—
Sexual attacks on children (molestation)			
20	25	-	borderline/avoidant/dependent
21	23	+	borderline/sadistic (paranoid)
22	35	-	borderline/sadistic (narcissistic/histrionic/antisocial)
23	27	-	antisocial
24	41	-	schizoid/schizotypal/avoidant (antisocial)
25	24	-	antisocial/sadistic (borderline)
26	24	-	antisocial/histrionic/avoidant (borderline)
27	36	+	schizoid/avoidant
28	22	-	dependent (antisocial)
29	42	-	(avoidant)
30	35	-	(sadistic)

included no forensic departments!) sadistic personality disorders were found extremely rarely. Only two cases out of 716 were included in the study because of a suspected personality disorder.

Dividing our sample according to offenses against adult victims and offenses against children (group 1 and 2 in Table 1 against group 3 in Table 1) we could again find no significant differences in the distribution of diagnoses. The same is true for a comparison between impulsive offenders (marked + in Table 1) and non-impulsive offenders. Diagnoses were distributed nearly equally in both sub-groups (schizoid, schizotypal and obsessive compulsive disorders were given so rarely that they do not count for any sort of comparison).

It seems important to us that in the group of sadistic personality disorders we found 3 patients rather impulsive in their offenses and 6 patients without impulsivity in carrying out their offenses: they planned their attacks rather carefully, taking different viewpoints into consideration. Table 2 shows the distribution of DSM-III-R personality disorders diagnoses in detail. Table 2 indicates that *avoidant* and *sadistic* personality disorders were the most frequently found in our sample. Since the frequency of occurrence of sadistic personality disorder is the focus of this paper, we will concentrate on the way this diagnosis is given, how it is combined with other personality disorders and on the presumed consequences for treatment and prognoses.

Diagnosis of Sadistic Personality Disorder

The definition of sadistic personality disorder by DSM-III-R is given by 8 criteria, from which at least four must be scored as positive in order to make a definitive diagnosis. (An item is scored positively only if the patient is able to give examples for the item in question.) For a probable diagnosis, a positive score of three items (instead of four) is required.

All nine patients with a definite diagnosis admitted that they got others to do what they wanted by frightening them and that they tended to restrict the autonomy of people with whom they were close (Table 3). Seven of the nine sadistic patients had used physical cruelty or violence to dominate, and/or were amused by or took pleasure in the suffering of others, and/or have lied to harm or inflict pain on others.

Table 2. Distribution of 51 diagnoses among 23 patients

N (patients)	23
N (diagnoses)	51
Character of diagnosis	
Personality disorder close to "psychoses"	
Paranoid	6
Schizoid	2
Schizotypal	1
"Extraverted" personality disorders	
Antisocial	7
Borderline	7
Histrionic	4
Narcissistic	3
"Introverted" personality disorders	
Avoidant	9
Dependent	2
Obsessive-compulsive	1
Passive-aggressive	0
Sadistic	9

It is necessary to consider that the query in the interview is not for single instances, but for frequent occurrences, commencing with the onset of adolescence. One then gets the impression that the sadistic habit in these patients has to be tackled on a more general basis than the sexual one. This sadistic habit does not only lead to one form of offense.

The proportions of sadistic personality disorder in the three offense groups we studied were:

□ *Table 3. Frequency of observation of criterion behaviors in sadistic offenders [N = 9]*

Criterion behavior	
Has used physical cruelty or violence to dominate	77.8 % (7)
Humiliates or demeans people in presence of others	33.3 % (3)
Treated or disciplined others unusually harshly	22.2 % (2)
Amused by or takes pleasure in suffering of others	77.8 % (7)
Has lied to harm or inflict pain on others	77.8 % (7)
Gets others to do what he wants by frightening them	100.0 % (9)
Restricts autonomy of people with whom he is close	100.0 % (9)
Fascinated by violence, weapons, injury, or torture	66.7 % (6)

- Sexual killing, 2 out of 5 patients;
- Rape, 3 out of 14 patients;
- Attacks on children, 3 out of 11 patients.

It is important to know that you cannot judge by merely taking the character of the offense into consideration, regardless of the existence of a sadistic personality disorder. Even sexual killing may be a result of a circumscribed conflictual situation or breakthrough of impulse — especially in adolescents shortly after puberty. On the other hand, sexual molestation of children without any violence used may be a result of sadistic personality disorder too. Since a combination of 2 or 3 personality disorder-diagnoses is the rule, it is important to take these possibilities of combinations for the sadistic personality disorder into consideration as well. From Table 4 it is obvious that we are often confronted with a combination of borderline and narcissistic pathology as well as antisocial personality in the sadistic personality disorder.

A short case vignette of a patient with sadistic personality disorder is presented. The patient was admitted to Justizanstalt Mittersteig for having molested his stepson and on other occasions his stepbrother (Case No. 22 on our first table).

□ *Table 4. Combination of Sadistic personality disorder with other disorders*

Sadistic [only]	2
Sadistic/borderline	2
Sadistic/antisocial	1
Sadistic/paranoid	1
Sadistic/narcissistic/antisocial	1
Sadistic/narcissistic/antisocial/avoidant	1
Sadistic/narcissistic/paranoid/borderline	1

Case Illustration

The patient is a rather well-adapted truck-driver of 37, with an adequate income. His previous convictions were for minor offenses against property and threats against other drivers during a heavy argument in traffic. He used a weapon to intimidate his rival. He lived in a long-lasting relationship with a woman intellectually superior to him, but dominated by him by outbursts of shouting or actions such as smashing plates and food if not cooked according to his taste. He succeeded in convincing his wife to participate in group sex and all sorts of sexual paraphilic activities (frequency of regular intercourse was not substantially reduced by the paraphilic activities). He was sure his wife was enjoying all these activities, too. On a few occasions, for instance, he succeeded in persuading his wife to seduce the patient's 15-year-old stepbrother and then to have intercourse with the boy while the patient penetrated him anally.

After the birth of a child, his wife refused most of his sexual requests and therefore he became more and more interested in the young stepson, then 12 years old. He seduced him for his pleasure, admitting that it was partly out of revenge against his wife. This brought him to prison and therapy. It is outside the scope of this presentation to describe the history of this patient, himself abandoned by his mother at the age of 2 and later a victim of seduction by an adult man and women, but it is important for treatment considerations.

DISCUSSION

As a reaction to a previous follow-up study (Berner, Karlick-Bolten, 1986), where the diagnosis of personality disorder was a criterion for unfavourable outcome, we decided for further follow-up studies to differentiate this diagnosis according to today's habits of psychiatric diagnosing and used a standardized interview for personality disorders in DSM-III-R — the Loranger PDE. Two thirds of thirty consecutively-admitted forensic patients with sex offenses in their history had at least one diagnosis of personality disorder. The distribution of personality disorders differed little from comparable distributions in a general outpatient clinic. Although antisocial personality disorder was expected to be a high in the sex offender sample, it was not; only seven cases had elevated scores. But a real exception was the high rate of sadistic personality disorders (9 out of 30 patients). This result is comparable with the result of a survey done by R. Spitzer et al. (1991) to prove the validity of sadistic personality disorder diagnosis on the basis of questionnaires answered by 279 members of the American Academy Psychiatry and Law. Approximately fifty percent of the respondents had at some time evaluated in a forensic setting a subject who exhibited behavior that met the criteria for the disorder. Four percent of the cases seen in the preceding year by those respondents met the criteria for the disorder. Spitzer concludes that the diagnosis is probably not rare under special circumstances and that it has both descriptive and construct validity.

We were not able to present special research data on the life event history of the mentioned patients with sadistic personality disorder to confirm the finding that these patients frequently have a history of childhood abuse and parental loss. Even though our clinical impression would support these findings, our findings of the importance of the sadistic personality disorder in our sample have to correlate to *therapeutic strategies*:

The complicated personality structure of our patients makes it obvious that we should concentrate our therapeutic strategies more on impulse control and reality testing than sexual preferences itself. The most important aspect of therapeutic aims is the capacity of object-relationship. Our psychotherapeutic strategies are divided into two groups: One following more closely *"cognitive therapy,"* in the sense of Beck's (1990) cognitive therapy (of personality disorders), and the second following Kernberg's approach to psychotherapy as exemplified in his book *Psychodynamic Psychotherapy of Borderline Patients* (Kernberg, Selzer, Koenigsberg, Carr, and Appelbaum, 1989).

Besides the diagnosis sadistic personality disorder most of the above-mentioned patients are disturbed corresponding to avoidant PD and antisocial PD with a connotation of borderline PD (in the DSM-III-R sense); therefore, we concentrate on the strategies developed especially for these disorders. If you take the antisocial personality as an example, it is important not only to encourage certain behaviors, or extinguish others, but to work with the patient on certain *attitudes* which cause behaviors. According to Beck and Freeman (1990) these attitudes for the antisocial personality disorder are:

- *Justification*: "Wanting something or wanting to avoid something justifies my actions."
- *Thinking is believing*: "My thoughts and feelings are completely accurate, simply because they occur to me."
- *Personal infallibility*: "I always make good choices."
- *Feelings make facts*: "I know I am right because I feel right about what I do."
- *The impotence of others*: "The view of others are irrelevant to my decisions, unless they directly control my immediate consequences."
- *Low-impact consequences*: "Undesirable consequences will not occur to me or will not matter to me."

In cognitive therapy with "avoidant personality disorder," which is one of the two most highly represented personality disorders, we have to work on the patient's dysfunctional beliefs about themselves and about others, mostly predicting rejection, which causes dysphoria followed then by real rejection.

It is of extreme importance to make these habits clear to the patient to convince him of its counter-productive effects and make clear that believing in them is a flight from reality testing. It is obvious that such clarifications are only possible on the basis of a good patient/therapist contract.

This patient/therapist's contract is conceptualized in cognitive therapy in the form of certain characteristics the therapist should bear in mind during therapy — it should give him an attitude-facilitating therapeutic-relationship. These characteristics helping therapists to have the desired therapeutic relationship are:

- Self-assurance
- Objectivity!
- A relaxed and nondefensive interpersonal style
- A clear sense of personal limits
- A strong sense of humor (Beck et al., 1990)

According to our own opinion and that of some of our colleagues at Mittersteig, the therapeutic relationship is not profound in cognitive therapy. Especially mechanisms of transference and countertransference cannot be overlooked in most therapeutic endeavours. Therefore, a group of therapists are following Kernberg's strategies (1989) to tackle all aspects of unconscious or preconscious attempts of the patient to manipulate the therapist and bring him or her to action. Kernberg recommends having a hierarchy of themes in mind which have to be tackled by the therapist according to their priority in the hierarchy, even if they only came to the fore in outlines.

This list is an example of the concreteness of therapeutic strategies in Kernberg's "confrontation-clarification" style of psychodynamic psychotherapy, as detailed in *Hierarchy of Thematic Priority* (Kernberg et al., 1989):

- Suicide or homicide threats
- Overt threats to treatment continuity (e.g., financial difficulties, plans to leave town, requests to decrease session frequency)
- Dishonesty or deliberate withholding in sessions (e.g., lying to the therapist, refusing to discuss certain subjects, silences occupying most of the sessions)
- Contract breaches (e.g., failure to meet with an auxiliary therapist when agreed upon, failure to take prescribed medication)
- In-session acting out (e.g., abusing office furnishings, refusing to leave at end of session, shouting)
- Between-session acting out
- Nonaffective or trivial themes
- Transference manifestations

  a. Verbal references to therapist
  b. "Acting-out" (e.g., positioning body in overtly seductive manner)
  c. As inferred by therapist (e.g., references to other doctors)
- Nontransferential affect-laden material

However, these different concepts for psychotherapy with patients suffering from PD are only the basis for what we had to develop for the group of patients described above — those with the circumscribed form of sadistic PD. Logically the form of transference developing in such cases has to be of sadomasochistic character and this is a special challenge for our therapists.

We do not believe that we are in the position to recommend a full-fledged therapeutic progam for these cases. We are in a stage of experimentation, too. The following list seems to be a contribution to developing therapeutic strategies:

- Be aware of the attempts by the patients to dominate the therapeutic situation.
- Beware of fighting back or give in to dominating the situation yourself.
- Don't lie about feelings the patient succeeds in eliciting from you (perhaps against your will). Don't try to reach the same grandiose sense of yourself the patient is struggling for.
- Be open in showing the patient your borders, your limited possibilities, without being too modest and falling into the dominated part of the relationship.
- Having reached a point outside the Domination-Submission line in the relationship, working through of pleasure gained from Domination-Submission becomes possible.
- Explore the defense-character of the wish to dominate-submit.

CONCLUSION

The diagnosis "personality disorder" or "psychopathy" or "sociopathy" in forensic settings is incorrect and should be differentiated according to modern diagnostic entities. In a sample of 30 consecutively admitted sex-offenders at J.A. Mittersteig, we found 23 patients belonging to the DSM-III categories of personality disorders. The diagnosis of antisocial personality disorder in this group of patients played a less important role than "sadistic personality disorder" (9 patients), which was diagnosed in a much higher rate than expected by comparisons with general outpatient samples. This is a finding corresponding to the opinion of Spitzer et al. (1991) that under certain circumstances a high rate of such disturbances may be found.

A case example shows how a sadistic attitude may influence more than one area in the life of a patient and has to be treated according to these multiple situational possibilities. Our own therapeutic strategies therefore are following Beck's cognitive therapy developed especially for personality disorders and Kernberg's psychodynamic therapy developed for borderline patients. Besides this, we are especially concerned with possible collusions in the sadomasochistic realm and are developing strategies to make therapists aware of this danger and able to work with such patients.

REFERENCES

Beck, A.T., & Freeman, A. (1990). *Cognitive therapy of personality disorders*, New York-London: The Guilford Press.

Berner, W., & Karlick-Bolten, E. (1986). *Verlaufsformen der Sexualkriminalitat*, Stuttgart: Enke.

IPDE: "International Personality Disorder — Examination" designed by A. Loranger for WHO, used in an international comparative study of personality disorders by ADAMHA/WHO. *See* Loranger, A.W. The WHO/ADAMHA international pilot study of personality disorders: Background and purpose. *Journal of Personality Disorders*, 1991, 5 (3), 296-306.

Kernberg, O., Selzer, M.A., Koenigsberg, H.W., Carr, A.C. & Appelbaum, A.H. (1989). *Psychodynamic psychotherapy of borderline patients*, New York: Basic.

Loranger, A.W. (1988). Personality disorder examination (PDE) manual. Yonkers, NY: DV Communications.

Loranger, A.W., Hirschfeld, R.M.A., Sartorius N., & Regier D.A. (1991). The WHO/ADAMHA international pilot study of personality disorders: Background and purpose. *Journal of Personality Disorders 5*(3), 296-306.

Murphy, W.D., Coleman, E.M., & Haynes, M.R. (1986). Factors related to coercive sexual behavior in a nonclinical sample of males. *Violence Vict. 1*(4), 255-278.

Spitzer, R.L., Feister, S., Gay, M. & Pfohl, B. (1991). Results of a survey of forensic psychiatrists on the validity of the sadistic personality disorder diagnosis. *Am. J. Psychiatry 148*(7), 875-879.

AUTHORS' NOTES

Wolfgang Berner, MD, Peter Berger, MD, Karin Guitierrez, MD, Bettina Jordan, MD, and Katharina Berger, MD, are affiliated with the Justizanstalt Mittersteig in Vienna. *Address correspondence* to Dr. Wolfgang Berner, Justizanstalt Mittersteig, Bereichsleitung fur Psychiatrie und Psychotherapie, Mittersteig 25, A- 1050 Wien, Austria.

SEX OFFENDER TREATMENT: PSYCHOLOGICAL AND MEDICAL APPROACHES. Pp. 39-47.

☐ ATTITUDINAL DETERMINANTS

Aggression Against Women by Men: Sexual and Spousal Assault

Ann Marie Dewhurst
Mental Health Clinic, University of Regina

Robert J. Moore
Campion College, University of Regina

Dennis P. Alfano
University of Regina

ABSTRACT The present research approached sexual and spousal assault from a perspective that integrated both feminist and psychodynamic theory. Men from four research groups — Sexual Offender (SO, $n = 19$), Batterer (B, $n = 22$), Violent Community Comparison (VCC, $n = 10$), and Community Comparison (CC, $n = 21$) — were compared on their responses to a questionnaire including demographic, personality, and attitudinal variables. The following hypotheses were tested: (1) the SO and B Groups would demonstrate similar personality and attitudinal characteristics and differ from the CC Group; (2) members of the community who reported violence (VCC) would resemble the SO and B Groups and differ from the CC Group. Data were analyzed using multivariate analysis of covariance and discriminant function analysis. As expected, the B Group shared many characteristics with the SO Group but differed in being less tolerant of minor irritations and frustrations, and more likely to be despondent and to ruminate over potential interpersonal harm. SOs were more likely to endorse the belief that interpersonal violence is an acceptable part of relationships than were Bs. The VCC Group responded in a similar but less deviant manner than the B Group. The SO and B Groups differed from the CC Group on several variables. The VCC and CC Groups differed on only one variable. The discriminating variables correctly classified 75% of the participants in the study. *Hostility toward women* and *Depression* were the two best discriminating variables, suggesting that a combined feminist-psychodynamic approach may be helpful in understanding male aggression against women.

Sexual and spousal assault have been identified as the two major crimes by men against women in our society (Gelles & Straus, 1979). Victimization rates for both types of offences have been cited at between 10 and 30 percent of adult women (MacLeod, 1980; Genteman, 1984; Hanneke, Shields & McCall, 1986). Given this frequency, any woman could be the victim of either offence and the offender could be any man from any socio-economic level in the community (Field, 1978; Hamberger & Hastings, 1985; Stark-Adamec & Adamec, 1982). Many men report attitudes and beliefs which condone aggression against women (Malamuth, 1981). While not all men act on these beliefs, numerous men who are physically and/or sexually abusive are not apprehended and can continue to perpetrate their abusive behaviour without sanction (Ponich, 1984).

In terms of actual aggressive behaviour, sexual and spousal assault both involve intimidation, threats and physical abuse. Even the settings for the assault may be similar (Finkelhor & Yllo, 1985). Both of these offences and the men who perpetrate them have been studied independently by a variety of researchers utilizing, for the most part, either a feminist or psychodynamic orientation. This implies that these offences and the men who commit them are distinct; however, few researchers have compared both populations of abusive men or considered both perspectives in the same study.

Feminists consider aggression against women to be a manifestation of a patriarchal social system which seeks to discriminate against women and which perpetuates the myth that men are superior to women (Clark & Lewis, 1977; Dobash & Dobash, 1979; Gondolf, 1983; Gross, 1978). They maintain that the belief structure used to repress women is conveyed in attitudes such as sexual conservatism, adversarial sexual beliefs, and acceptance of interpersonal violence (Burt, 1980; Check, 1985; Check & Malamuth, 1983; Field, 1978; Graff & Chartier, 1988; Gross, 1978; Koss, Gidyez & Wisniewski, 1987; Scott & Tetreault, 1986; Stark-Adamec & Adamec, 1982). While sexist attitudes are not a sufficient condition for the occurrence of aggression against women, their presence increases the likelihood of women being victimized (Malamuth, 1981).

In contrast, supporters of the psychodynamic perspective contend that personality factors specific to the individual facilitate the commission of aggressive acts. The individual utilizes violence as a means to deal with deep-seated resentments and fears that may or may not be available to the offender's conscious thought processes. Gondolf (1983) summarized this perspective by stating that men act aggressively against women in order to express infantile hostility and womb envy; such men are hateful and fearful of women. Aggression is one possible response which the offending man may use to express pent up emotions and cope with stressful personal situations (Farrington, 1986; Finkelhor & Yllo, 1987; Gelles & Straus, 1979; Groth, 1979; Rappaport & Burkhart, 1984).

Although both feminist and psychodynamic theorists acknowledge hostility as a central aspect of aggression against women by men, in isolation, each perspective fails to address critical aspects of the issue. On the one hand, feminist theory does not address why two men from similar environments do not both offend, while, on the other hand, the psychodynamic approach is insufficient to explain why two men with similar personality traits do not both abuse women. Further, neither theory adequately accounts for the individual man's choice of offence style.

An alternative perspective would consider both these frameworks. Comparing the personality traits, attitudes and beliefs of men who batter, men who perpetrate sexual assault, and non-abusive men may facilitate the emergence of a clearer picture of the man's choice to be abusive.

RESEARCH METHODS

Two hypotheses were tested in this research: (1) The attitudes and personality characteristics of men who batter and men who perpetrate sexual assault against adult women will be similar and differ from a community sample of men who do not self-disclose violence against women; (2) The attitudes and personality characteristics of men from the community who self-disclose physical or sexually assaultive behaviour toward women and men who have been formally identified as perpetrators will be similar and differ from non-disclosing community men.

Participants

Participants in the Sexual Offender Group (SO, n = 19) were recruited from federal and provincial correctional facilities located in Saskatchewan, Canada where they were serving sentences for sexually assaulting adult women. This group may not be representative of rapists in general, as most men who sexually assault adult women do not enter the criminal justice system (Clark & Lewis, 1977). The men in the Batterer Group (B, n = 22) were volunteers from community-based treatment programs for men who batter. Community respondents were classified into the Community Comparison Group (CC, n = 22) or the Violent Community Group (VCC, n = 10) based upon the presence or absence of self-reports of violence against a current and/or previous partner. Respondents from the community were recruited from a large local employer and from men's service organizations. Seventy-five men initially volunteered to complete the questionnaire package; however, three respondents from the SO Group were not included in subsequent analyses due to substantial missing data. The remaining 72 men ranged in age from 19 to 60 years with an average age of 35 years.

Questionnaire

All respondents were approached through group presentations and volunteers were asked to complete a questionnaire including demographic and life history items, the Hostility Toward Women Scale (Check, 1985), the Basic Personality Inventory (Jackson, 1989) and Burt's (1980) Acceptance of Interpersonal Violence, Sex Role Stereotyping, and Adversarial Sexual Beliefs Scales. Each man completed the questionnaire in private and returned it to the researcher or a research assistant. All responses were kept anonymous and confidential.

RESULTS

Demographic and Life History Variables

The four research groups did not differ significantly on the variables of age, having a best friend, or the number of friends regularly associated with. Members of the SO Group reported significantly less education ($F(3,68) = 5.31$, $p = .05$), a higher incidence of employment as skilled or unskilled labourers, and a greater likelihood of experiencing a period of being unemployed for more than two years since the age of 18 than individuals in the other three groups. Participants in the other three groups tended to have stayed in school longer, to have fewer periods of unemployment, and to be involved in farming, skilled labour, or professional occupations.

The SO and B Groups indicated drinking (Chi-square = 11.88, $p = .01$) and drug (Chi-square = 8.89, $p = .01$) problems more frequently than either the VCC and CC groups.

Significantly fewer men in the CC Group witnessed violence in their families of origin than men in the other three groups (Chi-square = 12.71, $p = .05$). Although 17% of the men in the study indicated that they had been sexually abused in some manner at least once as a child, there were no significant differences between the groups in the incidence of such experiences. The men in the SO, B, and VCC Groups indicated a higher occurence of corporal punishment as a child than did members of the CC Group.

Personality and Attitudinal Variables

A significant multivariate analysis of covariance (level of education as the covariate) supported overall differences between the groups on the personality and attitudinal variables (Wilks' Lambda = 0.21; $F(3,67) = 2.25$, $p = .05$).

Univariate analyses of covariance derived from the multivariate analysis followed by post-hoc testing using Duncan's Multiple Range Test indicated that the hypotheses tested in this study were partially confirmed. The SO Group differed from the B Group on only 3 variables: Acceptance of Interpersonal Violence, Interpersonal Problems and Anxiety. Members of the SO and the B Groups differed from the non-violent CC group on five variables: Hostility toward Women, Depression, Alienation, Impulse Expression and Deviation. On the other hand, the ten men from the community who self-reported perpetrating spousal assault (VCC) differed from the Sexual Offender Group on only two variables: Interpersonal Problems and Deviation. The two community comparison groups differed on only one variable addressed in this study, Interpersonal Problems. There were no differences between any of the four research groups on the following variables: Sex-Role Stereotyping, Adversarial Sexual Beliefs, Hypochondriasis, Denial, Persecutory Ideas, Thought Disorder, Self-depreciation and Social Introversion. (See Table 1).

A standard linear discriminant function analysis was performed to determine the extent to which the personality and attitudinal variables were able to correctly classify participants in their appropriate groups (Chi-square (48) = 103.6, p = .01). Eight-four percent of the SO Group, 73% of the B Group, 60% of the VCC Group, and 76% of the CC Group were appropriately classified; overall 75% of the participants were correctly grouped. The Depression and Hostility Toward Women Scales were the most useful variables in discriminating between the research groups.

DISCUSSION

The attitudes toward women and the behaviour reported by the men in the SO Group were congruent: they distrusted, were angry at, and sexually assaulted women. Although the men in the B Group revealed greater hostility toward women than the men in the two community comparison groups, this was not reflected in their responses to the attitudinal measures. It may be that men who batter act out aggressively from situational intolerance and general frustration, coupled with a thinking pattern which tends towards pessimism, suspicion and catastrophizing, particularly about their partners. These negative ruminations may be the motivation for their behaviour rather than the more anti-social orientation of the men who perpetrate sexual abuse of adult women.

Feminist theorists would have predicted that the two attitudinal scales, Hostility Toward Women and Acceptance of Interpersonal Violence, would distinguish between the men who perpetrated violence against women and the non-violent men of the community.

TABLE 1
Comparison of Group Means on Personality and Attitudinal Variables

	PARTICIPANT GROUPS								
	Sexual Offenders		Batterers		Community Comparison		Violent Community Comparison		
VARIABLES	M	SD	M	SD	M	SD	M	SD	F(3,68)
HOSTILE [1]	7.73	5.28	7.36	4.11	4.00	2.23	6.40	3.70	2.86*
STEREO [2]	41.63	9.56	47.23	6.87	47.76	9.74	43.56	10.77	1.12
ACCEPT [3]	31.72	7.29	37.45	3.00	36.71	4.36	34.00	3.91	3.34*
ADVERSE [4]	46.11	13.72	48.00	7.40	49.24	9.93	43.10	11.59	1.61
HYPOCHONDR. [5]	4.56	4.44	6.12	3.96	4.57	3.43	4.00	3.13	1.85
DEPRESSION [5]	4.47	2.55	6.27	3.30	2.87	2.39	2.50	1.58	8.83*
DENIAL [5]	5.90	3.23	5.27	2.73	6.05	2.50	5.60	2.55	0.33
INTER. PRO. [5]	6.57	2.52	11.00	3.74	6.71	3.52	9.50	3.66	8.53**
ALIENATION [5]	5.16	3.35	5.77	4.40	2.71	2.61	4.90	2.23	3.06*
PERS. IDEA [5]	5.79	4.08	5.55	3.71	3.43	3.19	4.00	2.21	1.08
ANXIETY [5]	6.00	3.73	8.96	4.21	5.86	3.41	5.80	4.10	4.13**
TH. DISORD. [5]	2.90	3.25	2.73	2.14	1.71	1.42	1.20	0.63	1.91
IMPULSE EXP. [5]	6.42	3.91	8.32	3.27	4.91	3.35	6.90	3.35	3.97**
SOCIAL INTR. [5]	4.95	3.27	6.96	4.03	4.52	3.54	4.40	2.37	2.57
SELF-DEPREC. [5]	2.74	3.65	2.96	3.06	1.19	1.40	1.00	1.16	1.69
DEVIATION [5]	3.79	2.10	3.95	2.08	1.86	1.93	2.20	1.03	4.37

*$p<0.05$ **$p<0.01$

1 HOSTILITY TOWARDS WOMEN SCALE
2 SEX ROLE STEREOTYPING SCALE
3 ACCEPTANCE OF INTERPERSONAL VIOLENCE SCALE
4 ADVERSARIAL SEXUAL BELIEFS SCALE
5 BASIC PERSONALITY SCALE

However, psychodynamic theory seems best able to account for the differences between groups on the personality variables. The results of the discriminate function analysis tends to support the use of both of these theoretical frameworks. The two best discriminating variables were Depression and Hostility Toward Women, a personality and an attitudinal variable, respectively.

In review, aggression against women by men may be facilitated by the misogynist values of a male dominated culture. However, the dynamics which influence an individual's choice of offence style, battering or sexual abuse, may be more related to the personality characteristics of the offender.

REFERENCES

Burt, M. (1980). Cultural myths and supports for rape. *Journal of Personality and Social Psychology, 38*(2), 217-230.

Check, J.V.P. (1985). *The Hostility Toward Women Scale*. Unpublished doctoral dissertation, University of Manitoba, Winnipeg.

Check, J.V.P., & Malamuth, N.M. (1983). Sex-role stereotyping and reactions to depictions of stranger versus acquaintance rape. *Journal of Personality and Social Psychology, 45*(2), 344-356.

Clark, L.M.G., & Lewis, D.J. (1977). *Rape, the price of coercive sexuality*. Toronto: The Women's Press.

Dobash, R.E., & Dobash, R. (1979). *Violence against wives: A case against the patriarchy*. New York: The Free Press.

Farrington, K.M. (1980). Stress and family violence. In M.A. Straus & G.T. Hotaling (Eds.), *The social causes of husband- wife violence*. Minneapolis: University of Minnesota Press.

Field, H.S. (1978). Attitudes toward rape: A comparative analysis of police, rapists, crisis workers and citizens. *Journal of Personality and Social Psychology, 36*(2), 156-179.

Finkelhor, D., & Yllo, K. (1985). *Licence to rape: Sexual abuse of wives*. New York: The Free Press.

Gelles, R.J., & Straus, M.A. (1979). Determinants of violence in the family: toward a theoretical integration. In W.R. Burr, R. Hill, F.I. Nye, & I.L. Reiss (Eds.), *Contemporary Theories About the Family, Vol. 1*. New York: Free Press.

Gentemann, K.M. (1984). Wife beating: Attitudes of a non- clinical population. *Victimology: An International Journal*, 2(1), 1-10.

Gondolf, E.W. (1985). Anger and oppression in men who batter: empiricist and feminist perspectives and their implications for research. *Victimology, 10*, 311-324.

Graff, L., & Chartier, B. (1988). Hostility toward women and men's responses to sexual stimuli. *Canadian Psychology*: *29*(2a), Abstract No. 315.

Gross, A.E. (1978). The male role and heterosexual behaviour. *Journal of Social Issues, 34*(1), 87-105.

Groth, N.A., (1979). *Men who rape: The psychology of the offender.* New York: Plenum.

Hamberger, L.K., & Hastings, J.E. (1986). Personality correlates of men who abuse their partners: A cross validation study. *Journal of Family Violence, 1*(4), 323-341.

Hanneke, C., Sheilds, N., & McCall, G. (1986). Assessing the prevalence of marital rape. *Journal of Interpersonal Violence, 1*(3), 350-362.

Jackson, D.N. (1989), *Basic Personality Inventory.* London, Ont.: Sigma Assessment Systems.

Koss, M., Gidyez, C., & Wisniewski, N. (1987). The scope of rape: Incidence and prevalence of sexual aggression and victimization in a national sample of higher education students. *Journal of Consulting and Clinical Psychology, 55*(2), 162-170.

MacLeod, L. (1980). *Wife battering in Canada: The vicious circle.* Ottawa: Canadian Government Publishing Centre.

Malamuth, N. (1981). Rape proclivity among males. *Journal of Social Issues, 37*(4).

Ponich, P., (1984). *Evaluation of an anger management program for male batters.* Unpublished Master's thesis: University of Calgary.

Rapapport, K., & Burkhart, B. (1984). Personality and attitudinal characteristics of sexually coercive college males. *Journal of Abnormal Psychology, 93*(2), 216-221.

Scott, R., & Tetreault, L. (1986). Attitudes of rapists and other violent offenders toward women. *Journal of Social Psychology, 127*(4), 375-380.

Stark-Adamec, C., & Adamec, R.E. (1982). Aggression by men against women: Adaptation or aberration. *International Journal of Women's Studies, 5*(1), 1-21.

Straus, M.A. (1979). Measuring intra-family conflict and violence: The Conflict Tactics (CT) Scale. *Journal of Marriage and the Family, 41*, 75-88.

AUTHORS' NOTES

Ann Marie Dewhurst, MA, is at Regina Mental Health Clinic, Regina, Saskatchewan, Canada.

Robert J. Moore, PhD, is a professor of psychology at Campion College, University of Regina, Regina, Saskatchewan, Canada.

Dennis P. Alfano, PhD, is at the University of Regina.

Correspondence should be addressed to Ann Marie Dewhurst, MA, Regina Mental Health Clinic, 1942 Hamilton Street, Regina, Saskatchewan, Canada S4P 3V7.

SEX OFFENDER TREATMENT: PSYCHOLOGICAL AND MEDICAL APPROACHES. Pp. 49-58.

□ PSYCHODYNAMICS

Dissociative Experiences of Sexual Offenders

A Comparison Between Two Outpatient Groups and Those Found to be Falsely Accused

S. Margretta Dwyer
University of Minnesota

B. R. Simon Rosser
University of Minnesota

Steven Sawyer
Project Pathfinder, St. Paul, MN

ABSTRACT The Dissociative Experiences Scale (Bernstein & Putnam, 1986), a 28-item self report questionnaire which distinguishes between subjects with a dissociative disorder and those without, was administered to 71 sex offenders who presented for treatment at a clinic at a major university medical school, a community based outpatient program, and 14 men who were falsely accused of sexual abuse. Outpatient sex offenders in both programs scored in the range attributed to the general population. Neither outpatient sample had significantly different scores from each other, although it was hypothesized they would. The trend for persons falsely accused of child sexual abuse was to score lower than the offenders, and lower than the general population.

Dissociation is a lack of integrated thoughts, feelings experiences with consciousness and memory. It is also a cognition in which the mental functioning is disintegrated, and operates in a compartmentalized manner outside the awareness sphere or memory recall (Ludwig, 1983). For example, when violations of a person's basic value system occur, the mind blocks out these violations by repression or other similar means in order to function (Ludwig, 1983). Dissociative experiences are common in the general population and are not necessarily pathological. Pathology depends on severity of dissociative experiences, or the degree to which distress interferes in daily functioning. For years dissociative syndromes have been described in the literature (Ellenberger, 1970; Cocores, Santa, & Patel, 1984; Putnam, 1985), and a strong linkage between dissociative symptoms and traumatic experiences has been documented (Putnam, 1985). Dissociation can occur in a minor or major pathological form (Hilgard, 1977; Ludwig, 1983; Nemiah, 1980; Spiegel, 1963; West, 1967) and is therefore seen on a continuum by most experts.

Norton, Ross & Novotny (1990) indicated in their study that the more irrational a person's thinking, the higher their DES score. It is believed that 5 to 10 percent of the general population may have dissociative disorders and since it is that common, dissociative symptoms probably occur in a range of psychiatric disorders, just as anxiety and depression are components of different diagnositic disorders (Ross, Joshi & Currie, 1990).

THE CHARACTER OF DISSOCIATION

The DSM-III-R (1987) names five categories of dissociation:

- Multiple Personality Disorder (300.14)
- Psychogenic Fugue (300.13)
- Psychogenic Amnesia (300.12)
- Depersonalization Disorder (300.60)
- Dissociative Disorder Not Otherwise Specified (300.15)

Through the authors' observations of sex offenders in two outpatient programs, it was believed that categories 3, 4 and 5 of the dissociation diagnosis from DSM-III-R could apply at various times.

The sudden inability of a person to recall important personal information may be attributed to the psychogenic amnesia dissociative disorder *(300.12)*. This disorder may be circumscribed or localized for a prescribed period of time, usually the first few hours following a profoundly disturbing event (DSM-III-R).

In depersonalization dissociative disorder *(300.60)* a person's own reality is temporarily lost: There is a feeling of detachment from his own mental processes or body. It is as if the patient is in a dream (DSM-III-R).

The dissociative disorder not otherwise specified *(300.15)* can be manifested in six ways according to the DSM-III-R. Usually for patients it will manifest in trance states, i.e., altered states of consciousness with markedly diminished or selective responsiveness to environmental stimuli.

Sexual Offenders and Dissociation

Misdiagnosis of dissociative features can hinder treatment for sex offender patients. During evaluation many sex offenders are denied entry into treatment because of "too much denial" or "lying about the offenses," when in fact they may not be lying, but the interviewing psychologist/psychiatrist has missed the sex offenders' dissociative experiences.

Dissociation's role in the psychological life of sexual offenders has been a mystery, since they are known to suffer "trance-like" states at various times, but different from psychogenic fugue states discribed in the DSM-III. (Fugue states are disturbances in the normally *integrative* functions of identity, memory, or consciousness [DSM-III-R,1987; p.269].)

In a study by Bliss and Larson (1985) two thirds of the sexual offenders reported dissociation from self before or at the time of their crime. They describe themselves as in a hynotic state. Self-hypnotic dissociative experiences can extend to amnesia, which induce an altered state allowing performance of acts which ordinarily would be repulsive or anathema. During initial offender evaluations perpretrators often speak, in a variety of ways, of an altered state.

This paper has four aims: First, to discover whether the degree of dissociation experienced by sex offenders significantly differs from dissociation scores of the general population. It is hypothesized that offenders should have significantly higher levels of dissociation. Second, the study explores whether offenders differ from those falsely accused in degree of dissociation; on the rationale that those falsely accused would report significantly less dissociative experiences than identified sex offenders. Third, it was hypothesized that offenders from one outpatient group experiencing more stress due to demographic factors (having less education, less economic power and greater unemployment) would have higher dissociation scores. Finally, because dissociation appears to decline with age in the general population (Ross, Joshi & Currie, 1990), it was hypothesized that older offenders would score lower than younger offenders.

METHOD

Measures

Bernstein and Putnam (1986) developed the Dissociative Experiences Scale (DES) to measure awareness of the degree of dissociation in a person's life. This 28-item self-report questionnaire asks subjects to rate themselves on a scale denoting frequency (0-100% of time) that they experience a number of common dissociative experiences. It yields one global score of dissociation.

Scale questions were developed using data from interviews with patients meeting DSM-III criteria for dissociative disorders (Bernstein and Putnam, 1986). Questions pertain to disturbance in awareness, memory, cognitions and feelings of depersonalization associated with such phenomena as *deja vu*. Test-retest and split-half reliability coefficients indicate that the test is reliable, while item-scale score correlation indicate good internal consistency and scale construct validity. Post-hoc comparisons (using Kruskal-Wallis tests), of eight psychiatric populations demonstrated criterion-referenced scale validity.

While the scale has been used to measure dissociation in the general population (Ross, Joshi & Currie, 1990), to date no scores have been published on the dissociative levels of identified sex offenders.

Subjects

Seventy-one men, who by self-admission met the legal definition of sex offender, comprised the experimental group. Most were court referrals although some volunteered to seek treatment for sex offending. Thirty-three (45.8%) were diagnosed as pedophiles (exclusive and non-exclusive types), the remainder 38 (54.2%) were incest offenders, exposers, voyeurs, and obscene phone callers. Forty-eight men were evaluated at a sex offender program which is part of a major midwestern university school of medicine sexuality program, while 23 were evaluated at another sex offender program which is community-based.

Only those offenders who qualified for outpatient treatment were included in the sample. To qualify, offenders needed to be of normal IQ, verbalize a desire to change their offending behavior, and admit to at least one offense. A diagnosis of severe psychopathology, such as an antisocial personality disorder, or evaluation that the person was significantly violent precluded being accepted for treatment in the outpatient settings.

In addition, 14 men falsely accused of sex offending were evaluated at the major university site. The falsely accused population was a selected group also, in that they had the money to seek extensive evaluations to eliminate reasonable doubt as to their innocence (the final decision for these cases was determined by a court of law). None of the 14 falsely accused had been arrested, tried, or convicted. The majority of the falsely accused were seeking divorce and custody of a child or children when the accusations arose.

The mean-age of all subjects was 38 years, and the range was 20 to 69 years. Seventy-five (88%) were Caucasian, the remainder being Afro-American, Native American, or of Hispanic decent. Approximately half of the participants were married at the time of the study. None of the three groups differed significantly in age, race, or marital status.

Procedure

All the participants filled in a battery of psychological and psychosexual questionnaires as part of their evaluation for sex offending treatment. The falsely accused did likewise. All subjects filled in their testing at either of the two evaluation sites involved in the study. Subjects were required to indicate their permission for their testing to be used for results on a separate signed permission form.

Once a subject had completed all the tests, the testing was returned to the testing department for scoring. The DES was then scored in accordance with the manual instructions (Bernstein and Putnam, 1986).

ANALYSIS AND RESULTS

A one-way analysis of variance was used comparing all three means, with an alpha level of .05 determined *a priori* as significant. The Newman-Keuls test was used and it was determined that if significant results were found, contrasts would be obtained. Given the exploratory nature of the study and the relative importance of a type-I versus type-II error, no adjustments were made for multiple testing.

No significant difference was found between the two outpatient sex offender groups (Table 1). They scored within the realm of the general population (Table 2). The falsely accused scored much lower than either offender group (Table 1).

Data compiled in a decade age break-down for the offenders (Table 3) indicated a declining in scores by 1% for each decade, matching Ross, Joshi & Currie, 1990 findings of reduction by age. The sample for the falsely accused was too small to report in this manner.

DISCUSSION

Because the samples of sex offenders and those falsely accused are both self-selected, these results must be interpreted with caution. In addition, the number of subjects enlisted in the study suggest that further studies replicating this one are warranted before generalizations to wider sex offender populations can be made. Nevertheless, a number of interesting conclusions can be made, based upon these results.

The first hypothesis, namely, that sex offenders would have significantly higher levels of dissociation than those reported in the general population, was not supported by this study. This may be a genuine finding. The general population was never screened for mental disorders.

Table 1. Means & medians of the 3 comparison groups

	N	Mean	Median	Probability
Pathfinder Program [community-based]	23	10.8	8.4	NS
Program in human sexuality (University based)	48	10.1	7.4	NS
Falsely Accused	14	6.5	4.1	Trend

The simplest explanation for these results is that the DES does not accurately identify the type of dissociation experienced by offenders. For example, it may be that offenders dissociate but are not sufficiently aware of the dissociation to record (at least on the DES) and so are not distinguished from the general population. If so, it can be concluded that dissociation is a term for processes not necessarily accessible by observation or testing, but known only by their consequences (Gruenewald, 1986) as regards to offenders.

Since offenders often describe the feelings of "out of touch about the behavior" and "unable to recall what happened," a neurological model called transient global amnesia could apply. This occurs with brief episodes of amnesia while a person performs simple ordinary tasks (Pincus & Tucker, 1985; Tucker & Nepe, 1988). Further, it is known that dissociative experiences are linked to childhood abuse or trauma (Chu & Dill, 1990). Since many offenders suffer from abuse it was expected this would also elevate their scores.

Table 2. General population data

	N	Mean	Median
*General population**	1,055	10.5	7.0

**Ross, Joshi & Currie Study, 1990*

Table 3. DES Scores for sex offenders by decade

Age	20-29	30-39	40-49	50-59	60-69
Mean	11.5	10.6	9.4	8.7	7.2
Median	7.5	9.8	9.0	3.8	7.0
N =	21	19	17	5	6

The DES test discriminates subjects with multiple personality disorders from other diagnostic groups and general population; it does not, however, measure degree or severity. But it can give a self-report indication of "the *felt* fugue states," although in the case of offenders this apparently was not the case.

An example of this is offenders reporting situations where they spent long periods of time (often 3-4 hours or more) engaging in seeking out a victim or in actual offending, and report loss of time reference or are unable to chronicle events due to "memory loss." One subject was a 28-year-old man convicted of exposing. He reported numerous incidents of spending 4-6 hours per day driving in his car, masturbating, and looking for women to exhibit to. He also reports frequent incidents of "losing track of time" both at work and at home. While this "memory loss" has been the source of many arguments with his spouse, his DES score was 11.4 — only 1% above general population scores.

The offender's dissociation enables him to operate in a compartmentalized way, usually outside total consciousness and sometimes outside of memory recall. It is believed that people who dissociate use this phenomena to cope with unpleasant events (Bliss, 1984; Norton, Ross, & Novotny, 1990). Because offenders' states of dissociation are limited in time and frequency, they may be under-reported on the DES. It may be that the DES is better able to distinguish multiple disorders and fugue states than other types of dissociative disorders. Individuals experiencing mild states of dissociation, such as those reported during sexual offending, may not be distinguished by the DES.

There was a *trend* for the falsely accused to score much lower than sex offenders, thus supporting the second hypothesis; however, it was not significant at the .05 level. The finding that those falsely accused scored not only lower than offenders, but much lower than the mean for the general population is interesting. Although the sample is small and hence the finding is tentative, it may suggest that the investment to present oneself as "innocent" may lead this group to present as "better than normal" or to "cover up." Replication must be done with a much larger sample.

The hypothesis that those experiencing more stress due to demographic factors of education, unemployment, etc., did not bear out. Both offending groups' mean scores were within .07% of each other.

The fourth hypothesis, that DES scales are inversely correlated with age, appears supported in this study as each decade's score was reduced by 1% for each age group. This supports other studies which have stated that dissociation lessens with age.

REFERENCES

Bernstein, E., & Putnam, F. (1986). Development, reliability, and validity of a dissociation scale. *J. of Nervous & Mental Disease, 174*(12), 727-735.

Bliss, E.L., & Larson, E.M. (1985). Sexual criminality and hypnotizability. *J. of Nervous & Mental Disease, 173*(9), 522- 526.

Bliss, E.L. (1984). A symptom profile of patients with multiple personalities, including MMPI results. *J. of Mental & Nervous Disorders 171*, 197-202.

Carlson, E., & Bernstein, E. (1991). Measuring dissociation with DES scale. Paper presented at Dissociation Workshop for Mind & Body Network, Palo Alto, CA.

Chu, J.A., & Dill, D.L. (1990). Dissociative symptoms in relation to childhood physical and sexual abuse. *Am. J. Psychiatry 147*(7), 887-892.

Cocores, J., Santa, W., & Patel, M. (1984). The Ganser syndrome: Evidence suggesting its classification as a dissociative disorder. *J. Psychiatric Med. 14*, 47-56.

Ellenberger, H.F. (1970). *The discovery of the unconscious: The history and evolution of dynamic psychiatry*. New York: Basic.

Gruenewald, D. (1986). Dissociation: Appearance and meaning. *Am. J. of Clinical Hypnosis* 29(2), 116- 122.

Hilgard, E.R. (1977). *Divided consciousness: Multiple controls in human thought and action.* New York: Wiley.

Ludwig, A.M. (1983). The psychobiological functions of dissociation. *Am. J. Clin. Hypnosis 26*, 93-99.

Nemiah, J.C. (1980). Dissociative disorders. In: A.M. Freedman, H. Kaplan (Eds.), *Comprehensive textbook of psychiatry* (3rd ed., pp. 1544-1561). Baltimore: Williams & Wilkins.

Norton, G.R., Ross, C.A., & Novotny, M.F. (1990). Factors that predict scores on the Dissociative Experiences Scale. *J. of Clinical Psychology 46*, 273-277.

Pincus, J., & Tucker, G. (1985). *Behavioral Neurology*, 3rd ed. New York: Oxford University Press.

Putnam, F.W. (1985). Dissociation as a response to extreme trauma. In: R.P. Kluft (Ed.), *The childhood antecedents of multiple personality*. Washington: American Psychiatric Press.

Rook, K.S., & Hammer, C.L. (1977). A cognitive perspective on the experience of sexual arousal. *J. of Social Issues 33*, 7-29.

Ross, C.A., Joshi, S., & Currie, R. (1990). Dissociative experiences in the general population. *American J. of Psychiatry 147*, 1547-1552.

Spiegel, D. (1984). Multiple personality as a post-traumatic stress disorder. *Psychiatr. Clin. North Am. 7*, 101- 110.

Tucker, G.J., & Neppe, V.M. (1988). Critical review and update: Neurology and psychiatry. *Gen. Hospital Psych. 10*, 24-33. @REFER = West, L.J. (1967). Dissociative reaction. In: A. D. Freedman, H.I. Kaplan (Eds.), *Comprehensive textbook of psychiatry*. (2nd ed., pp. 885-899). Baltimore: Williams & Wilkins.

AUTHORS' NOTES

S. Margretta Dwyer, MA, is coordinator of the sex offender treatment program at the Program in Human Sexuality and psychologist and instructor, Department of Family Practice and Community Health, Medical School, University of Minnesota.

B. R. Simon Rosser, PhD, is an assistant professor at the Program in Human Sexuality at the University of Minnesota.

Steven Sawyer, LICSW, is at Project Pathfinder, St. Paul, MN.

Correspondence should be addressed to the first author at the Program in Human Sexuality, Department of Family Practice and Community Health, 1300 South 2nd Street, Suite 180, Minneapolis, MN 55454.

SEX OFFENDER TREATMENT: PSYCHOLOGICAL AND MEDICAL APPROACHES. Pp. 59-74.

□ MEASUREMENT & APPRAISAL

The Utility of the MMPI-2 with Pedophiles

Jim Mann
Federal Correctional Institution, Butner, N.C.

Walter Stenning
Texas A&M University

Christopher Borman
University of Texas at San Antonio

ABSTRACT The Minnesota Multiphasic Personality Inventory (MMPI) has been revised and restandardized on new national norms. One of the criticisms of the MMPI-2 is that the restandardization sample was more highly educated and of a higher socio-economic status (SES) than the average adult population (Adler, 1990). This criticism calls into question the utility of the MMPI-2 with incarcerated sex offenders who are often high school drop outs and come from lower SES levels. Furthermore, there is a question of the similarity of MMPI-2 results across pedophile samples composed of different educational and social backgrounds. It is unclear if past MMPI results with incarcerated sex offenders will generalize to MMPI-2 interpretations. The present study examined MMPI-2 profiles of incarcerated pedophiles in three types of sex offender treatment programs (SOTP) — state prison (n = 60), federal prison (n = 24), and military confinement facility (n = 25) — each offering a different educational and social composition. The overall mean MMPI-2 profile for the combined groups presented an unelevated profile with a high point on Scale 4 (T63). The two most common elevated profiles (greater than T64) were spike 4 and spike 0, but the total of these profiles included only 16.51 percent (n = 18) of the subjects. No two-point code types had a frequency greater than four. Multivariate statistics revealed that the three SOTP profiles were significantly different. Profiles broken down by scales indicated significant differences on scales K, 1, and 5. These results are discussed in light of previous MMPI research with pedophiles.

Across the nation sex offender treatment programs are developing in order to reduce the injury of child sexual abuse by preventing the perpetrator from re-offending (Pallone, 1990). A key element of sex offender treatment programs is reliable assessment. Identifying the social, sexual, and personality characteristics of sex offenders enables the clinician to develop treatment plans that are general enough to fit a specific class of sex offender while flexible enough to intervene on an individual basis. Without adequate assessment of sex offenders, it is unlikely that effective treatment programs can be developed (Earls & Quinsey, 1985; Korchin & Schuldberg, 1981).

Effective assessment of pedophiles should cover a number of areas including psychopathology, personality characteristics, attitudes and beliefs, interpersonal style, coping strategies, neuropsychological deficients, psychosexual development, and sexual arousal patterns (Barbaree, 1991; Langevin, 1991; Mayer, 1988; Salter, 1988). The Minnesota Multiphasic Personality Inventory (MMPI) has been a widely used instrument to assess psychopathology and personality characteristics in pedophiles (Hall, Maiuro, & Vitaliano, 1986; Lanyon, 1968; Panton, 1979). Recently, the MMPI has been revised with new norms and the addition of new or reworded items (Butcher, Dahlstrom, Graham, Tellegen, & Kaemmer, 1989). This revised version, MMPI-2, has been supported by Butcher et al. as an improved test which will yield more accurate clinical interpretations of clients without losing the richness of the original version. Others, however, have critiqued the MMPI-2 more negatively stating that this revised test has lost much of the flavor of the original version and therefore should be used with caution (Adler, 1990). Because of the frequent use of the MMPI with pedophiles, its replacement by the MMPI-2 should be carefully investigated.

In revising the MMPI, the normative base was enlarged from a generally rural Minnesota sample to a large, nation-wide sample designed to approximate the 1980 census. In addition, items have been deleted or reworded, new items were added to facilitate the construction of fifteen new content scales measuring specific personality characteristics and psychiatric symptoms, and linear T-scores have been replaced by uniform T-scores (Butcher, 1990). The problem facing clinicians using the MMPI- 2 is that it is unclear how these changes will effect the responses and profiles of special populations such as sex offenders. The Pedophilia (Pe) scale serves as an example of how the MMPI-2 revisions have impacted some of the past MMPI research with pedophiles. As an early attempt to assess pedophilia, Toobert, Bartelme, and Jones (1959) empirically identified MMPI items which discriminated pedophiles from nonpedophiles in a prison population. These items became the Pe scale. Because four of the twenty-four Pe items (or about 17% of the scale) were dropped from the MMPI-2, the reliability and validity of the scale is called into question.

One of the criticisms of the MMPI-2 is that its new normative base was more educated and from a higher socio-economic status (SES) than the average adult population presented in the 1980 census (Adler, 1990). Because many incarcerated pedophiles are poorly educated and come from lower SES backgrounds, it is unclear how well the MMPI-2 norms will generalize to this population. Likewise, the educational and SES level of pedophiles differ across SOTPS. One cannot assume that there is a single MMPI-2 profile characteristic of most pedophiles (Hall, Maiuro, Vitaliano, & Proctor, 1986). Without further research we cannot be certain how to interpret MMPI-2 profile elevations (Greene, 1989). While the MMPI has been one of the commonly used assessment instruments with sex offenders in the past, there is no guarantee that the MMPI-2 profiles of sex offenders will be consistent with past research and clinical observations. To answer these questions, a MMPI-2 normative base for sex offenders needs to be developed. This normative base will serve as a point of reference by which clinicians can compare their clients who are referred for pedophilia.

The purpose of this study was to examine the utility of the revised MMPI with incarcerated pedophiles by (1) providing a small normative base or clinical point of reference, (2) comparing these results with past MMPI research, and (3) investigating the degree of similarity/dissimilarity among MMPI-2 profiles of pedophiles in different SOTPS.

METHODOLOGY

Subjects

Inmates from the Sex Offender Treatment Program (SOTP) of the Texas state prison system (n = 60), Federal Bureau of Prisons (n = 24), and a military confinement center (n = 25) served as subjects (total n = 109). All of the subjects were male pedophiles. The state and federal prison subjects voluntarily entered the SOTP, while the military subjects were mandated to enter the SOTP as a part of their adjudication.

Procedures

Upon entering their respective SOTP, each inmate was administered the MMPI-2. Demographic data consisting of social history and offense information was obtained from prison records and pre-sentencing reports. One of the variables of interest was socio-economic status (SES). In order to quantify SES, the Occupational Status Scores (Nam & Powers, 1983) that most closely corresponded with the subject's primary occupation were used. Occupational status scores range from 01 (farm laborers) to 99 (physicians). The occupational status score for military enlisted servicemen was 38 which was assigned to all of the subjects in the military SOTP sample.

To explore differences in demographic characteristics among the SOTP samples, nominal data (race, marital status, history of drug and alcohol abuse, prior criminal convictions, victims' sex and relationship to offender) were analyzed by Pearson Chi-Squares. Analysis of variance was performed on the interval demographic data such as age, education, occupational status, and victim's age.

To see if the MMPI-2 profiles of the SOTP samples were dissimilar, multivariate analysis of variance (MANOVA) was used. Univariate statistics were employed to analyze differences among the clinical scales across the three SOTP groups. To provide clinical utility and comparison with previous MMPI studies, raw scores were converted to K-corrected T-scores using the conversion table in the MMPI-2 manual (Butcher et al., 1989, Table A-1). The frequency of spike and two-point code-types were examined to explore the possibility of profile configuration patterns.

RESULTS

Demographic Characteristics

The subjects in this study provided a cross-section of incarcerated pedophiles participating in SOTPS. Table 1 provides demographic information about the three SOTP samples. Statistical differences among the SOTP samples were found in several demographic variables. The state SOTP was primarily composed of lower educated and low socio-economic status (SES) subjects with a mean education level of 10.37 years and a mean occupational status score of 29.87. Most of the state SOTP subjects were from unskilled and skilled occupational backgrounds such as general laborers and mechanics. These subjects had a higher frequency of prior criminal records for crimes other than sex offenses (66.33%) than the other two SOTP samples.

In comparison the federal prison SOTP subjects were the most educated ($M = 13.29$) and had the highest occupational status scores ($M = 49.13$). The federal SOTP subjects represented a cross section of society's occupations by containing laborers, truck drivers, teachers, managers, and doctoral level professionals. They had the highest mean age ($M = 41.29$) of the three SOTP samples and all but one were White males. The federal subjects appeared more predatory. They had higher incidents of prior sex offense convictions and sought victims outside the family more often than subjects in the other two SOTPS.

The military SOTP sample fell in between the other two SOTP samples with a high school education ($M = 12.08$) and a similar occupational background with the military ($M = 38$). All of the military SOTP subjects were enlisted men ranging in rank from E-3 to E-6 (mode = E-6). The military subjects had the lowest number of prior convictions and the highest incidence of alcohol related problems. Subjects in the military and state SOTPS were similar in that their victims were predominately female and fairly equally divided between incest and nonincest cases.

TABLE 1
Demographics of SOTP Samples

Variable	State	Federal	Military	F	p
Mean Age (SD)	35.88 (9.30)	41.29 (12.14)	33.32 (7.69)	4.42	0.01
Mean Education (SD)	10.37 (2.29)	13.29 (3.10)	12.08 (1.32)	15.00	<0.01
Mean Occupation Status Score (SD)	29.87 (18.73)	49.13 (29.89)	38.00 (0.00)	8.34	<0.01
Mean Age of Victim	9.47	9.96	9.40	0.23	0.80

Variable	State	Federal	Military	ChiSq	p
Percent White	53.33	95.83	72.00	24.05	<0.01
Percent Married	55.00	41.67	56.00	7.30	0.51
Percent with Prior Convictions (nonsex)	66.33	29.17	32.00	15.90	<0.01
Percent with Prior Sex Offenses	15.00	62.50	0.00	33.57	<0.01
Percent with History of Drug Abuse	15.00	4.17	24.00	3.86	0.15
Percent Alcoholic	15.00	12.50	48.00	12.87	<0.01
Victim Preference: Percent				34.48	<0.01
Female	90.00	33.33	88.00		
Male	8.33	50.00	12.00		
Both	1.67	16.67	0.00		
Targeted Victims: Percent				20.27	<0.01
Within Family	56.67	12.50	48.00		
Outside Family	40.00	58.33	44.00		
Both	3.33	29.17	8.00		

Statistical Analysis of the MMPI-2 Scales

In order to provide generalized normative information about the MMPI-2 profiles of incarcerated pedophiles, the validity and clinical scores of the three SOTP samples were combined. The K-corrected T score means and standard deviations of the validity and clinical scales of the three SOTPS and the combined sample are presented in Table 2. If plotted the combined SOTP sample would show an unelevated clinical profile with Scale 4 (T63) as the highest point and a low point on Scale 5 (T48). The remaining scales ranged from T51 to T58. Of the validity scales the L Scale was most elevated (T58) while the K Scale was lowest (T51).

MANOVA procedures indicated that the MMPI-2 profiles of the three SOTP samples were not statistically alike. When clinical and validity scales were examined separately through analysis of variances, differences were found in scales K, 1, and 5.

Graham (1977) has pointed out the interpretative usefulness of examining code types with the MMPI. A code type is a profile configuration with one or more scales clinically elevated. Butcher et al. (1989) state that scores equal to or greater than T65 denote clinical significance in the MMPI-2. Therefore, the two highest K-corrected clinical scales above T64 are listed as two-point code types in this study. Likewise, a profile with a single clinical scale exceeding T64 is considered a clinically significant spike. Frequencies and percentages of the most repeated clinical scale two-point code types and spikes are listed in Table 3. A wide variety of profile configurations were obtained with none standing out clearly as predominate. No scale elevations above T65 were noted on 27.52% (n = 30) of the profiles while a single elevation (spike) was present in 28.44% (n = 31) of the profiles. The remaining profiles recorded at least two scales at or above T65. The most frequent profiles were spike 4 and spike 0. However, the total for these profiles amounted to only 16.51% (n = 18) of the subjects. Of the clinically elevated two-point code types, four code types (24/42, 20/02, 34/43, and 40/04) accounted for 14.68% of the profiles, each with a frequency of four. The remaining code types had a frequency of three or less. Although no code type was more predominate than another, Scale 4 was widely represented as one of the elevated scales.

TABLE 2
MMPI-2 Means and Standard Deviations of the SOTP Samples

MMPI-2 Scale	State Mean (SD)	Federal Mean (SD)	Military Mean (SD)	F Mean (SD)	p	Combined Mean (SD)
L	59.58 (11.94)	53.54 (12.19)	59.28 (11.00)	2.39	0.10	58.18 (11.94)
F	55.07 (12.08)	53.71 (9.77)	51.96 (10.96)	0.67	0.51	54.06 (11.33)
K	47.95 (10.66)	55.08 (9.33)	54.08 (11.30)	5.39	0.01	50.93 (10.95)
1	59.02 (13.02)	54.79 (12.53)	51.28 (10.40)	3.69	0.03	56.31 (12.67)
2	57.93 (11.69)	56.04 (9.40)	54.20 (11.06)	1.05	0.35	56.66 (11.10)
3	52.45 (12.43)	55.92 (11.73)	51.92 (10.11)	0.90	0.41	53.09 (11.78)
4	61.33 (10.38)	64.17 (10.87)	64.16 (10.30)	0.99	0.38	62.61 (10.46)
5	45.63 (8.48)	57.00 (10.73)	46.56 (10.53)	12.87	<0.01	48.45 (10.48)
6	54.92 (13.24)	58.88 (10.56)	53.40 (10.57)	1.37	0.26	55.44 (12.17)
7	54.68 (12.07)	56.25 (7.92)	51.40 (8.35)	1.40	0.25	54.28 (10.55)
8	57.43 (14.43)	59.79 (10.20)	55.36 (10.40)	0.74	0.48	57.48 (12.73)
9	52.83 (11.87)	46.96 (8.05)	51.72 (8.14)	2.78	0.07	51.28 (10.54)
0	56.50 (11.51)	54.79 (10.96)	54.40 (12.03)	0.38	0.67	55.64 (11.45)

TABLE 3

Frequency of K-Corrected Spike
and Two-Point Code Type Profiles

Profile Code Type	Frequency	Percent of Total
Unelevated	30	27.52
Spike 1	5	4.59
Spike 4	11	10.09
Spike 0	7	6.42
20/02	4	3.67
24/42	4	3.67
34/43	4	3.67
40/04	4	3.67

NOTE: Only frequencies greater than three are reported.

DISCUSSION

Because of revisions and restandardization, it is uncertain how well past MMPI research can be applied to MMPI-2 cases. The primary purpose of this study was to establish the utility of the revised MMPI with incarcerated pedophiles by providing a normative base from a cross section of incarcerated pedophiles.

Comparing Results With Past MMPI Research

Examination of the combined SOTP sample across MMPI-2 K-corrected clinical scales revealed that the code types varied widely. Scales 4, 0, and 1 were the most frequent scales involved in spike profiles and no two-point code types had a frequency greater than four. Furthermore, there was a high frequency of unelevated profiles.

While these results share some similarities with past MMPI research with pedophiles, there are some noteworthy differences as well.

The demographic diversity and profile variability of the SOTP samples support the conclusions of Hall, Maiuro, Vitaliano, and Proctor (1986) that pedophiles are as different as they are alike. Past research with pedophiles report no consistent MMPI profile. Likewise, in this study there were a wide variety of profiles within each SOTP sample ranging from unelevated to floating profile configurations.

An elevated Scale 4 with other scales varying widely has been the most consistent finding across studies with pedophiles (Armentrout & Hauer, 1978; Duthie & McIvor, 1990; Erickson, Luxenberg, Walbek, & Seely, 1987; Kirkland & Bauers, 1982; Panton, 1979; Scott & Stone, 1986). The results of this study tend to support these past observations with the MMPI on Scale 4. A moderately elevated Scale 4 suggests a mildly non-conforming individual who may get into trouble through periodic impulsive behavior and occasional poor social judgment (Butcher, 1990; Lachar, 1974). As Scale 4 elevations increase, interpersonal problems, conflicts with authority, and social alienation also are likely to increase (Graham, 1977).

The primary difference between past MMPI research and the MMPI-2 results in this study was the frequency of unelevated profiles and overall lower elevations in T-scores. However, Butcher et al. (1989) state that MMPI-2 profiles in general have been found to be lower as a result of the restandardization process. Another MMPI-2 finding in the SOTP profiles not often discussed in past MMPI research with pedophiles is the somewhat frequent elevations on scales 0 and 1. Whether these findings are a result of restandardizing the MMPI or an artifact of these samples will need further investigation. Elevations on Scale 0 are associated with social introversion, submissiveness, social inadequacy, and discomfort around members of the opposite sex (Butcher, 1982; Graham, 1977; Greene, 1980). An elevated Scale 0 supports an etiological view of pedophilia suggesting that male pedophiles have difficulty relating to adult females thereby blocking appropriate sexual outlets (Araji & Finkelhor, 1986). Likewise, limited social skills have been observed in pedophiles by several clinicians and researchers (Langevin, Paitich, Freeman, Mann, & Handy, 1978; Overholser & Beck, 1986; Segal & Marshall, 1985). Groth, Hobson & Gary (1982) suggested that shyness and social inadequacy force some pedophiles to withdraw from adult relationships and seek children with whom to gratify their social and sexual needs.

Etiological theory and clinical observations suggest that Scale 0 should be elevated in many pedophiles. In the combined SOTP sample of this study, Scale 0 was a frequent elevation. Nevertheless, only 18.39% (n = 20) of the combined SOTP sample had Scale 0 elevated in a spike or two-point code type.

Within the combined sample 12.84% (n = 14) of the subjects had Scale 1 elevated in a spike or two-point code type. Scale 1 measures the degree of undue concern about one's health. Moderate elevations may suggest a tendency to express anxiety in the form of physical complaints (Graham, 1977; Reilley & Reilley, 1991). Peters (1976) found that pedophiles reported an unusually large number of physical complaints and general health concerns on the somatic scale of the Cornell Medical Index. Peters concluded that pedophiles internalize their emotional problems which may later manifest themselves as somatic problems. Pedophiles erect a number of defenses to avoid dealing with their sexual deviancy (Groth, Hobson, & Gary, 1982). Somatization may be a further defense mechanism which allows them to avoid facing their sexual deviancy.

Comparing MMPI-2 Profiles Across SOTP Samples

In spite of the demographic differences among the three SOTP samples, the basic configuration of the MMPI-2 profiles of each SOTP sample was similar in that elevations were generally within average limits and there was a moderate rise on Scale 4. In the state and military SOTP profiles, the L Scale rose moderately (T59) and Scale 5 dipped below T50. This profile is somewhat similar to the MMPI profile found in pedophiles by Smith, Monastersky, and Deisher (1987) which was characterized by an elevated L Scale and a depressed Scale 5. Smith and his colleagues described these pedophiles as naively denying difficulties and projecting a hypermasculine identification which served as an overcompensation for their sexual behavior with children. However, socio-cultural factors may influence a low Scale 5 score accounting for the hypermasculine identification. Graham (1977) noted that Scale 5 in the MMPI tended to be lower in individuals with less education or from lower SES backgrounds. Butcher (1990) found the same trend with the MMPI-2. The state and military SOTP subjects averaged the lowest Scale 5 scores as well as the lowest education and occupational status scores. In contrast, the federal SOTP, with the highest mean education and occupational status scores, resulted in a significantly higher Scale 5 (T57). This observation suggests that Scale 5 of the MMPI-2 continues to be influenced by education and/or SES in pedophiles.

In addition to education and SES factors, sexual orientation has been associated with clinically significant elevations (greater than T64) in Scale 5, especially when accompanied with an elevation on Scale 4. Duthie & McIvor (1990) and Singer (1970) found that the 45/54 code type was frequently present in homosexual pedophiles. It could be hypothesized that the rise on Scale 5 in the federal sample was due to the high frequency of federal subjects having homosexual or bisexual pedophilia preferences. However, an examination of the two-point code types of the federal SOTP subjects revealed no 45/54 code types. Only four subjects in the state and military SOTPS had this code type, but in each profile there were multiple elevations with at least one other scale more predominately elevated than Scale 4 or Scale 5.

Elevations on Scale 1 were most frequent in the state SOTP sample; all of the spike 1 profiles were in this sample. Also, the state SOTP sample had the highest mean elevation on the L Scale and the lowest education and SES levels. While street-wise, the state SOTP subjects were often psychologically naive and had difficulty expressing themselves and discussing their problems in group therapy. Their naivety and verbal difficulties may have resulted in somatization as a viable defense mechanism.

Another distinction of the state SOTP sample was that it had a moderate elevation on the L Scale (T60) and a considerably lower score on the K Scale (T48). Elevations on the L Scale suggest a naive form of defensiveness in which the subject attempts to make a positive impression by not endorsing obvious weaknesses that most individuals will admit (Butcher, 1990; Graham, 1977). Defensiveness and impression management are common in pedophiles (Lanyon & Lutz, 1984). However, low K Scale scores in lower educated/lower SES subjects, such as the state SOTP subjects, may be indicative of self-criticism (Lachar, 1974). Therefore, item endorsement may be a process of balancing the bad with the good in order to not appear too sick, but sick enough to volunteer for treatment. Upon examining the elevation on Scale 1 (T59) in the state SOTP sample, it appears that the subjects may have been more willing to admit to health related concerns rather than psychological problems in order to achieve that balance.

Treatment Planning Considerations

The conclusions of past MMPI research with pedophiles appear to be generalizable to MMPI-2 profile interpretations if one remembers to interpret lower scores as clinically significant. While the MMPI-2 can identify problems in general psychopathology, it does not offer much insight into the nature of his/her sexual deviancy. It is recommended that the MMPI-2 be used to assess possible strengths and weaknesses that could impact the treatment process. High levels of depression, anxiety, poor treatment motivation, and social alienation are examples of symptoms that can be uncovered with the MMPI-2 and dealt with specifically as part of the sex offender treatment process. Interpreting the MMPI-2 in light of previous MMPI research may suggest further treatment considerations which focus on inappropriate coping skills or interpersonal relationships that influence the pedophile's deviant behavior. For example, elevations on Scale 0 may suggest a feeling of heterosexual inadequacy in adult relationships (Segal & Marshall, 1985). When Scale 1 is elevated, examination of problems relating to internalization of unpleasant feelings may be a concern.

Defensiveness needs to be assessed in light of what problems the pedophile is willing to initially admit. There is likely to be a tendency in pedophiles to selectively endorse some problem areas while not endorsing others. This may be especially true in profiles with an elevated Scale L and low Scale K. As with the MMPI, the MMPI-2 validity scales are influenced by education and social status. Butcher (1990) suggested interpreting defensiveness with the MMPI-2 K Scale only if it is greater than T70 in well educated/high SES subjects. Likewise, elevations in Scale 5 tend to be associated with increases in education and SES.

As a final caution one needs to remember that pedophiles represent a variety of demographic, personality, and motivational variables. Many of these variables are addressed by the MMPI-2 scales while others are not. In spite of the similarities among the averaged profiles within this study, there were subtle differences as well. No one MMPI-2 profile fits the majority of pedophiles.

Recommendations for Future Research

This study has been exploratory in nature in order to examine the type of MMPI-2 profiles generated by incarcerated pedophiles. Due to the small sample size of the separate SOTPS, further comparisons with other samples of pedophiles are needed. Out-patient pedophiles should be examined with the MMPI-2 to exclude the effects of incarceration. The potential MMPI-2 differences between subjects who volunteer for sex offender treatment versus those who are mandated into treatment or refuse treatment should be addressed as well. Furthermore, the effects of education and socio-economic levels on MMPI-2 profiles require further investigation with pedophiles.

CONCLUSIONS

The results of this study suggest that there is no characteristic MMPI-2 profile with which to diagnose pedophilia. However, these results, as well the results of past MMPI studies with pedophiles, demonstrate a wide range of psychological problems. At this time the best use of the MMPI-2 with pedophiles is in treatment planning. The utility of the MMPI-2 with incarcerated pedophiles will ultimately be measured in its ability to assist in treatment which, in turn, can be measured in lower recidivism rates.

REFERENCES

Adler, T. (1990, April). Does the "new" MMPI beat the "classic"? *APA Monitor, 21*, 18-19.

Araji, S., & Finkelhor, D. (1986). Abusers: A review of the research. In D. Finkelhor (Ed.), *A source book on child sexual abuse* (pp. 89-118). Beverly Hills: Sage.

Armentrout, J.A., & Hauer, A.L. (1978). MMPI's of rapists of adults, rapists of children, and non-rapist sex offenders. *Journal of Clinical Psychology, 34*, 330-332.

Barbaree, H. (1991, November). A multi-dimensional assessment of risk for re-offense in sexual offenders: Clinical applications. Paper presented at annual conference of the Association for the Treatment of Sexual Abusers, Ft. Worth.

Butcher, J.N. (1990). *The MMPI-2 in psychological treatment.* New York: Oxford University Press.

Butcher, J.N., Dahlstrom, W.G., Graham, J.R., Tellegen, A., & Kaemmer, B. (1989). *MMPI-2: Manual for administration and scoring.* Minneapolis, MN: University of Minnesota Press.

Duthie, B., & McIvor, D.L. (1990). A new system for cluster- coding child molester MMPI profile types. *Criminal Justice and Behavior, 17,* 199-214.

Earls, C.M., & Quinsey, V.L. (1985). What is to be done? Future research on the assessment and behavioral treatment of sex offenders. *Behavioral Sciences and the Law, 3,* 377-390.

Erickson, W.D., Luxenberg, M.G., Walbek, N.H., & Seely, R.K. (1987). Frequency of MMPI two-point code types among sex offenders. *Journal of Consulting and Clinical Psychology, 55,* 566-570.

Graham, J.R. (1977). *The MMPI: A practical guide.* New York: Oxford University Press.

Greene, R. (1989, October). *Introducing the MMPI- 2.*Workshop sponsored by Belle Park Hospital, Houston.

Groth, A.N., Hobson, W.F., & Gary, T.S. (1982). The child molester: Clinical observations. *Social Work and Child Sexual Abuse, 1,* 129-144.

Hall, G.C., Maiuro, R.D., Vitaliano, P.P., & Proctor, W.C. (1986). The utility of the MMPI with men who have sexually assaulted children. *Journal of Consulting & Clinical Psychology, 54,* 493-496.

Kirkland, K.D., & Bauers, C.A. (1982). MMPI traits of incestuous fathers. *Journal of Consulting and Clinical Psychology, 38,* 645-649.

Korchin, S.J., & Schuldberg, D. (1981). The future of clinical assessment. *American Psychologist, 36,* 1147-1158.

Lachar, D. (1974). *The MMPI: Clinical assessment and automated interpretation.* Los Angeles: Western Psychological Services.

Langevin, R. (1991, November). A complete assessment package for the sex offender. Paper presented at the annual conference of the Association for the Treatment of Sexual Abusers, Ft. Worth, TX.

Langevin, R., Paitich, D. Freeman, R., Mann, K., & Handy, L. (1978). Personality characteristics and sexual anomalies in males. *Canadian Journal of Behavioral Science, 10,* 222-238.

Lanyon, R.I. (1968). *MMPI: A handbook of MMPI group profiles.* Minneapolis, MN: Land Press.

Lanyon, R.I., & Lutz, R.W. (1984). MMPI discrimination of defensive and nondefensive felony sex offenders. *Journal of Consulting & Clinical Psychology, 52,* 841-843.

Mayer, A. (1988). *Sex offenders: Approaches to understanding and management.* Holmes Beach, FL: Learning Publications.

Overholser, J.C., & Beck, S. (1986). Multimethod assessment of rapists, child molesters, and three control groups on behavioral and psychological measures. *Journal of Consulting & Clinical Psychology, 54,* 682-687.

Pallone, N.J. (1990). *Rehabilitating Criminal Sexual Psychopaths: Legislative Mandates, Clinical Quandaries.* New Brunswick, NJ: Transaction Books.

Panton, J.H. (1979). MMPI profile configurations associated with incestuous and non-incestuous child molesters. *Psychological Reports, 45*, 335-338.

Peters, S.D. (1988). Child sexual abuse and later psychological problems. In G.E. Wyatt & G.J. Powell (Eds.), *Lasting effects of child sexual abuse* (pp. 101-118). Newbury Park, CA: Sage.

Reilley, R.R., & Reilley, B.A. (1991). *MMPI-2: Tutorial workbook.* Austin, Texas: Pro-ed.

Salter, A.C. (1988). *Treating child sex offenders and victims.* Beverly Hills: Sage.

Scott, R.L., & Stone, D.A. (1986). MMPI profile constellations in incest families. *Journal of Consulting & Clinical Psychology, 54*, 364-368.

Segal, Z.V., & Marshall, W.L. (1985). Heterosexual social skills in a population of rapists and child molesters. *Journal of Consulting & Clinical Psychology, 53*, 55-63.

Singer, M. (1970). Comparison or indicators of homosexuality on the MMPI. *Journal of Consulting & Clinical Psychology, 34*, 15-18.

Smith, W.R., Monastersky, C., & Deisher, R.M. (1987). MMPI-based personality types among juvenile sexual offenders. *Journal of Clinical Psychology, 43*, 422-430.

Toobert, S., Bartelme, K., & Jones, E. (1959). Some factors related to pedophilia. *International Journal of Social Psychiatry, 4*, 272-279.

AUTHORS' NOTES

Jim Mann, PhD, is at the Federal Correctional Institution Sex Offender Treatment Program, P.O. Box 1000, Butner, NC 27509.

Walter Stenning, PhD, is at Texas A&M University.

Christopher Borman, EdD, is at the University of Texas at San Antonio.

The authors express appreciation to Judy O'Brien of the Texas Department of Corrections and Brad Burg of the Charleston Navy Brig and their staffs for their support in the data collection process.

Correspondence should be addressed to the first author.

SEX OFFENDER TREATMENT: PSYCHOLOGICAL AND MEDICAL APPROACHES. Pp. 75-88.

☐ CLINICAL PROCESSES: PHARMACOTHERAPY & PSYCHOTHERAPY

An Exploratory Study of the Role of Psychotropic Medications in the Treatment of Sex Offenders

Eli Coleman
University of Minnesota

John Cesnik, M.D.
University of Minnesota

Anne-Marie Moore
University of Minnesota

S. Margretta Dwyer
University of Minnesota

ABSTRACT Sixteen patients who had been treated with psychotherapy and pharmacotherapy for sex offenses in an outpatient clinic for sex offenders from 1988 to 1991 were contacted to participate in a retrospective study of their treatment. These subjects had been part of an outpatient treatment program for sex offenders and had either been arrested and convicted of sexual offenses or had been engaging in illegal behavior involving a paraphilia (pedophilia, exhibitionism, voyeurism, and obscene phone calls). During the course of their treatment, they had been referred to one of our physicians for evaluation for pharmacotherapy because of a lack of response to psychological treatment, intense and recurrent sexual obsessions, difficulty in controlling their paraphilic urges, and concomitant and unremitting symptoms of anxiety and depression. Thirteen patients agreed to participate in the study and were administered the Hamilton Anxiety and Depression Scales, the Beck Depression Inventory, and the Yale-Brown Obsessive-Compulsive Scale. The patients were also asked to respond to a semi-structured interview. There was a significant reduction in scores on all measures. Generally we found a reduction in anxiety and depression, a greater ability to engage in the process of psychotherapy, a decrease in paraphilic obsessions, an increased control over paraphilic compulsive sexual behavior, a reduction in other non-paraphilic compulsive sexual behavior, a reduction in non-sexual obsessive-compulsive behaviors, an increased understanding of their cycle of compulsive sexual behavior and improved concentration, memory, and other cognitive processes.

This study was designed to explore new applications of some psychotropic medications in the treatment of sex offenders. While antiandrogren therapy (medroxyprogesterone and cyproterone acetate) has to date been recognized as the most effective pharmacotherapy with paraphiliacs—especially in treating sex offenders (Cooper, 1986), we have been interested in the effectiveness of some other medications which might prove to be as effective in controlling sexual obsessions and compulsions as well as treating underlying psychiatric disorders. This study confirms a small but growing case report literature which suggests that a variety of serotonergic antidepressants might be effective in treating paraphilias (Pearson, 1990; Kafka and Coleman, 1991; and Kafka, 1991).

John Money (1986) describes antiandrogens as the "erotic tranquilizers" which have a direct effect on the erotosexual pathways in the limbic brain. While there are many different pathogenic pathways that result in a paraphilia, we have hypothesized that, in many cases, the obsessive and compulsive nature of the paraphilias may be best characterized as an anxiety disorder (Coleman, 1990; 1991). A paraphiliac's compulsive sexual behavior is driven by anxiety-reduction mechanisms. Many of these patients meet the *Diagnostic and Statistical Manual of Mental Disorders* of the American Psychiatric Association (DSM-III-R) criteria for generalized anxiety disorder or dysthymia. We further hypothesize that such anxiety disorders may be generated by childhood trauma such as abuse or a sexually restrictive environment.

Our hypotheses stem from the distinct similarity between obsessive compulsive disorders and the paraphilias. While paraphilias are specifically excluded in DSM-III-R classification from obsessive compulsive disorder or the impulse control disorders, there has been recent speculation that obsessive-compulsive disorders may include the impulse control disorders and the paraphilias. Rapoport (1989) has argued that trichotillomania (compulsive hair-pulling) is better understood as an obsessive-compulsive disorder (OCD) rather than as an impulse control disorder, as it is currently classified. She has effectively treated individuals with trichotillomania with the serotonergic antidepressant *clomipramine*, which has been also found to be effective in treating obsessive-compulsive disorders (Swedo, Leonard, Rapoport, Lenane, Goldberger and Cheslow, 1989). Rapoport (1989) has stated, "Perhaps the new biology of OCD will one day lead to a reclassification of some other disparate behaviors under a broader category of compulsive syndromes." Other experts in OCD research agree. Jenike (1989) has stated, "A number of other disorders may be related to obsessive-compulsive disorder, among them bowel and urinary obsessions, eating disorders, compulsive gambling, compulsive sexual behaviors, body dysmorphic syndrome, and monosymptomatic hypochrondiasis."

The obsessive-compulsive model has lead us to a clearer understanding of compulsive sexual behavior (CSB) and has suggested treatment methods, including certain pharmacotherapies. In 1988, we successfully treated a case of autoerotic asphyxia with lithium carbonate (Cesnik and Coleman, 1989). We demonstrated prompt interruption in compulsive autoerotic asphyxiation following initiation of lithium carbonate treatment at a relatively low dose (600 mg/day). In addition, the comorbid dysthymic and avoidant personality disorder greatly improved. Why lithium carbonate? Lithium enhances presynaptic serotonergic functioning. Serotonergic medications have been found to effectively treat obsessive-compulsive disorder. Lithium was being used in a number of different centers to treat a variety of non-affective disorders which had similar symptomatology such as: aggressive conduct disorder, alcoholism, eating disorder, and post-traumatic stress disorder (van der Kolk, 1986). We were impressed by the fact that lithium was not only able to control obsessive thoughts and compulsive behaviors, but to improve symptoms of anxiety and depression.

Because of fluoxetine's selective serotonergic activity, we also began to treat a number of patients with this medication. Fluoxetine works by inhibiting serotonin reuptake. It has been reported to be effective in treating individuals with generalized anxiety disorder, social phobia, dysthymia, eating disorder, and obsessive-compulsive disorder and has become the leading anti-depressant medication used in the United States.

We quickly found fluoxetine to be as effective in treating CSB as lithium carbonate. Beginning in 1988, we began treating psychosexual disorders with comorbid obsessive-compulsive disorder with lithium carbonate and fluoxetine. In particular, we focused on patients with paraphilic and nonparaphilic compulsive sexual behavior. We also reported on eliminating self-mutilating, obsessive and compulsive behavior in two cases of extreme gender dysphoria (Coleman and Cesnik, 1990). We have been impressed with the anxiolytic and antidepressant properties of these medications and with their ability to reduce obsessions and compulsions.

Many paraphiliacs and nonparaphilics with compulsive sexual behavior report anxiety symptoms originating in their childhood or adolescence. These anxiety symptoms may be associated with histories of childhood trauma, including abuse and restrictive sexual environments (Anderson and Coleman, 1991). We began to speculate that these traumatic experiences were amplified by an underlying or evolving anxiety disorder. In anxiety-driven paraphilias, their obsessive thoughts and compulsive drives were "hard wired" in the pathways of the brain. This helped explain the resistance of their pathology to psychotherapy. We began using serotonergic medications with individuals with paraphilic CSB, not only to help interrupt their cycle of obsessive-compulsive behavior, but also to reduce symptoms of anxiety and depression which interfered with their ability to engage in therapy. We found that the combination of pharmacotherapy and psychotherapy was more successful than therapy alone.

After several years of utilizing serotonergic medications, we were troubled by a few patients' lack of progress in therapy and their general cognitive dysfunctions. In one case, we conducted an extremely thorough neurological examination, including EEG and SPECT. Findings were negative. However, after the patient experienced continued difficulties, we decided to add an anti-epileptic to his pharmacotherapy regimen. In another patient with similar symptomatology, we decided to try an anti-epileptic also.

Through a systematic retrospective analysis, this study was designed to test our hypothesis that this combination of psychotherapy and pharmacotherapy was effective in treating a group of sex offenders with obsessive and compulsive sexual behavior.

METHOD

Subjects

Sixteen patients who had been treated or were being treated with psychotherapy and pharmacotherapy for sex offenses in an outpatient clinic for sex offenders from 1988 to 1991 were contacted to participate in a retrospective study of their treatment. Thirteen patients agreed to participate in this study. Nine of the subjects had offended against children and were diagnosed as pedophiles. All except one of the pedophiles had been arrested for their offending behavior. Two of the subjects were diagnosed as exhibitionists, although neither of these subjects had been arrested for their paraphilic behavior. One subject had been arrested for voyeurism. The last subject had been arrested for criminal sexual assault with an adult female. However, his primary pattern of offending behavior had involved voyeurism and making obscene and harassing phone calls to women.

During the course of their treatment, patients had been referred to our physicians for evaluation for pharmacotherapy because of a lack of response to psychological treatment, intense and recurrent sexual obsessions, difficulty in controlling their paraphilic urges, and concomitant and unremitting symptoms of anxiety and depression.

Instruments

Each of the subjects were administered the Hamilton Anxiety and Depression Scales (Hamilton, 1959, 1960, 1967), the Beck Depression Inventory (Beck, Ward, Mendelson, Mock and Erbaugh, 1961), and the Yale-Brown Obsessive-Compulsive Scale (Goodman, Rasmussen, Price, Mazure, Heninger, and Charney, 1986). Measures were obtained for pre-medication as well as current functioning. The patients were also asked to respond to a semi-structured interview; these interviews were conducted by an independent examiner to ensure greater objectivity. Patients were asked to respond to the following questions:

- How is therapy helping you with symptoms of anxiety? depression? obsessive thoughts? compulsive behavior?
- How is the medication helping you with symptoms of anxiety? depression? obsessive thoughts? compulsive behavior?

- How do you feel the medication affected the progress of your psychotherapy?

RESULTS

The patients' diagnoses and medications are shown in Table 1. Premedication and current scores on all measures can be seen in Table 2. The observed signficance levels (or the probability of obtaining an F statistic as large as would be found with equal population means) were very small (= .01) and therefore statistically significant.

The statements reported by the subjects on the effects of medication on symptoms of anxiety, depression, obsessive thoughts, compulsive behaviors and their progress in psychotherapy reflected positive effects in all of these areas. While no negative effects were reported, a few subjects reported no change in some of the categories. The following statements were made on the effects of the medication on anxiety:

- "I feel better overall and have a better outlook on life. It smooths the rough edges for me. I feel better about myself."
- "I'm not afraid of making mistakes. I am able to collect my thoughts better; I don't look at things as finalistic as I used to."
- "I can think more clearly. Things don't become such a big problem anymore. Also, things don't seem so strange or hard to look at now."
- "I am better able to take chances, i.e., social risks."
- "I'm more laid back now and less meticulous."
- "Anxiety is not as strong; it has tapered off. I am able to handle things better now."
- "It slowed me down so I could deal with my issues."
- "It gave me strength to do the things I want to do."
- "It's largely responsible for me to better handle stressful situations."

The following are some statements reflecting the decrease in symptoms of depression:

- "My quality of life is much better."
- "I don't feel so hopeless. I don't dwell on failure and I sleep better."
- "I am less sad. I have more energy to do my work."
- "It's easier to see friends leave town for the school year. I don't get so bummed out about things like this anymore."
- "If I feel bad, I don't turn to other (self-destructive) behaviors."

Table 1

Paraphilia Diagnosis	Comorbid Psychiatric Diagnoses	Medications
Pedophilia	Dysthymia	Lithium to Fluoxetine
Pedophilia	Generalized Anxiety Disorder	Lithium
Pedophilia	Dysthymia Alcohol Dependence (remission)	Lithium
Pedophilia	Generalized Anxiety Disorder	Fluoxetine
Pedophilia	Dysthymia	Lithium
Pedophilia	Dysthymia Cannabis Dependence (remission)	Fluoxetine Carbamazepine
Pedophilia	Dysthymia	Fluoxetine
Pedophilia	Dysthymia Alcohol Dependence (remission)	Fluoxetine
Pedophilia	Dysthymia	Fluoxetine to Imipramine Carbamazepine
Exhibitionism	Generalized Anxiety Disorder	Fluoxetine
Exhibitionism	Dysthymia	Fluoxetine
Voyeurism	Dysthymia	Fluoxetine
Voyeurism	Dysthymia	Fluoxetine
Voyeurism Obscene Phone Call Rape	Dysthymia	Fluoxetine

Table 2

Pre-Medication and Current Scores

	Mean Score	Std. Deviation	Sig. *
Beck Depression, Pre-Medication	15.54	9.23	0.0002
Beck Depression, Current	3.38	3.69	
Hamilton Anxiety, Pre-Medication	15.46	8.31	0.0002
Hamilton Anxiety, Current	4.54	3.10	
Hamilton Depression, Pre-Medication	24.69	8.82	0.0000
Hamilton Depression, Current	5.08	3.90	
Yale-Brown Obsessions, Pre-Medication	12.15	3.67	0.0000
Yale-Brown Obsessions, Current	4.38	2.39	
Yale-Brown Compulsion, Pre-Medication	13.46	3.05	0.0000
Yale-Brown Compulsion, Current	4.46	3.13	
Yale-Brown Obsession & Compulsion, Pre-Medication	25.62	6.20	0.0000
Yale-Brown Obsession & Compulsion, Current	8.85	4.54	

* F-Probability from One-Way Analysis of Variance Procedure

- "It made me wake up, be more attentive and avoid the 'traps' that I used to fall into."
- "I am able to avoid the lows that were incapacitating."
- "Feelings of depression are no longer all consuming. The medication has settled me down."
- "I am about half as depressed as I used to be."
- "It is largely responsible for my ability to confront things head on, analyze them and resolve my problems and move on."

In response to the question regarding the effects of the medication on obsessive thoughts, the subjects reported:

- "I experience them less frequently. I am able to dismiss them when they pop into my head."
- "They're not as strong and the images are less appealing."
- "I have more control. I can get rid of my thoughts that I don't want. I'm not constantly in my head thinking."
- "They occur much less frequently."
- "It's tapered off. If they do arise, I am able to not cross that fine line."
- "Lithium helped me get rid of some of my obsessive thoughts."
- "I was able to control myself more."
- "Sexual obsessive thoughts have decreased about 90%. Other obsessive thoughts have decreased by about 50%."
- "They are no longer all-consuming. The medication has settled me down."

When asked how the medication helped with compulsive behaviors, the subjects stated:

- "I don't look forward to performing the behaviors. I am better able to control them. Behaviors occur less frequently and they are much less a priority than they use to be."
- "I'm doing much less acting out."
- "I have more control."
- "I don't have the need to perform them much any more."
- "Decreased, but I don't know if I should attribute this to therapy or medication."
- "I don't perform the behaviors anymore. I now fight them instead of giving into them."
- "I follow girls around less because my sexual urges and drive are down."
- "It helped me be more cautious, helped me to slow myself down so I can think before I act."
- "They have virtually been eliminated."

Finally patients were asked how their medication effected the progress of their psychotherapy. These are some of their responses:

- "It stopped my anxiety-type symptoms and gave me more energy. I didn't get stuck in the low slumps that I used to."
- "My mind is less cluttered. I feel less apprehensive and can think clearly. I am able to solve problems versus dwelling on them and getting stuck like I used to."
- "It calmed me down. It allowed me to cope with and address my problems. I feel less panicky."
- "I can communicate better with others. I can understand people's intentions and meanings of what they say. I can remember past events more clearly. I'm not hyperactive, i.e., wanting to change the topic all the time. I enjoy having an increase in my cognitive skills."
- "I am able to think more clearly and progress through treatment more efficiently."
- "I don't know how to separate the medications from the therapy, but I do feel more in control now."
- "Personally, I haven't noticed a difference, but several others have commented on the changes they've seen."
- "It helped me calm down. It helped me deal with my depression, stress and anxieties. It helped me control my behavior and thoughts so I don't get lost in all of it. I am able to avoid places, behaviors and thoughts that I want to avoid. I am able to use forethought and analyze the situation before reacting to it impulsively."
- "I didn't like the way lithium suppressed my sexuality, but it helped me learn there *is* a way to control urges."
- "Before, I didn't 'get into' therapy. After, I started participating and listening to feedback and I was able to control my impulses more."

DISCUSSION

In this retrospective study of the role of pharmacotherapy, patients reported that they found serotonergic medications to be effective in:

- Reduction of anxiety and depression
- Decrease in paraphilic obsessions
- Increased control over paraphilic compulsive sexual behavior
- Reduction of other non-paraphilic compulsive sexual behavior
- Reduction of non-sexual obsessive-compulsive behaviors
- Improved concentration, memory, and other cognitive processes
- Greater ability to engage in the process of psychotherapy

We feel these results are very promising. We are initiating the necessary systematic prospective studies of these medications.

It should be emphasized that all sex offenders do not suffer from obsessive and compulsive disorder. This behavior seems to be more likely in pedophiles, exhibitionists, voyeurs, and obscene phone callers and less common in incest perpetrators. Not all patients need or would benefit from pharmacotherapy. The severity of the patient's obsessions and compulsions and comorbidity with other psychiatric disorders must be considered. For example, at the time of this report only 13 of the 43 sex offenders in our treatment program are receiving pharmacotherapy as an adjunct to their psychotherapy. The remainder respond favorably to psychotherapy without medication.

While the use of antiandrogens has been proven effective in treating a variety of sex offenders, our clinical experience illustrates some advantages of lithium carbonate and fluoxetine and, in a few cases, carbamazepine.

Advantages

- Relatively low resistance to be willing to try these medications
- Minimal known side effects
- Relatively high patient compliance
- Relative ease in prescribing and administering

Disadvantages

- Reliance on patient's report of taking medication
- Lack of FDA approval of these medications for treating compulsive sexual behavior

The relative advantages and disadvantages of lithium versus fluoxetine in the treatment of paraphilic and nonparaphilic compulsive sexual behavior are still somewhat unclear. In our patients, both lithium and fluoxetine acted quickly in their anxiolytic and anti-depressive effects, reducing paraphilic and nonparaphilic compulsive sexual behavior. Lithium is not FDA approved for the treatment of generalized anxiety disorder, dysthymia or obsessive-compulsive disorder. The use of this medication has to be carefully justified and patients must give informed consent. This medication is given in 300 mg. doses and must be taken several times a day (depending on prescribed dosage). Lithium blood levels and thyroid function must be monitored regularly. Dosage adjustments are more common with lithium.

Fluoxetine treatment demonstrates therapeutic effects at 20 mg. per day, which is administered once a day, usually in the morning. Adjustments in dosage are less common. With both medications, the physician must be alert to the potential of developing unpleasant side effects, an increase in anxiety and/or depression, and a desire to discontinue medication without informing the physician or treatment personnel. By giving the patient a drug holiday, changing dosage or medication, unpleasant side effects can often be eliminated.

In anxious patients, it is often difficult to assess for attention deficit disorders or other cognitive dysfunctions. Once reductions in anxiety occur, this assessment is made easier. In the few cases, where we identified cognitive dysfunctions, these were greatly improved with the combination of fluoxetine and the anti-epileptic carbamazepine. Since temporal lobe involvement in many paraphiliacs is suspected, further exploration of the effectiveness of anti-epileptics is suggested.

Several patients in our study reported discontinuing their medication at some point in their therapy. They cited overall improvement and a desire to see if they could manage without the medication. However, in most all of the cases, patients decided to resume pharmacotherapy because of a resurgence in their symptoms. In some cases, the patients were not able to recognize this and were advised by their therapists to resume pharmacotherapy. It is unclear how long these patients will need or benefit from these medications. Some patients have been taking them for three years. We have yet to find patients who do as well off the medication once they start taking it. However, most of the patients in this study were still involved in psychotherapy. It could be that with the completion of their treatment and a significant length of time on medications, their need for the medication would be reduced or eliminated. Further investigation will shed light on this question.

In the meantime, we report the successful use of lithium carbonate and fluoxetine in treating the obsessive and compulsive behavior of paraphilic sex offenders. A few patients have also benefitted from the anti-epileptic medication carbamazepine. While this study is obviously exploratory, these findings add to the hope of finding improved therapeutic solutions to these patients' problems.

REFERENCES

American Psychiatric Association. (1987). *Diagnostic and Statistical Manual of Mental Disorders-III-R*. Washington: American Psychiatric Association.

Anderson, N. and Coleman, E. (1991). Childhood Abuse and Family Sexual Attitudes in Sexually Compulsive Males: A Comparison of Three Clinical Groups. *American Journal of Preventive Psychiatry & Neurology*, *3*(1), 8-15.

Beck, A. T., Ward, G. H., Mendelson, M., Mock, J., and Erbaugh, J. (1961). An inventory for measuring depression. *Archives of General Psychiatry, 4*, 561-571.

Cesnik, J. and Coleman, E. (1989). Use of lithium carbonate in the treatment of autoerotic asphyxia. *American Journal of Psychotherapy, 43*, 277-286.

Coleman E. and Cesnik, J. (1990). Skoptic Syndrome: The treatment of an obsessional gender dysphoria with lithium carbonate and psychotherapy, *American Journal of Psychotherapy, 44(2)*, 204- 217.

Coleman, E. (1990). The obsessive-compulsive model for describing compulsive sexual behavior. *American Journal of Preventive Psychiatry and Neurology*, *2*, 9-13.

Coleman, E. (1991). Compulsive sexual behavior: New concepts and treatments. *Journal of Psychology and Human Sexuality, 4(2)*, 37-52.

Cooper, A. J. (1986). Progesterone in the treatment of male sex offenders: A review. *Canadian Journal of Psychiatry, 31*, 73-79.

Goodman, W. K., Rasmussen, S. A., Price, L. H., Mazure, C., Heninger, G. R. and Charney, D. S. (1986). *Yale-Brown Obsessive Compulsive Scale*. New Haven, CT: Departments of Psychiatry, Yale and Brown Universities.

Hamilton, M. (1959). The assesment of anxiety states by rating. *British Journal of Medical Psychology, 32*, 50-55.

Hamilton, M. (1960). A rating scale for depression. *Journal of Neurology, Neurosurgery, and Psychiatry, 12*, 56-62.

Hamilton, M. (1967). Developments of a rating scale for primary depressive illness. *British Journal of Social and Clinical Psychiatry, 12, 56-62.*

Jenike, M. A. (1989). Obsessive-compulsive and related disorders: A hidden epidemic. *New England Journal of Medicine, 321*, 539-540.

Kafka, M. P. (1991). Successful antidepressant treatment of nonparaphilic sexual addictions and paraphilias in men. *Journal of Clinical Psychiatry, 52(2)*, 60-65.

Kafka, M. P. and Coleman, E. (1991). Serotonin and paraphilias: The convergence of mood, impulse and compulsive disorders. (Letter). *Journal of Clinical Psychopharmacology, 11(3)*, 223-224.

Money, J. (1986). *Lovemaps: Clinical Concepts of Sexual/Erotic Health and Pathology, Paraphilia, and Gender Transpositions in Childhood, Adolescence, and Maturity*. New York: Irvington.

Pearson, H. J. (1990). Paraphilias, impulse control, and serotonin. (Letter). *Journal of Clinical Psychopharmacology, 10*, 233.

Rapoport, J. (1989). The biology of obsessive-compulsive disorders. *Scientific American, 260*, 83-89.

Swedo, S. E., Leonard, H. L., Rapoport, J. L., Lenane, M. C. Goldberger, E. L, and Cheslow, D. L. (1989). A double-blind comparison of clomipramine and desipramine in the treatment of trichotillomania (hair pulling). *New England Journal of Medicine, 321*, 497-501.

van der Kolk, B. A. (1986). Uses of lithium in patients without major affective illness. *Psychopharmacology, 37*, 683- 684.

AUTHORS' NOTES

Eli Coleman, PhD, is director and associate professor in the Program in Human Sexuality at the Department of Family Practice, Medical School, University of Minnesota.

John Cesnik, MD, formerly assistant professor at the Department of Family Practice and Community Health at the University of Minnesota, is now a staff physician at Humboldt General Hospital, Winnemucca, Nevada.

Anne-Marie Moore, MC, is a counselor at the Program in Human Sexuality at the University of Minnesota.

S. Margretta Dwyer, MA, is coordinator of the sex offender treatment program at the Program in Human Sexuality, Department of Family Practice and Community Health, Medical School, University of Minnesota.

Address correspondence to the first author, 1300 S. 2nd Street, Suite 180, Minneapolis, MN 55454.

SEX OFFENDER TREATMENT: PSYCHOLOGICAL AND MEDICAL APPROACHES. Pp. 89-108.

☐ BEHAVIOR DYNAMICS & PHARMACOTHERAPY

Buspirone and Paraphilic Sexual Behavior

J. Paul Fedoroff, M.D.
Clarke Institute of Psychiatry, University of Toronto

Ingrid C. Fedoroff
Department of Psychology, University of Toronto

ABSTRACT In a review of the literature concerning buspirone's effect on sexual functioning three hypotheses are presented: 1. Buspirone's facilitation of sexual functioning is not due solely to its anxiolytic effects; 2. Buspirone facilitates non-paraphilic arousal but inhibits paraphilic sexual arousal; 3. Buspirone's efficacy in reducing paraphilic arousal is related to its efficacy in reducing obsessive-compulsive disorder symptoms. Evidence in support of these hypotheses is presented and suggestions for further research are provided.

The ideal medication for the treatment of paraphilic disorders would be one that can be easily and reliably administered with no adverse side effects. It would be not only effective in suppressing aberrant sexual behaviors but also in augmenting or facilitating normophilic sexual behaviors. To date, most research has focused on the anti-androgenic medications. The two most commonly used are medroxyprogesterone acetate (Provera[R]) and cyproterone acetate (Androcur[R]). Although their precise mechanisms of action appear to be different, both medications are associated with a reduction in peripheral testosterone levels and an accompanying decrease in paraphilic sexual interests and behaviors.

Unfortunately both medications also suppress non-paraphilic sexual behaviors, have numerous serious side-effects, and their efficacy in preventing relapse has yet to be subjected to large scale double blind treatment trials. In addition, patients frequently are reluctant to take these medications and many physicians are uncomfortable prescribing them (Langevin, Wright, and Handy, 1988). The side effects of infertility and feminization make them particularly unacceptable as treatment options for sex offenders who are often young males with insecurities about their own sexual abilities. Finally, a direct causal relationship between anti-androgens' effects on testosterone and the suppression of paraphilic sexual behaviors has never been proven and there is now an increasing body of literature to suggest that neurotransmitter systems that do not primarily affect sex hormones have important influences on the development and expression of normal and abnormal sexual behaviors.

Several reviews of the effects of monoamines on abnormal behaviors in general (van Pragg, Asmis, Kahn, Braun, Harkauy Friedman and Wetzler, 1990) and sexual behaviors in particular (Meyerson and Malmnas, 1978; Everitt and Hansen, 1983) have been published. However, there have been few attempts to relate non-hormonal pharmacologic research findings to paraphilic behavior. The purpose of this paper is to review the current evidence suggesting that buspirone hydrochloride may represent the first of a new generation of pharmacologic treatments for paraphilias and other atypical sexual behaviors. In addition, three hypotheses concerning the possible mechanism of action of buspirone will be presented.

Buspirone hydrochloride (familiar as Buspar[R]) is a synthetic form of azaspirodecanedione (Wu, Rayburn, Allen, Ferguson, Kissel, 1972). In early pharmacologic trials it was found to have stimulating effects on both dopaminergic and noradrenergic neuroreceptors while also suppressing serotonergic neurotransmitter systems (Eison and Temple, 1986). Electrophysiologic studies in the rat have shown that buspirone administration results in the inhibition of the spontaneous firing of serotonergic neurons in the dorsal raphe through stimulation of 5-HT_{1A} autoreceptors (Vander Maelen and Wilderman, 1984). Evidence also suggests that chronic treatment with buspirone results in a reduction or down-regulation of serotonin binding sites in the frontal cortex of rats (Taylor, Becker, Crane, Hyslop, Riblet and Temple, 1983). Subsequent studies in humans found buspirone to have anxiolytic properties which were somewhat unexpected since it has an antagonistic effect on gamma-aminobuteric acid receptors and no cross-tolerance with traditional anxiolytic medications such as diazepam (Eison and Eison, 1984). In spite of some reports that buspirone is less effective than benzodiazepines in reducing anxiety, it has been marketed as a potentially useful alternative to the benzodiazepines for treatment of generalized anxiety disorder (GAD) particularly since it is non-addictive (Cole, Orzack, Beake, Bird and Bar-Tal, 1982) and less sedating than are the traditional benzodiazepines (Newton, Marunycz, Alderice and Napolieto, 1986).

Hypothesis 1: Buspirone's facilitation of sexual functioning is not due solely to its anxiolytic effects

Interest in buspirone's potential usefulness in the treatment of sexual dysfunction was stimulated by a study reported by Othmer and Othmer (1987a) in which ten adult out-patients with GAD were treated with buspirone in an open-label design. At the start of the trial, nine of the ten study participants reported impaired sexual functioning. However, by the end of the four week trial, eight had normalized their sexual interest, arousability and performance as measured by the Sexual Evaluation Scale (Othmer and Othmer, 1987b). In addition, improvement in sexual function appeared to be independent of improvement in anxiety as measured by the Hamilton anxiety scale or severity of illness as measured by a Clinical Global Impressions Scale. Given the limitations of this study (small sample size, open-label, non-randomized design), Hypothesis 1 that buspirone's facilitation of sexual functioning is not due solely to its anxiolytic effects is supported. However the results of this study are insufficient to allow more than speculation regarding the mechanism by which improvement in sexual function in their subjects was achieved.

Further support for Hypothesis 1 is provided by a case study involving a man with GAD and transvestic fetishism who was treated with alprazolam and buspirone in a modified A-B-A design (Fedoroff, 1988). This man reported that he could relieve his chronic

□ *Mean number of paraphilic journal entries and number of pages written per month on buspirone (buspirone begun midway through month number four). Note: These data previously presented in tabular form in: Fedoroff, J.P. (in press). Buspirone hydrochloride in the treatment of an atypical paraphilia. Archives of Sexual Behavior.*

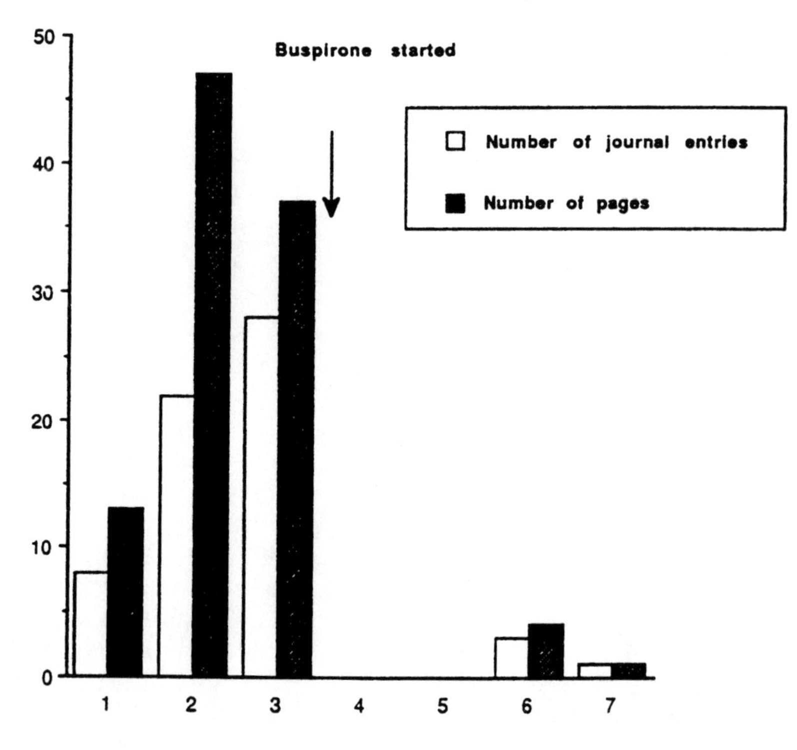

anxiety by drinking alcohol or by dressing in his wife's clothing (especially lingerie). He was initially treated with alprazolam (Xanax[R]) 0.25 mg, four times daily and on this regime his anxiety symptoms diminished although his urges to cross-dress and frequency of cross-dressing did not change. Because of the patient's complaints of drowsiness while taking alprazolam, he was switched to buspirone 5 mg four times daily. Nine days after starting buspirone, the patient reported an unexpected decrease in his urge to cross-dress and within three weeks he stopped cross-dressing completely. While taking buspirone there was also a concurrent increase in his sexual interest in his wife (that she confirmed). Frequency of sexual intercourse with his wife increased from once every two to three months before starting treatment with buspirone to once weekly while taking buspirone. Prior to treatment the patient had found it difficult during sexual relations with his wife to achieve an erection or reach orgasm unless he fantasized about being cross-dressed. While taking buspirone the patient found that he did not have to fantasize about being cross-dressed in order to become sexually excited and his wife found him less "distracted" during sexual intercourse. This is unlike the usual reports of patients treated for paraphilic disorders with anti-androgens in which reduction in paraphilic symptoms are accompanied by a reduction in non-paraphilic functioning.

After taking buspirone for three months he was asked to stop this medication by his therapist in order to determine whether it was still required. The patient reported feeling "edgier" within one week of stopping buspirone and both he and his wife noted a decrease in his non-paraphilic sexual interest toward his wife accompanied by a concomitant increase in his paraphilic urges to cross-dress. Buspirone was restarted which again resulted in a prompt decrease in transvestic urges accompanied by an increase in non-paraphilic sexual interest and activity.

Following this case report, a question was raised about the relationship between the patient's anxiety disorder and his cross-dressing behavior (Fishbain, 1989). Specifically, could the fact that the cross-dressing behavior stopped while the patient took buspirone but not alprazolam be explained by postulating that buspirone had controlled the patient's anxiety symptoms more adequately than alprazolam did (i.e., a refutation of Hypothesis 1 above)?

This seems unlikely for several reasons. First, when he was asked six months after discharge from treatment, the patient without hesitation not only identified alprazolam as being the more effective of the two medications in terms of reducing his anxiety but also stated that only buspirone seemed to decrease his urge to cross-dress. Both of these observations were confirmed by his wife (Fedoroff, 1989). Secondly, there have now been several studies suggesting that benzodiazepines are either as effective or more effective than buspirone in alleviating anxiety symptoms (Fieghner, Merideth and Hendrickson, 1982). Thirdly, prior to therapy, the patient had resorted to drinking alcohol when he felt anxious. Although he said that alcohol was very effective in making him feel less anxious, he frequently would cross-dress after drinking (that is at times when he was feeling *less* anxious but perhaps more disinhibited than usual).

Prospective randomized studies in which both frequency of non-paraphilic and paraphilic sexual arousal and activity in multiple types of sexual dysfunctions and paraphilias, using standardized measures of anxiety will be needed to more adequately test Hypothesis 1.

Hypothesis 2: Buspirone facilitates non-paraphilic arousal but inhibits paraphilic sexual arousal

In the previous study, the finding of a progressive improvement in the patient's non-paraphilic sexual functioning (sexual interest in his wife) together with a progressive decrease in his paraphilic sexual interests (cross-dressing) suggests a second hypothesis that buspirone facilitates non-paraphilic arousal but inhibits paraphilic sexual arousal.

Further data relating to these first two hypotheses are provided by a recently reported case study involving a young man who voluntarily presented for treatment following discharge from an alcohol detoxification center with the chief complaint of anxiety in social situations (Fedoroff, in press). As a result of his anxiety he claimed to also have a sexual problem although he would not elaborate on the exact nature of his difficulties during the early months of treatment. He met DSM-III-R criteria for social phobia and alcohol dependency in partial remission. Although there was insufficient information to confirm whether he had met criteria for major depression while in hospital, he did not meet criteria for major depression at the time of his initial out-patient clinic interview. He had been prescribed doxepin (Sinequan[R]) during his hospitalization but the patient claimed it had not helped either his anxiety or his "sexual problem."

The patient was initially maintained on 175 mg of doxepin at bedtime but because of complaints from the patient that he was feeling too sedated, this medication was gradually tapered. The initial clinical impression was that the patient did not like this medication and likely was non-compliant with its use since a serum level drawn while he was prescribed 175 mg at night was only 23 mcg/L with normal laboratory values being 100-300 mcg/L. Since there had been no improvement in the patient's social phobia with psychotherapy alone he was prescribed buspirone which was increased to 5 mg four times daily. Within two weeks of beginning buspirone the patient reported a marked decrease in his symptoms of anxiety to the point that he was able to resume work. Over the next few weeks he began speaking more openly about the nature of his sexual problem. He confessed that for at least the past four years he had been "obsessed" (his own word) with violent sexual thoughts concerning his older adoptive sister. His descriptions of these thoughts were very similar to true obsessions in that they were recurrent, persistent impulses and images which he experienced as intrusive and unwanted.

However, since beginning buspirone his paraphilic fantasies had decreased in frequency and intensity. Since he was able to reassure us that he was in no danger of acting on his paraphilic fantasies and since he had no known past history of dangerous activity he was continued on buspirone as an out-patient.

Although he had been asked, it was not until three months later that the patient admitted that he also had a "compulsion" (patient's phrase) which accompanied his paraphilic "obsessions." Beginning mid-way through his first month of out-patient treatment he had started writing out his sexual obsessions on scraps of paper. He explained that he felt a need to write out each sexual thought as it occurred. He was asked to bring these notes to the clinic and the next week he arrived with a shopping bag full of scraps of paper, neatly bound together with elastic bands. Since each entry was carefully dated it was possible to calculate the number and length of each paraphilic note (Figure 1). While these data require cautious interpretation, there appears to be a definite decrease in the frequency and length of paraphilic notes associated with the start of treatment with buspirone. In addition, there also was a change in the quality of the notes. Whereas the early notes were written in the present tense as though the paraphilic activities were actually happening or about to happen, later notes were more reflective, describing the patient's horror of the fantasies.

During treatment, the patient began a short-lived relationship with a woman that included sexual intercourse. The patient had never had sexual intercourse before and he reported relief when he discovered that he didn't need to resort to his paraphilic fantasies to become sexually aroused with this woman. Because of the previous report of buspirone's efficacy in treating transvestic fetishism (Fedoroff, 1988), the patient was carefully reassessed for symptoms suggestive of this disorder. In spite of specific questioning regarding symptoms of transvestism the patient continued to deny any interest in cross-dressing. However, when a careful review was conducted of his extensive past psychiatric records the medical notes revealed that he had once been arrested for breaking and entering a house. In the police report (a copy of which was in the hospital records), the arresting officer had noted that the only item stolen from the house was a pair of women's underwear. When the patient was shown this report and asked to comment, he sheepishly admitted that he had broken into several houses in the past for the sole purpose of obtaining women's panties which he would use to cross-dress in and masturbate with when he got home. Asked why he had not reported this earlier he replied that he had been too embarrassed since he thought it would cause his therapist to think he was a homosexual. He was unable to say whether buspirone had any affect on his urges to cross-dress since he claimed that he had stopped cross-dressing years before, after he had been arrested.

There are several important points to made about this case. The first is the fact that this patient was a very poor informant who clearly had great difficulty in talking about sex. It is interesting that he seems to have had less difficulty discussing his violent heterosexual fantasies than his transvestic behaviors which he (incorrectly) regarded as something that most homosexuals engage in. This pattern of confessing to paraphilias which the patient considers "more normal" or of waiting until they begin to recover before revealing the true nature of the paraphilia to the therapist has been noted by others (Cesnik and

Coleman, 1989); Fedoroff, Hanson, McGuire, Malin and Berlin, in press).

Secondly, although it must be acknowledged that this patient may have been a somewhat unreliable informant, it is difficult to explain why he would spontaneously report that buspirone had helped alleviate a previously undisclosed paraphilia if it had not been truly effective. The reliability of this case is further supported by the fact that he kept records of the frequency of his paraphilic fantasies without being asked and with no knowledge that they would ever be used to assess his progress in treatment.

In addition, although the therapist was aware that the patient had "sexual difficulties," he did not realize they were paraphilic in nature making it less likely that the patient's improvement was due to an "expectancy effect" especially since buspirone had been prescribed for the purpose of treating his anxiety disorder and not his undisclosed paraphilia.

This case provides no information to refute or confirm Hypothesis 1 since there is insufficient information to comment on whether or not improvement in the patient's anxiety symptoms and sexual functioning were independent. In this case they were most likely inter-related.

However, alcohol (which the patient reported to be helpful in reducing his anxiety symptoms) failed to reduce his paraphilic fantasies. Again, while this does not completely support Hypothesis 1, it suggests that anxiety reduction alone was not sufficient to improve his sexual function. The patient's report that paraphilic arousal decreased while non-paraphilic arousal and function were facilitated supports Hypothesis 2.

Confirmation of Hypothesis 2 will require studies similar to those required to test Hypothesis 1 with the addition of specific measures of both non-paraphilic and paraphilic sexual function. In addition to self reports, standardized phallometric protocols which would allow for more careful measurements of both types of sexual function would be helpful.

Hypothesis 3: Buspirone's efficacy in reducing paraphilic arousal is related to its efficacy in reducing OCD symptoms, potentially through its effects on serotonergic neurotransmitter systems

What is especially interesting about the case described immediately above is the apparently obsessional character of his paraphilic fantasies (aversive, repetitive, unable to be ignored) and the compulsive nature of his need to write out his fantasies on carefully dated pieces of paper. The relationship between obsessive compulsive disorder (OCD) and the paraphilias or atypical sexual behaviors has recently received increased attention (Cesnik and Coleman, 1989; Jenike, 1989; Pearson, 1990). Although the DSM-III-R specifically forbids making a diagnosis of OCD if the obsessions or compulsions are entirely of a sexual nature, there is no research to support this exclusion. The DSM-III-R states that it is inappropriate to label as obsessional drives such as eating, sleeping and sex which are considered "pleasurable" in themselves (Skodol, 1989, p. 301). However, phenomenologically, patients with paraphilias frequently state that their paraphilic sexual interests are *not* pleasurable (hence the reason that many voluntarily seek treatment). Conversely, there are now reports that some patients with non-sexual OCD find their symptoms sufficiently "pleasurable" that they refuse treatment that they have found to be effective in relieving their OCD symptoms (Thoren, Asberg, Cronholdn, et al., 1980). This issue is of more than academic interest since most effective pharmacologic treatments of OCD have been shown to affect primarily serotonin neurotransmitter systems (though the precise reason for their effectiveness is still not resolved (Zohar, Insel, Zohar-Kadouch, et al., 1988). Several reports and studies have now shown that buspirone is effective in reducing symptoms of OCD (Pato, Pigott, Hill, Grover, Bernstein and Murphy, 1990; Watts and Neil, 1988). If buspirone's effectiveness in inhibiting paraphilic sexual arousal is due to its effect on serotonin it could be predicted that its effectiveness in treating paraphilias would correspond to its effectiveness in treating OCD symptoms since both are postulated to be associated with changes in central nervous system serotonin activity.

Taken together, a third hypothesis is suggested, that buspirone's efficacy in reducing paraphilic arousal is related to its efficacy in reducing OCD symptoms (presumably, though not necessarily, via effects on central nervous system function). The case described above would support this hypothesis since the decrease in his compulsive writing corresponded to the decrease in his paraphilic fantasies.

In a preliminary and on-going study to test Hypothesis 3 (Fedoroff, in preparation) a group of ten men with transvestic fetishism who had not received treatment were administered the Yale Brown Obsessive Compulsive Scale (YBOCS) (Goodman, Price, Rasmussen, Mazure, Fleishman, Hill, Heninger and Charney, 1989a). The YBOCS is a ten item clinician-administered scale designed to assess symptom severity and response to treatment. Scores are not influenced by the type or number of obsessions and compulsions present (Goodman, Price, Rasmussen, Mazure, Fleishman, Hill, Heninger and Charney, 1989b). When participants were asked to answer questions about their transvestic behavior (technically not usually allowed due to the exclusion of sexual behaviors from the definition of obsessions or compulsions) the mean total YBOCS total score +/- standard deviation was 19.6+/-7.8 with an obsession subscore of 8.7+/-4.6 and compulsion subscore of 10.9+/-3.9. While caution is needed in interpreting these data since technically transvestic symptoms are associated with sexual arousal and therefore not allowable as OCD symptoms, these scores are indicative of considerable symptomatology and severity of both obsessional thinking and compulsive behavior associated with cross-dressing in this group. Further work in progress will further quantify the relationship between COD symptoms in transvestites and other paraphilic disorders.

If Hypothesis 3 is correct, it would be predicted that other medications with efficacy in treating OCD should also be effective in treating paraphilic disorders. Recently, a 32 year old married male who met DSM-III-R criteria for transvestic fetishism requested treatment at the Clarke Institute Clinic. He was unwilling to enter an on-going double blind treatment trial of buspirone so he was offered an alternative treatment consisting of weekly psychotherapy involving individual, couple's therapy and behavioral therapy components on an out-patient basis. After four weeks of treatment his urges to cross-dress had not changed. In addition he now reported difficulty sleeping. He asked if there was a non-pharmacologic treatment for his insomnia and he was advised to try drinking heated milk. Heated milk has been reported to improve sleep presumably due to the presence of the soporific effect of L-tryptophan (the metabolic precursor of serotonin) which is present in heated milk (Murphy, Mueller, Garrick, Aulack, 1986). The next week he reported an improvement in his sleep. The following week he also reported a reduction in his urge to cross-dress. In fact, he had been so surprised and alarmed by this sudden change in his transvestic interests that he cross-dressed "just to see if I could get turned on but it didn't work. I just felt silly." His total YBOCS score which had been 21 (11 obsession subscale and 10 compulsion subscale) fell to 2 (1 obsession subscale and 1 compulsion subscale) for a total change of 90%. This is a highly significant change in YBOCS scores and was confirmed by the patient's and wife's report that he had never before been so disinterested in cross-dressing. Unfortunately, in this case, the patient's interest in sexual activity with his wife remained low. He continued to suffer from inability to ejaculate or reach orgasm during sexual intercourse (retarded ejaculation). Interestingly, retarded ejaculation is a frequent side-effect of serotonergic medications (Zajecka, Fawcett, Schaft, Jeffriess and Guy, 1991). In this case, however, retarded ejaculation preceded initiation of treatment with heated milk.

This case provides support for Hypothesis 3 which predicted that other anti-obsessional, serotonergic medications (such as tryptophan) may decrease paraphilic behavior. It is notable that in this case, unlike in the two cases reported above who were treated with buspirone, decrease in paraphilic function did not appear to be accompanied by a change in non-paraphilic function. This finding that the patient's paraphilic interests decreased without any major change in his non-paraphilic interest provides partial support for Hypothesis 2 since the two sexual behaviors appear to be independent. However, the possibility that some of the decrease in paraphilic behaviors were due to an undetected decrease in his non-paraphilic sexual interest cannot be excluded.

Further support for Hypothesis 3, that buspirone inhibits paraphilic or atypical sexual arousal through serotonergic mechanisms comes from a recent report in which a series of nine men who presented with the DSM-III-R diagnosis of non-paraphilic sexual addiction were treated with the serotonin re-uptake blocker fluoxetine or lithium or imipramine (Kafka, 1991). Although this was a small series and several of the patients also met criteria for other psychiatric disorders, there was a trend suggesting a decrease in the compulsive nature of the sexual behavior in men treated with fluoxetine.

In addition, Coleman and Cesnik (1990) have recently reported the successful treatment of two men with the unusual paraphilia described originally by Money as the scoptic syndrome (Money, 1988). Patients with this syndrome typically are convinced that their lives would be better if they were castrated. Both reported a decrease in their paraphilic interests when they were treated with lithium. While its mechanism of action is still not completely understood, lithium is generally considered to have serotonergic activity. Of particular interest is the authors' descriptions of the two men as "obsessional." Had it not been for the sexual characteristics of their complaints, these patients would likely be classified as having a variant of the "body dysmorphic syndrome" which itself has been reported to respond to treatment with serotonergic medications. The similarities between body dysmorphic disorder and obsessive-compulsive disorder and their similar response to treatment with serotonergic medications has been noted previously (Brady, Austin and Lydiard, 1990).

In yet another report, a patient with an atypical fetish (sexual arousal induced predominantly by the sight or thought of muscular people) was successfully treated with fluoxetine (Lorefice, 1991). Again, change in anxiety was considered to be independent of change in abnormal sexual fantasies in support of Hypothesis 1. The successful treatment of this paraphilia with fluoxetine which is a highly selective serotonergic medication supports Hypothesis 3. Unfortunately there is insufficient information about the change in the patient's non-paraphilic sexual arousal before or after treatment to allow comment on Hypothesis 2.

Further support for the hypothesis that buspirone may affect sexual behavior is also found in studies of populations with low serotonin metabolites. For example, investigators have commented on the unusual psychiatric presentation of patients with evidence of low serotonergic function as evidenced by low or reduced levels of the major metabolite of serotonin 5-hydroxyindoleacetic acid (5HIAA) (Gerner, Fairbanks, Anderson, Young, Scheinin, Linnoila, Hare, Shaywitz, Cohen, 1984; Brown, Goodwin, Ballenger, Goyer and Major, 1979; Linnoila, Virkkunen, Scheinin, Nuutila, Riman and Goodwin, 1983; Roy, Adinoff and Linnoila, 1988). Patients with reduced 5HIAA have been described as having an increased incidence of mood disorders, impulsivity, compulsivity and aggression. For example, in a recent report of two patients found to have extremely low cerebral spinal fluid 5HIAA levels (Leckman, Goodman, Riddle, Hardin and Anderson, 1990), both were described as impulsive with many symptoms suggestive of an obsessive-compulsive disorder. The first was a 24 year old man with Tourette's syndrome with "a compulsive need to touch objects and other people, and to touch himself in a stereotypic fashion including inappropriate touching of his genitals." This behavior is very similar to that of patients with frotteurism which involves sexual arousal from touching or rubbing against a non-consenting person, usually in a public place. The second was a 28 year old female who had presented to a surgeon with the request that both her arms be amputated to prevent her from acting on her violent obsessions involving the harm of innocent and "vulnerable" people. This unusual presentation has similarities to the paraphilia known as apotemnophilia in which individuals are sexually aroused by thoughts of amputation (Money, Jobaris and Furth, 1977).

In spite of extensive research, the relationship between serotonergic treatments and sexual behaviors is still unresolved. However, there is now a considerable literature supporting the hypothesis that sexual behavior in male rats is inhibited when intracerebral serotonin levels are raised and sexual behavior is increased when levels of serotonin are decreased (Meyerson and Malmnas, 1978; Everitt, 1978 for reviews). The reason for this association is not known. Of particular interest is the recent finding that a sub-group of dorsal raphe neurons associated with a specific pattern of behavior in cats described as compulsive grooming behavior involving oral-buccal movements (Jacobs, Wilkinson and Fornal, 1990). Preliminary evidence suggests that the neurons facilitating these behaviors become more active in the presence of "arousing stimuli." Buspirone is known to bind to neuroreceptors on neurons in the dorsal raphe (Vander Maelen, and Wilderman, 1984) and buspirone appears to specifically inhibit related head shaking behaviors induced by pharmacologic stimulation of 5-HT_2 receptors (Lucki and Ward, 1986). Further research into the relationship between buspirone's effect on these "compulsive" behaviors and other sexual behaviors would be helpful.

Some of the research involving the effect of serotonin on sexual behavior has already yielded promising results. For example, p-chlorophenylalanine (PCPA) is a compound which inhibits the synthesis of serotonin. In male rats it has been shown to increase the rate of achieving intromission (Everitt, Fuxe and Hokfelt, 1974) and shorten the time taken to ejaculate (Gessa and Tagliamante, 1974). In sexually inexperienced male rats given PCPA, the percentage reaching ejaculation when paired with estrous females is also increased (Tagliamonte, Tagliamonte and Gessa, 1971). In addition, the frequency of male to male mounting is increased (Tagliamonte, 1969). These PCPA studies also demonstrate the importance of taking more than just the primary pharmacologic action of a test compound into consideration. For example, in spite of the large number of experiments such as these implicating decreased levels of serotonin with increased sexual activity, the possibility that PCPA is acting through another mechanism has not been excluded since PCPA is known to stimulate adrenal activity and to interact with other neurotransmitter systems (Clemens and Gladue, 1979). Interpretation is further complicated by the growing recognition that so-called serotonergic medications may have different effects depending on which part of the brain they are found, which serotonergic receptor(s) they stimulate, and what other neurotransmitters and hormones they influence. The development of drugs with more specific effects on individual neurotransmitter pathways will certainly aid in testing the hypotheses which have been presented.

SUMMARY AND CONCLUSIONS

A number of reports from the human and animal literature have been presented which relate to the possible effect that buspirone may have on non-paraphilic and paraphilic sexual arousal. Taken together, there is considerable circumstantial evidence supporting Hypothesis 1 that buspirone's effects on facilitating non-paraphilic sexual arousal, though not yet proven, appear to be independent of its effects on anxiety symptoms. This hypothesis in no way obviates the importance of anxiety symptoms in transvestites or other paraphilic disorders. Further studies to examine the effect that anxiety has in terms of facilitating or inhibiting paraphilic and non-paraphilic sexual arousal and function are needed.

While reports supporting Hypothesis 2 that buspirone may inhibit paraphilic sexual arousal but not non-paraphilic sexual arousal are still at the stage of case reports, this is a potentially very important finding. It challenges the current view that the best way to suppress paraphilic sexual behavior is by suppressing all sexual interest with anti-androgen medications. Future studies to verify this hypothesis are important. In addition, studies in which buspirone is added to other more standard pharmacologic agents may also be instructive.

Hypothesis 3 suggests that buspirone's efficacy in reducing paraphilic arousal is related to its efficacy in reducing OCD symptoms through its effect on serotonergic central nervous system pathways. This is the least well proven of the three hypotheses presented, in part because it rests on the first two hypotheses. It is recognized that the argument may appear to be somewhat circular: i.e, if paraphilic symptoms are redefined as OCD symptoms then it is not surprising that paraphilic patients appear to have OCD. However, reconceptualizing paraphilias as "adult onset OCD syndromes" may have important treatment implications since several medications which are effective in relieving symptoms of OCD also appear to be effective in reducing paraphilic symptoms. At the same time there are many phenomenologic similarities between some paraphilias and some OCD's. Studies to investigate whether measures of obsessionality such as the YBOCS score predict response to treatment with buspirone will be extremely important since there currently is no reliable method of predicting response to any form of treatment in paraphilic patients. In addition, studies to ascertain the prevalence of true obsessions and compulsions in paraphilic patients and the prevalence of paraphilias in OCD patients will be needed to rule out the possibility that some patients with paraphilias respond to treatment with buspirone because their true OCD symptoms diminish (this is similar to the question raised by Fishbain (1989) regarding the relationship between anxiety reduction and improvement in sexual functioning discussed under Hypothesis 1 above).

In conclusion, prospective studies employing more sophisticated methodology and standardized assessment instruments are now needed to more formally test the hypotheses outlined in this paper. Current research findings also support the need to further investigate the utility of sub-classifying paraphilia diagnoses according to severity of "obsessiveness," using scales such as the YBOCS and others.

others. In addition, treatment studies using buspirone and other serotonergic medications in other paraphilias are needed. Studies designed to measure the efficacy of buspirone in preventing relapse are especially important.

Finally, it must be emphasized that current diagnostic criteria for the paraphilias are based primarily on observable behaviors. It is well known that behaviors nearly always have multiple etiologies. For example, patients may cross-dress because they are transvestites, ego-dystonic homosexuals, schizophrenics, or are intoxicated (to name just a few diagnoses). It is highly improbable that a single pharmacologic agent will be found to treat all cross-dressers (even those with the same diagnosis). Studies of patients who do not respond in the expected way to treatment with buspirone are as important as "positive studies." It is most likely that increased knowledge about the underlying etiology of sexual disorders will result in improved therapies including, but not limited to, new pharmacologic treatments.

REFERENCES

Brady, K.T., Austin, L., and Lydiard, R.B. (1990). Body dysmorphic disorder. The relationship to obsessive compulsive disorder. *The Journal of Nervous and Mental Disease*, 178, 538-540.

Brown, G.L., Goodwin, F.K., Ballenger, J.A., Goyer, P.F., and Major, L.F. (1979). Aggression in humans correlates with cerebrospinal fluid amine metabolites. *Psychiatry Research*, 1, 131-139.

Cesnik, J.A., and Coleman, E. (1989). Use of lithium carbonate in the treatment of autoerotic asphyxia. *American Journal of Psychotherapy*, 43, 277-286.

Clemens, L.G., Gladue, B.A. (1979). Neuroendocrine control of adult sexual behavior. In: D.M. Schneider (Ed.). *Reviews of Neuroscience*, (pp. 73-103). New York, N.Y.: Raven Press.

Cole, J.O., Orzack, M.H., Beake, B., Bird, M. and Bar-Tal, Y. (1982). Assessment of the abuse liability of buspirone in recreational sedative users. *Journal of Clinical Psychiatry*, 43, 69-74.

Coleman, E., and Cesnik, J. (1990). Scoptic syndrome: the treatment of an obsessional gender dysphoria with lithium carbonate and psychotherapy. *American Journal of Psychotherapy*, 44, 204- 217.

Diagnostic and statistical manual of mental disorders, third edition, revised. (1987). Washington, D.C., American Psychiatric Association.

Eison, A.S. and Temple, D.S. (1986). Buspirone: review of its pharmacology and current treatment perspectives on its mechanism of action. *American Journal of Medicine*. 80(suppl 3B), 1-9.

Eison, M.S., and Eison, A.S. (1984). Buspirone as a midbrain modulator: anxiolysis unrelated to traditional benzodiazepine mechanisms. *Drug Development Research*, 4, 109-119.

Everitt, B.J., (1978). A neuroanatomical approach to the study of monoamines and sexual behavior. In: J.B. Hutchison (Ed.), *Biological determinants of sexual behavior*. Chichester: John Wiley & Sons. Chapter 17 (pp. 555-574).

Everitt, B.J., Fuxe, K., and Hokfelt, T. (1974). Inhibitory role of dopamine and 5-hydroxy-tryptamine in the sexual behavior of female rats. *European Journal of Pharmacology*, 29, 187-191.

Everitt, B.J. and Hansen, S. (1983). Catecholamines and hypothalamic mechanisms. In: David Wheatley (Ed.). *Psychopharmacology and sexual disorders*. Oxford: Oxford University Press, British Association of psychopharmacology monograph No. 4: Chapter 1 (pp. 3-14).

Fedoroff, J.P. (in press). Buspirone hydrochloride in the treatment of an atypical paraphilia. *Archives of Sexual Behavior*.

Fedoroff, J.P. (1988). Buspirone in the treatment of transvestic fetishism. *Journal of Clinical Psychiatry*, 49, 408- 409.

Fedoroff, J.P. (1989). Buspirone and transvestic fetishism (reply to letter). *Journal of Clinical Psychiatry*, 50, 437.

Fedoroff, J.P. (in preparation). Obsessive-compulsive symptoms in men with transvestic fetishism.

Fedoroff, J.P., Hanson, A., McGuire, M., Malin, H.M., and Berlin, F.S. (in press). Simulated paraphilias — a preliminary study of patients who imitate or exaggerate paraphilic symptoms and behaviors. *Journal of Forensic Psychiatry*.

Feighner, J.P., Merideth, C.H. and Hendrickson, G.A. (1982). A double-blind comparison of buspirone and diazepam in out-patients with generalized anxiety disorder.

Fishbain, D.A. (1989). Buspirone and transvestic fetishism. *Journal of Clinical Psychiatry*. 50, 436-437.

Gerner, R.H., Fairbanks, L., Anderson, G.M., Young, J.G., Scheinin, M., Linnoila, M., Hare, T.A., Shaywitz, B.A., Cohen, D.J. (1984). CSF neurochemistry in depressed, manic and schizophrenic patients compared with that of normal controls. *American Journal of Psychiatry*, 141, 1533-1540.

Gessa, G.L. and Tagliamonte, A. (1974). Role of brain monoamines in male sexual behavior. *Life Sciences*, 14, 425- 436.

Goodman, W.K., Price, L.H., Rasmussen, S.A., Mazure, C., Fleishman, R.L., Hill, C.L., Heninger, G.R. and Charney, D.S. (1989). The Yale-Brown Obsessive Compulsive Scale: I — Development, use, and reliability. *Archives of General Psychiatry*. 46, 1006-1011.

Jacobs, B.L., Wilkinson, L.O. and Fornal, C.A. (1990). The role of brain serotonin. A neurophysiologic perspective. *Neuropsychopharmacology*, 3, 473-479.

Jenike, M.A. (1989). Obsessive-compulsive and related disorders — a hidden epidemic. *The New England Journal of Medicine*, 321, 539-541.

Kafka, M.P. (1991). Successful antidepressant treatment of nonparaphilic sexual addiction and paraphilias in men. *Journal of Clinical Psychiatry*, 52, 60-65.

Langevin, R., Wright, P. and Handy, L. (1988). What treatment do sex offenders want? *Annals of sex research*, 1, 363-385.

Leckman, J.F., Goodman, W.K., Riddle, M.A., Hardin, M.T. and Anderson, G.M. (1990). Low CSF 5HIAA and obsessions of violence: report of two cases. *Psychiatry Research*, 33, 95-99.

Linnoila, M., Virkkunen, M., Scheinin, M., Nuutila, A., Riman, R., and Goodwin, F.K. (1983). Low cerebrospinal fluid 5- hydroxyindoleacetic acid concentration differentiates impulsive from non- impulsive violent behavior. *Life Sciences*, 33, 2609-2614.

Lorefice, L.S. (1991). Fluoxetine treatment of a fetish. *Journal of Clinical Psychiatry*, 52, 41.

Lucki, I. and Ward, H.R. (1986). Antagonism of serotonin- mediated behaviors in rats pretreated with the non-benzodiazepine anxiolytics buspirone and ipsapirone. *Society of Neuroscience Abstracts*, 12, 1236.

Meyerson, B.J. and Malmnas, C. (1978). Brain monoamines and sexual behavior. In: J.B. Hutchinson (Ed.) *Biological determinants of sexual behavior*, Chapter 16 (pp. 521-554). Chichester, John Wiley & Sons.

Money, J., Jobaris, R. and Furth, G. (1977). Apotemnophilia: Two cases of self-demand amputation as a paraphilia. *Journal of Sex Research*, 13, 115-125.

Money, J. (1986). Lovemaps: Clinical concepts of sexual/erotic health and pathology, paraphilia and gender transposition in childhood, adolescence and maturity. New York, Irvington.

Money, J. (1988). The scoptic syndrome: castration and genital self-mutilation as an example of sexual body-image pathology. *Journal of Psychology and Human Sexuality*, 1, 113-128.

Murphy, D.L., Mueller, E.A., Garrick, N.A., Aulack, C.S. (1986). Use of serotonergic agents in the clinical assessment of central serotonin function. *Journal of Clinical Psychiatry*, 147 (4, Suppl), 9-15.

Newton, R.E., Marunycz, J.D. Alderice, M.T. and Napolieto, M.J. (1986). Review of the side effect profile of buspirone. *American Journal of Medicine*, 80, 17-21.

Othmer, E., Othmer, S.C. (1987). Effect of buspirone on sexual dysfunction in patients with generalized anxiety disorder. *Journal of Clinical Psychiatry*, 48, 191-193.

Othmer, E., Othmer, S.C. (1987). Evaluation of sexual dysfunction. *Journal of Clinical Psychiatry*, 48, 191-193.

Pato, M.T., Pigott, T.A., Hill, J.L., Grover, G.N., Bernstein, S. and Murphy, D.L. (1990). Controlled comparison of buspirone and clomipramine in obsessive compulsive disorder. *American Journal of Psychiatry*, 148, 127-129.

Pearson, H.J. (1990). Paraphilias, impulse control and serotonin. *Journal of Clinical Psychopharmacology*, 10: 233.

Roy, A., Adinoff, B. and Linnoila, M. (1988). Acting out hostility in normal volunteers: Negative correlation with levels of 5HIAA in cerebrospinal fluid. *Psychiatry Research*, 24, 187-194.

Skodol, A.E. (1989). Problems in differential diagnosis: from DSM-III to DSM-III-R in clinical practice. Washington, D.C.: American Psychiatric Press, Inc.

Tagliamonte, A., Tagliamonte, P., Gessa, G.L. and Brodie, B.B. (1966). Compulsive sexual activity induced by p-chorophenylalanine in normal and pinealectomized male rats. *Science*, 166, 1433- 1435.

Tagliamonte, A., Tagliamonte, P. and Gessa, G.L. (1971). Reversal of pargyline-induced inhibition of sexual behavior in male rats by p-chlorophenylalanine. *Nature*, 230, 244-245.

Taylor, D.P., Becker, J.A., Crane, M., Hyslop, D.K., Riblet, L.A. and Temple, D.L. (1983). Chronic treatment with buspirone reduces type two serotonin binding sites. *Society of Neuroscience Abstracts*, 9, 435.

Thoren, P., Asberg, M., Cronholdn, et al. (1980). Clomipramine treatment of obsessive-compulsive disorder II. *Archives of General Psychiatry*, 37, 1286-1294.

van Praag, H.M., Asmis, G.M., Kahn, R.S., Braun, B.M., Harkauy Friedman, J.M. and Wetzler, S. (1990). Monoamines and abnormal behavior. A multi-aminergic perspective. *British Journal of Psychiatry*, 157, 723-734.

Vander Maelen, C.P. and Wilderman, R.C. (1984). Iontophoretic and systemic administration of the non-benzodiazepine anxiolytic drug buspirone causes inhibition of serotonergic dorsal raphe neurons in rats. *Federal Proceedings*, 43, 947.

Watts, V.S. and Neil, J.R. (1988). Buspirone in obsessive compulsive disorder. *American Journal of Psychiatry*. 145, 1606.

Wu, Y.H., Rayburn, J.W., Allen, L., Ferguson, H.C. and Kissel, J.W. (1972). Psychosedative agents — 2,8-(4-substituted 1- piperazinylalkyl)-8-azaspiro-(4,5)decane-7,9-diones. *Journal of Medical Chemistry*, 15, 477-479.

Zajecka, J., Fawcett, J., Schaft, M., Jeffriess, H. and Guy, C. (1991). The role of serotonin in sexual dysfunction: fluoxetine-associated orgasm dysfunction. *Journal of Clinical Psychiatry*, 52, 66-68.

Zohar, J., Insel, T.R., Zohar-Kadouch, R.C., et al. (1988). Serotonergic responsivity in obsessive-compulsive disorder: effects of chronic clomipramine treatment. *Archives of General Psychiatry*, 45, 167-172.

AUTHORS' NOTES

J. Paul Fedoroff, M.D., is Staff Psychiatrist in the Forensic Division, The Clarke Institute of Psychiatry of the University of Toronto.

Ingrid C. Fedoroff is at the Department of Psychology, University of Toronto.

Address for Correspondence: J. Paul Fedoroff, M.D., Clarke Insitute of Psychiatry, 250 College Street, Toronto, Canada M5T 1R8.

SEX OFFENDER TREATMENT: PSYCHOLOGICAL AND MEDICAL APPROACHES. Pp. 109-123.

□ CLINICAL PROCESSES: PHARMACOTHERAPY & GROUP THERAPY

Medroxy-Progesterone Acetate in the Treatment of Paraphilic Sexual Disorders

Rate of Relapse in Paraphilic Men Treated in Long-Term Group Psychotherapy With or Without Medroxy-Progesterone Acetate

J. Paul Fedoroff, M.D.
University of Toronto

Robert Wisner-Carlson, M.D.
Sheppard and Enoch Pratt Hospital, Baltimore

Sharon Dean
The Johns Hopkins Hospital

Fred S. Berlin, M.D., Ph.D.
The Johns Hopkins University

ABSTRACT Results are presented of an open retrospective study in which 46 male patients with paraphilic sexual disorders were followed for 5 or more years in the Johns Hopkins Sexual Disorders Unit. All patients received equivalent amounts of group psychotherapy. Of these, 17/46 (37%) relapsed. The rate of relapse among subjects receiving treatment with medroxy-progesterone acetate (MPA) was 4 out of 27 subjects (15%) whereas the rate of relapse among subjects not receiving MPA was 13/19 (68%) (Chi-square = 13.80; df = 1; $p = 0.0002$). The lower rate of relapse among subjects who were receiving MPA continued to be demonstrated when other variables were accounted for including age, race, marital status, employment, socioeconomic status, diagnosis, and sexual orientation. It is concluded that among paraphilic male out-patients treated with weekly psychotherapy for 5 or more years, the addition of MPA is associated with a decrease in the rate of relapse. Limitations of this study and suggestions for future research are discussed.

In recent years there has been a growing recognition of the need for more effective treatments of patients with paraphilic sexual disorders. Some treatments that have been proposed include intensive psychoanalysis (Rubins, 1969), behavioral and cognitive psychotherapy (McGuire, Carlisle and Young, 1965; Marshall and Barbaree, 1990), pharmacologic therapies (Berlin and Meinecke, 1981; Fedoroff, 1988) and even castration (Sturup, 1972) or psychosurgery (Roeder, 1966). However, in spite of the wide number of treatment regimes that have been proposed, there have been few scientific evaluations of their efficacy and many of the studies that have been carried out have serious methodologic flaws that have been reviewed elsewhere (Furby, Weinrott and Blackshaw, 1989; Kilmann, Sabalis, Gearing, Bukstel and Scovern, 1982). Perhaps the greatest amount of attention has focused on the treatment of paraphilias with the anti-androgen hormone medroxy-progesterone (MPA) which was first used for this purpose in North America by Money (Money, 1970). Although there have been numerous demonstrations of this hormone's efficacy in reducing serum testosterone levels in men (Bercovici, 1979), definitive proof on its efficacy in reducing relapse rates of paraphilic patients is still lacking.

In order to conduct a fair trial of the efficacy of MPA the sample studied must be sufficiently ill that therapy is considered necessary, the sample must be followed long enough for relapses to occur, the sample must be able to relapse (i.e., not be incarcerated or otherwise unable to commit sex offenses) and the sample must be sufficiently motivated to accept treatment. To meet these criteria we studied all paraphilic men admitted into the out-patient treatment program for sex offenders of the Johns Hopkins Sexual Disorders Unit (JHSDU) who remained in treatment for at least 5 years. The purpose of this paper is to present a preliminary report on a retrospective study of the treatment efficacy of a program of weekly group psychotherapy with or without MPA to test the hypothesis that the addition of MPA to patients' treatment regimes is associated with a reduced rate of relapse.

METHOD

Sample

All subjects included in this study were male patients accepted into out-patient treatment of the JHSDU. This is a clinic specializing in the treatment of patients with paraphilias. Out-patient treatment in the JHSDU typically consists of weekly group-psychotherapy as well as the option, if clinically indicated, of receiving intra-muscular (i.m.) MPA (300 to 500 mg weekly). To participate in the JHSDU program patients are required to attend psychotherapy sessions but are not required to receive MPA treatment without voluntarily giving informed consent. Only patients who were in continuous treatment for 5 or more years were included in this study. Out of a total of 395 patients who had been entered into the JHSDU program more than 5 years prior to December 31, 1989, 185 had been compliant with treatment and were discharged before receiving 5 years of treatment because they clinically were judged not to need further treatment. Another 38 patients were arrested before 5 years had expired. An additional 7 patients died before receiving 5 years of treatment (none from known complications of MPA). Twenty-two more moved out of state and were lost to follow-up. Finally, 88 patients were discharged because of refusal to receive MPA treatment. This left 55 patients who had completed 5 years of treatment. After excluding patients who had organic brain syndromes or who had incomplete records, there were 46 male patients who had met inclusion criteria for this study. All of these 46 patients were included in the present study.

Sources of Information

Retrospective hospital and clinic chart reviews were conducted on all 46 subjects. Each subject had at least one complete semi-structured psychiatric interview conducted by a resident psychiatrist and an attending psychiatrist. Wherever possible, all records from other psychiatric admissions were obtained and outside informants were interviewed. In addition, clinic notes included police and legal reports of known sex offenses. Regular progress notes were kept on all subjects by their respective out-patient therapists. Whenever therapists became aware that a subject had relapsed they completed a standardized form that included questions about how the therapist had become aware of the relapse, the characteristics of the relapse, and whether the patient was receiving MPA.

Operationalization of Criteria

Before beginning any data collection the following criteria were defined:

Definition of sexual disorder: All subjects met criteria for at least one paraphilic sexual disorder as defined according to DSM-III-R criteria (American Psychiatric Association, 1987). For purposes of description and analysis paraphilias were combined into three groups: Pedophilia, Exhibitionism and Voyeurism, and Other Paraphilias.

Definition of relapse: In order to minimize the chance of overlooking relapses, specificity was sacrificed to increase sensitivity by defining relapse broadly as "any inappropriate sexual behavior" whether or not it was the type for which the subject originally sought treatment. Use of force, threats, interference with other aspects of the subject's functioning, subjective distress, legal charges or confirmation of reported relapses were *not* required to satisfy the criteria for relapse. In addition, "sexual behavior" was defined broadly to include any behavior that the subject or rater (not necessarily both) considered sexual. For example, a report that a subject with pedophilia had visited a school yard would qualify as inappropriate sexual behavior even though this activity would not ordinarily be considered sexual. Relapses were classified as "self-reported" if the subject was the first to report the relapse to the treatment staff. If the clinic learned of a relapse from any other source prior to report by the subject, it was classified as *not* self-reported even if the subject later confessed.

Definition of treatment with MPA: For the purposes of this study, subjects whose hospital charts included a doctor's order for MPA and who attended the out-patient clinic at which the MPA was administered were assumed to have received MPA. Most subjects were prescribed i.m. MPA 300-500 mg weekly. Subjects who received oral MPA were included in the MPA group unless otherwise indicated.

Study Design

All charts were reviewed retrospectively and abstracted. Subjects were initially divided into two groups — those known to have relapsed at least once since starting treatment (Relapsers; N = 17) and those who were not known to have relapsed since starting treatment (Non-relapsers) (N = 29) as of January 1, 1990. The two groups were compared using Chi-square analysis and two-tailed, unpaired t-tests, as appropriate.

In addition, the study population was divided into those who were receiving weekly intramuscular MPA treatment (MPA Group) (N = 27) and those who were not receiving MPA (Non-MPA Group) (N = 19). The Non-MPA Group and MPA Group were also compared using Chi-square analysis or two-tailed, unpaired t-tests, as appropriate.

RESULTS

The diagnosis, type of relapse, outcome and MPA status at time of relapse for each subject known to have relapsed is shown in Table 1. The demographic characteristics and diagnoses for subjects known to have relapsed compared to subjects not known to have relapsed are shown in Table 2. There were no statistically significant differences between Relapsers and Non-relapsers in terms of age, race, years of education, employment, socioeconomic status as defined by the Hollingshead two factor method (Hollingshead and Redlich, 1958), marital status, previous arrests, years of follow-up, or known family history of psychiatric disorder (Table 2). In addition, there were no statistically significant differences between Relapsers and Non-relapsers in terms of number of subjects in each of the 3 diagnostic groups of paraphilias: *Pedophilia*, *Exhibitionist/voyeur*, or *Other paraphilias* (Table 2; Chi- square = 1.02; df = 2; p = NS). The Pedophile group was the only group large enough to allow a further subclassification into those who were attracted only to males (homosexual pedophiles (N = 15), and those who were attracted only to females (heterosexual pedophiles (N = 10). There were 4 bisexual

□ *Table 1: Diagnosis, type of relapse, outcome and MPA status of known relapsers*

ID No.	Group	Relapse Type	Outcome	MPA
1	*Other	Threatened Rape	Hospitalized	+
2	Exhibitionist	Indecent exposure	Arrested	-
3	Exhibitionist	Indecent exposure	Arrested	+
4	Pedophile	Pedophilic assault	Arrested	-
5	Pedophile	Pedophilic assault	Arrested	-
6	Pedophile	Pedophilic assault	Arrested	-
7	Pedophile	Pedophilic assault	Arrested	-
8	Voyeur	Voyeurism	Arrested	-
9	Pedophile	Pedophilic assault	Arrested	-
10	Pedophile	Invited boys to room	Discharged	+
11	Pedophile	Pedophilic assault	Arrested	-
12	Pedophile	Pedophilic assault	Arrested	-
13	Pedophile	Pedophilic assault	Arrested	-
14	Exhibitionist	Indecent exposure	Arrested	-
15	Exhibitionist	Indecent exposure	Started MPA	-
16	Pedophile	Invited boys to room	Discharged	-
17	Exhibitionist	Indecent exposure	Increased MPA	+

** See text definition of "other" paraphilia group.*

pedophiles. There were no statistically significant differences between the number of homosexual pedophiles who relapsed (N = 3) and the number of heterosexual pedophiles who relapsed (N = 5) (Chi-square = 2.48; df = 1; *p* = NS). In addition, the statistical difference in proportions of pedophiles who relapsed on MPA compared to pedophiles not receiving MPA was not changed by removing the 2 incestuous pedophiles from the analysis (Chi-square = 22.73; df = 1; *p* = 0.0001). Since there were no significant differences between the three diagnostic groups in terms of relapse, use of MPA or demographic variables, they were combined in subsequent analyses.

In the Non-relapse group, 22 (76%) were receiving i.m. MPA and 1 was receiving oral MPA at the time of follow-up. However, only 2 (12%) of the 17 in the Relapse group were receiving weekly i.m.

□ *Table 2: Demographic and diagnostic characteristics of subjects who relapsed or did not relapse at follow up*

	NO RELAPSE	RELAPSE
Number (N)	N = 29	N = 17
Demographic characteristics		
Age (Mean [standard deviation])	34 [11]	31 [9]
Race (% Black [number])	10 [3]	12 [3]
Education (Mean Years [standard deviation])	12 [3]	12 (4]
Employment (% with jobs [number])	55 [16]	71 [12]
Socioeconomic status (% Hollingshead 3- [Number])	52 [15]	53 [9]
Marital Status (% Married [N])	34 [10]	35 [6]
Family History of Psychiatric Illness (% positive [number])	41 [12]	56 [9]
Previous Arrests (% subjects [number of subjects])	52 [15]	35 [6]
Years Follow-up (Mean [standard deviation])	6.7 [2.4]	7.5 [2.3]
Diagnostic Characteristics (% [Number])		
Pedophilia	66 [19]	59 [10]
Exhibitionist/Voyeur	17 [5]	29 [5]
Other Paraphilias	17 [5]	12 [2]

There were no significant differences between No Relapse and Relapse groups on any of the variables listed in this table.

MPA. An additional 2 subjects in the Relapse group were receiving decreased doses of MPA (less than 300 mg i.m. per week). The remaining 13 subjects who relapsed did not receive MPA. A chi-square analysis comparing the number of subjects receiving MPA in the Non-relapse group (23/29) to the number receiving MPA in the Relapse group (4/17) was statistically significant (Chi-square = 1.38; df = 1; $p = 0.0002$).

Next, several possible differences in the course of treatment of Relapsers and Non-relapsers which could account for differences in use of MPA and relapse rate were investigated. Among Relapsers, the mean time to first relapse (years (SD)) was 4.7 years (2.3). This was

Table 3: Demographic and diagnostic characteristics of subjects receiving regular full dose MPA at follow-up (MPA Group) versus subjects not receiving MPA at follow-up (No-MPA Group)

	NO MPA	MPA
Number (N)	N = 19	N = 27
Demographic characteristics		
Age (Mean [standard deviation])	32.3 [9.3]	33.8 [10.9]
Race (% Black [number])	6 [1]	15 [4]
Education (Mean Years [standard deviation])	12.6 [3.5]	11.8 [2.9]
Employment (% with jobs [Number])	68 [13]	56 [15]
Socioeconomic status (% Hollingshead 3- [Number])	47 [9]	56 [15]
Marital Status (% Married [N])	42 [8]	30 [8]
Family History of Psychiatric Illness (% positive [number])	53 [10]	41 [11]
Diagnostic Characteristics (% [Number])		
Pedophilia	74 [14]	56 [15]
Exhibitionist/Voyeur	21 [4]	22 [6]
Other Paraphilias	5 [1]	22 [6]

There were no significant differences between No MPA and MPA groups on any of the variables listed in this table.

significantly less than the mean time that subjects in the Non-relapse group had been followed (6.65 years (2.4) (t = 2.69; df = 44; $p = 0.01$) suggesting that differences in relapse rate were not due to the Non-relapse group being followed for a shorter time.

Relapses were self-reported by 11 out of 17 (65%) of the Relapsers. Since self-report was the most common means of detecting relapse in this study, the possibility of differences in the frequency of self-reporting by subjects receiving MPA compared to subjects not receiving MPA was investigated. There was no significant difference between the number of subjects who self-reported while receiving MPA (2 out of 4) compared to the number who self-reported while not receiving MPA (9 out of 13) (Chi-square = 0.49; df = 1; $p = 0.48$).

Next, the possibility that there were important differences between those subjects who were receiving treatment with MPA (N = 27) and those not receiving MPA (N = 19) was investigated. No significant differences between these two groups were found in terms of age, race, education, employment, socioeconomic status, marital status, family history of psychiatric disorder, or diagnostic group (Table 3). In addition, there were no significant differences between No-MPA and MPA groups in terms of number of years follow-up, or years to first relapse (mean (SD): 6.7 years (1.4) vs 7.2 years (2.9) (t = 0.74; df = 44; $p = 0.46$); 4.5 years (2.0) versus 5.3 years (3.3) (t = 0.53; df = 15; $p = 0.60$) respectively).

However, significant differences were found between the No-MPA group and MPA group in terms of number of relapses (mean (SD) 1.5 (1.9) versus 0.33 (1.0) t = 2.8; df = 44; $p = 0.007$).

Finally, a greater proportion of subjects in the MPA group had had previous arrests prior to enrolment in the JHSDU than subjects in the No-MPA group (17/27 vs. 4/19 respectively, Chi-square = 7.9; df = 1; $p = 0.005$).

DISCUSSION

The major finding of this study, that a smaller proportion of subjects who received regular MPA relapsed compared to subjects who did not receive MPA, is summarized in Figure 1. Although this supports the hypothesis that regular MPA treatment decreases the risk of relapse there are several methodologic limitations of this study that require acknowledgement. Perhaps most important is the fact that neither subjects nor therapists were blind to the subject's medication status during therapy. It is possible that subjects who were more likely to relapse were selectively deprived of MPA treatment. However, this seems unlikely since there was no difference between groups in terms of variables which have been reported to increase the risk of relapse. These include: male sex, youth, race, single marital status, unemployment, low socioeconomic status (Amir, 1971; Chappell, Geis, Schafer and Siegel, 1971), previous arrests (Meyer and Romero, 1980), homosexual pedophilia (Sturgeon and Taylor, 1980) (particularly non-incestuous (Revitch and Weiss, 1962)), or exhibitionism (Cox, 1980). Moreover, the finding that subjects in the MPA group were significantly more likely to have been arrested prior to beginning treatment suggests that if anything, subjects with poorer past records were selected into the MPA group. Although compliance

□ *Figure 1: Number of subjects who relapsed (N = 17) and did not relapse (N = 29) graphed according to MPA status (Chi-square = 13.8; df = 1; p = 0.0002). See text for definition of "relapse."*

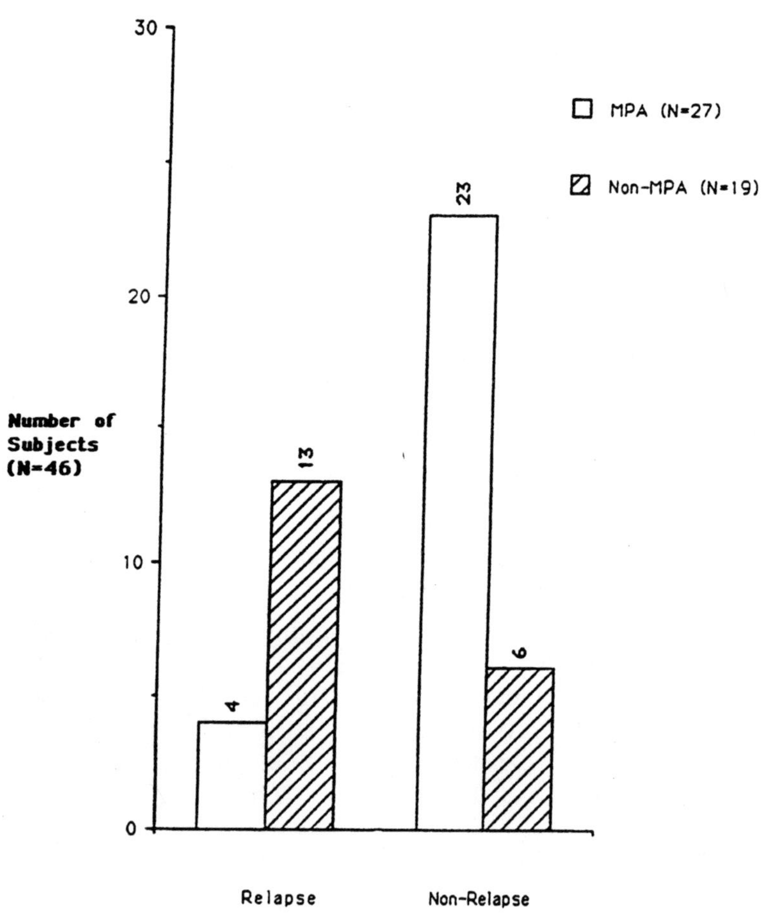

and motivation for treatment are also important predictors which were not possible to control for directly, it seems reasonable to assume that the sample selection criteria (5 years of continuous treatment) was sufficient to select only highly motivated subjects. Nonetheless, the possibility that subjects who volunteered for MPA treatment were even more motivated than subjects who received psychotherapy alone for 5 years cannot be ruled out.

Patient and therapist expectations about the efficacy of MPA is another important confounding influence. Although this problem can only be adequately controlled in a double blind prospective treatment design, the fact that the relationship between MPA status and relapse was the same across all groups analyzed in this study suggests that expectation effects alone are insufficient to account for the main finding of this study. It also suggests that the effect of MPA in addition to regular psychotherapy was sufficiently powerful to eliminate the differences in relapse rates usually observed between diagnostic groups.

In addition, the subjects included in this study were a highly selected sample. Subjects who were unwilling or unable to comply with the requirement of regular attendance at group psychotherapy sessions were excluded. It is possible that the *a priori* decision to eliminate subjects who had not attended psychotherapy sessions for 5 or more years selectively eliminated subjects who relapsed while taking MPA. However, the exclusion criteria for this study would also be expected to eliminate non-responders to psychotherapy alone. Fortunately, this is a testable hypothesis and the relapse rates of subjects who were excluded from this study will be the subject of a future report. Until these data have been analyzed generalizations from this study to other patient populations, particularly those treated for less than 5 years, must remain tentative.

Finally, any investigation of medication efficacy in the treatment of sexual disorders is limited by the ability of the investigators to accurately detect relapses. It is almost certain that undetected relapses occurred in this study sample. However, there is no *a priori* reason to suspect that these would be more likely to occur in the group treated with MPA. In fact, although multiple sources were used to detect relapses, most relapses were self-reported. This may reflect the highly selected nature of the sample, which demonstrated commitment to the JHSDU by staying in treatment for over 5 years.

However, there was no statistical difference between number of self-reports in the group treated with MPA and the group not treated with MPA.

Given these limitations, this study has several important findings. Subjects receiving MPA had lower rates of relapse than subjects who were not receiving MPA. There were no differences between Relapsers and Non-relapsers and no differences between subjects treated with MPA and subjects not treated with MPA on any of the main demographic or psychiatric variables studied. Taken together, these findings strongly support the hypothesis that lower relapse rates are associated with the addition of MPA to on-going long-term psychotherapy.

There are no clear guidelines in the literature about how long patients should continue to receive MPA. The finding that relapses in the study sample occurred at a mean of 4.7 years (2.3 SD) from the start of treatment suggests that long-term use of MPA should be considered. Moreover, the finding that only 4 patients who were treated with MPA relapsed suggests that MPA continues to be effective with chronic use.

Some investigators have suggested that arrest records are the only reliable way to assess relapse rates since paraphilic men will tend to deny many of their activities. The finding that most relapses in this study were detected through self-report by the subjects themselves contradicts this view and supports the hypothesis that risk taking even to the point of engineering their own capture may be characteristic of some patients with paraphilias who present for treatment in clinics (Money, 1986; Stollar, 1975). If this is true, it might be expected that paraphilic patients who are followed as long as in this study would have a high likelihood of self-reporting. However, there are several other possible reasons for the high rate of self-report in this sample. One reason for the high rate of self-report may be that the sample was an unusually compliant sub-group of the true population of paraphilics. Abel, et al (Abel, Mittleman and Becker, 1985; Abel, Becker, Cunningham-Rathner, Mittleman and Rouleau, 1988) found that when he was able to guarantee confidentiality to his subjects, they self-reported far more relapses than had been suspected. It is possible that chronic patients in the JHSDU came to trust the staff enough that they became more likely to self-report relapses. In any case, none of these explanations is sufficient to account for the higher rate of relapse (but not self-report) in subjects who were not receiving MPA at follow-up. Until further research is completed, it would seem that the best approach is to use multiple sources of information (as was done in this study).

In summary, this study found that patients in long-term psychotherapy with adjunctive MPA had lower rates of relapse than patients in psychotherapy without MPA. The design of this study was intentionally conservative to avoid falsely attributing effectiveness to MPA in preventing relapse by: (1) using a broad definition of "relapse," (2) following the subjects for more than 5 years, (3) accepting multiple sources of information about relapse, and (4) separately analyzing subjects with low expected relapse rates (incestuous and heterosexual pedophiles). Variables which have been reported to be associated with relapse were controlled both between Relapsers and Non-relapsers and between subjects treated with MPA and not treated with MPA. These factors included age, race, marital status, employment, socioeconomic status, and type of paraphilia. Further studies comparing the rate of relapse in paraphilic men followed for less than 5 years are required.

Finally, although this study appears to support the use of MPA in the treatment of sex offenders, it does not prove that MPA works. The fact that this study was an open, retrospective investigation carried out in a clinic that has considerable experience in the use of MPA as an adjunct to psychotherapy in the treatment of paraphilias limits the generalizability of this study. Replication of this study's findings in other patient groups utilizing a multi-center, double-blind treatment design is clearly needed.

REFERENCES

Abel, G.G., Mittleman, M.S. and Becker, J.V. (1985). Sex offenders: results of assessment and recommendations for treatment. In: Ben-Aron, M.H., Hucker, S.J. and Webster, C.D., eds. *Clinical Criminology: Current Concepts*, 191-205.

Abel, G.G., Becker, J.V., Cunningham-Rathner, J., Mittleman, M.S. and Rouleau, J.L. (1988). Multiple paraphilic diagnoses among sex offenders. *Bulletin of the American Academy of Psychiatry and the Law*, 16, 153-168.

American Psychiatric Association (1987). *Diagnostic and statistical manual of mental disorders, third edition, revised.*

Amir, M. (1971). *Patterns in forcible rape.*

Bercovici, J. (1979). Androgens and antiandrogens: mechanisms of action. In: Agarwal MK, ed. *Antihormones*, 307-317.

Berlin, F.S. and Meinecke, C.F. (1981). Treatment of sex offenders with anti-androgenic medication: conceptualization, review of treatment modalities and preliminary findings. *American Journal of Psychiatry*, 138, 601-607.

Chappell, D., Geis, G., Schafer, S. and Siegel L. (1971). A comparative study of offenses known to the police in Boston and Los Angeles. In: Henslin JM. ed. *Studies in the sociology of sex.*

Cox, D.J. (1980). *Exhibitionism: description, assessment and treatment*, 3-10.

Fedoroff, J.P. (1988). Buspirone hydrochloride in the treatment of transvestic fetishism. *Journal of Clinical Psychiatry*, 49, 408-409.

Furby, L., Weinrott, M.R. and Blackshaw, L. (1989). Sex offender recidivism: a review. *Psychological Bulletin*, 105, 3-30.

Hollingshead A.B. and Redlich, F.C. (1958). *Social class and mental illness—a community survey.*

Kilmann, P.R., Sabalis, R.F., Gearing, M.L., Bukstel, L.H. and Scovern, A.W. (1982). The treatment of sexual paraphilias: a review of outcome research. *Journal of Sex Research*, 18, 193-252.

Money J. (1970) Use of an androgen-depleting hormone in the treatment of male sex offenders. *Journal of Sex Research*, 6, 165-172.

Marshall, W.L. and Barbaree, H.E. (1990). Outcome of comprehensive cognitive-behavioral treatment programs. In: Marshall, W.L., Laws, D.R. and Barbaree, H.E., eds. *Handbook of sexual assault*, 363-385.

McGuire, R., Carlisle, J. and Young, B. (1965). Sexual deviations as conditioned behavior. *Behavioural Research Therapy*, 2, 185-190.

Meyer, L. and Romero, J. (1980). *A ten-year follow-up of sex offender recidivism.*

Money, J. (1986). *Lovemaps.*

Revitch, E. and Weiss, R.G. (1962). The pedophiliac offender. *Diseases of the nervous system*, 23, 73-78.

Roeder, F.D. (1966). Stereotaxic lesion of the tuber cinereum in sexual deviation. *Conferences in Neurology*, 27, 162-163.

Rubins, J. (1969). Sexual perversions. *American Journal of Psychoanalysis*, 29,94-105.

Stollar, R.J. (1975). *Perversion: the erotic form of hatred.*

Sturgeon, V.H. and Taylor J. (1980). Report of a five-year follow-up study of mentally disordered sex offenders released from Atascadero State Hospital in 1973. *Criminal Justice Journal*, 4, 31-63.

Sturup, G.K. (1972). Castration: the total treatment. In: Resnick, H.L.P. and Wolfgang, M.E., eds. *Sexual behaviors: Social, clinical and legal aspects*, 361-382.

AUTHORS' NOTES

J. Paul Fedoroff, M.D., is Assistant Professor of Psychiatry, University of Toronto, Toronto.

Robert Wisner-Carlson, M.D., is Staff Psychiatrist, The Sheppard and Enoch-Pratt Hospital, Baltimore.

Sharon Dean is Research Assistant, The Johns Hopkins Hospital, Baltimore.

Fred S. Berlin, M.D., PhD, is Associate Professor of Psychiatry, The Johns Hopkins University, Baltimore.

Address for Correspondence: J. Paul Fedoroff, M.D., Forensic Division, The Clarke Institute of Psychiatry, 250 College Street, Toronto, Ontario, Canada M5T 1R8.

SEX OFFENDER TREATMENT: PSYCHOLOGICAL AND MEDICAL APPROACHES. Pp. 125-139.

The Texas Experience with DepoProvera: 1980-1990

L.E. Emory, M.D.
University of Texas Medical Branch & Rosenberg Clinic, Galveston

C.M. Cole
University of Texas Medical Branch & Rosenberg Clinic, Galveston

W.J. Meyer, III, M.D.
University of Texas Medical Branch, Galveston

ABSTRACT We are reporting on our experience with treatment of sex offending behaviors with anti-androgen therapy (DepoProvera®) to control sex offending behaviors. In the last ten years, we have had the opportunity to compare a group of men who received DepoProvera to a group who had the same clinical and legal problems of sexual offenses but who refused pharmacological treatment. Both groups received group therapy, individual therapy, and sometimes family therapy. The goal of treatment was to prevent further victimization, develop personal insight, enhance self esteem, and to make restitution to society through successful probation and parole, working regularly, and meeting their adult responsibilities. Side effects of the medication can be serious and include formation of gall stones, weight gain, malaise, muscle cramps, and even diabetes. Outcome results indicate that possible factors signifying an increased likelihood of re-offense are high initial plasma testosterone, regressed behavior type, exhibitionism, continued substance abuse, and past history of major head trauma. Many of the professional and ethical issues surrounding DepoProvera treatment are serious considerations in establishing this type of treatment program.

A variety of different therapies for sex offenders has been attempted with varying degrees of success (Heim and Hursch, 1979). Anti-androgen therapy in the form of medroxyprogesterone acetate (MPA, DepoProvera) to control and ultimately eliminate sexual aggressiveness and deviancy in males has been used since 1966 in the United States (Money, 1968). Cyproteroneacetate, (CPA) (not available in the U.S.A.) has been used in Western Europe and Canada (Berlin and Coyle, 1981). Both MPA and CPA are powerful anti-androgens without the property of feminization (breast enlargement,female fat distribution, loss of male hair pattern, significant penile atrophy). Their main pharmacologic action is inhibition of testosterone production in the testes, but there is an initial effect on mood and affect that occurs before any reported changes in the person's plasma sex hormone concentration or sexual fantasies (Walker and Meyer, 1981; Money, 1986). Initial calmness and even sedation are often reported. These effects may be due to the recently discovered benzodiazepine action of progestational agents on the GABA receptors (Gee, 1988).

Since 1976 the University of Texas Medical Branch has had an active treatment program of sex offending behavior utilizing MPA. Earlier experience of the clinic was reported by Walker, Meyer, Emory and Rubin (1984). In 1980 the clinic moved from the medical school campus into the private community. In that private psychiatric clinic which is still associated with The University of Texas Medical Branch, 153 men have been interviewed and evaluated specifically for help in dealing with sex offending behavior from 1980 to the end of 1990. Most of the sex offending behaviors have had significant legal ramifications, and all behaviors have been psychologically devastating to the person presenting, as well as others. All the men requested to be evaluated as to suitability of medical treatment to control these unacceptable sexual practices.

The primary goal is to avoid any new victims. Other long-term goals are to establish a pair bond with someone over 18 who is receptive. Another objective is to have a job (or avocation for those retired) that provides structure and positive self worth. The current report concerns the 61 men who were offered MPA and presents the process for initial evaluation and treatment selection, a detailed description of both the psychotherapeutic and the pharmacological aspects of treatment, and reviews the side effects and behavior outcomes of treatment. Also, many of the professional and ethical issues involved in this type of therapy are discussed.

INITIAL EVALUATION AND SELECTION FOR TREATMENT

Patients considered for DepoProvera were self-referred or referred by family members, a physician or their attorney who was seeking some psychiatric aid in a defense strategy. Several men had written from prison for information and later contacted the clinic when they were released. Of the 61 men who were specifically recommended to receive MPA, DepoProvera, as a major component of their treatment plan, 40 men agreed to this therapy. The consent process and form enumerating the many side effects provided a significant barrier to accepting MPA. Those who accepted MPA were more likely to be either self-referred or referred by a physician than those who refused MPA. The median age of the patients was between 30 and 40. All were known to want or admitted to aberrant, illegal sexual behaviors listed in Table 1.

A number of parameters are considered to determine if the individual is suitable for MPA therapy. One selection factor for offering MPA therapy is the patient's psychological mind set: does the person admit the offense and does he have such compelling sexual fantasies, pressures, compulsions as to be overwhelming? Is his deviant imagery or fantasy for sexual gratifications/arousal so entrenched as to be used even in normal sexual activities with a consenting person? If he is driven by these paraphiliac thoughts, DepoProvera might be an appropriate form of therapy (Money, 1986).

The patient must comprehend that DepoProvera needs to be given over a long period of time, possibly 3-5 years and in conjunction with group therapy, individual psychotherapy and sometimes family therapy. Men in a pre-adjudication phase pressing for a rapid cure are refused. We know these men didn't develop this disorder overnight and it will take a long time for follow-up.

Another selection factor for DepoProvera may be contributing physical conditions. Inappropriate sexual behavior following head injury is often amenable to MPA therapy. A history of previous seizures is not a contraindication for therapy. DepoProvera does not

Table 1: Diagnostic Distribution of Offenders Offered DepoProvera

Type of Paraphilia	Total Number	Accepted Treatment
Pedophilia	37	23
Rape	7	7
Exhibitionism	16	10
Voyeurism	1	0
Sum	61	40

lower the seizure threshold; it can even be used as an adjunct in anticonvulsant therapy (Blumer and Migeon, 1975).

There are also conditions which exclude the use of DepoProvera. We also do not accept for DepoProvera therapy those people who admit the sexual offense, but blame drugs, alcohol, fatigue, or their own abused childhood. We do not accept those people who have severe dyssocial tendencies in their histories, e.g., brutal physical assault as a result of severe sado-sexual tendencies. For security reasons, we cannot handle these people in a private outpatient clinic setting.

For those who can't return to Galveston each week for the MPA injection, they must identify an accountable, reliable resource to administer the medication. If the logistics can't be worked out ahead, (a measure of commitment), we decline. In a few instances we have set up treatment protocols for patients living far away; they must agree to be in some type of regular counseling and return to see us every six months.

Medical exclusion criteria include high potential for developing diabetes, i.e., abnormal glucose tolerance test with insulin levels, or strong family history of diabetes (Meyer, Walker, Emory, Smith, 1985). One should be clinically very cautious if the patient has elevated serum cholesterol and triglycerides, or other conditions linked to an increased risk of gall bladder disease (Meyer, Weiner, Emory, Cole, Isenberg, Fagan, Thompson, 1992). We refused to treat one man with DepoProvera because he had a history of recurrent phlebitis, severe (Gagne, 1981).

Based on this initial 1 to 1-1/2 hour interview, we feel reasonably comfortable in recommending hospitalization for a complete physical, neuropsychological battery and hormonal testing, prior to initiating DepoProvera. Hospitalization is recommended because it allows intense observation of the patient, his response to rules and uniformity, and his ability to participate in a microcosm of society without acting out. The hospitalization also allows the offending patient to be comforted by his peers and to begin to make restitution to society by his acknowledgment of his crime.

Another benefit of inpatient stay is similar to the drug-dependent patient being admitted. The patient is in a safe environment to look at himself, crack the defenses of isolationism and denial, and spend very dedicated time confronting himself. In our experience, these initial goals cannot be accomplished in as timely a manner on an outpatient basis. A real limitation of our program is that it is all private. Therefore, one must have the financial resources to be admitted. The cost of laboratory work alone is over $300. Some Texas counties have paid for the outpatient counseling, but none has provided resources for DepoProvera therapy.

After admission to a psychiatric ward, the nursing staff are informed about the patient's history and therefore are receptive and able to answer questions at anytime. It takes three hospital days to obtain the baseline workup on a new DepoProvera patient: blood chemistry, thyroid panel, testosterone, gonadotropins, prolactin, lipid profile, gall bladder assessment (usually ultrasound with a fatty meal challenge), five-hour glucose tolerance test including insulin levels, and masturbated semen specimen. The physical exam is done to detect any physical abnormalities, including stretch phallic length and testicular size in reference to Prader beads. An electroencephalogram and possible brain CT scan may be done especially where clinical history suggests probable pathology.

During the hospital stay, we have the more senior patients on DepoProvera talk with the new patient. We also speak with the man's family members and encourage them to read the extensive consent form. We have taken every precaution to ensure that the patient is truly and thoroughly informed and that his consent is voluntary. After the evaluation period, the patient signs the consent and begins the treatment phase.

PSYCHOTHERAPEUTIC ASPECTS OF TREATMENT

An integral part of the treatment program involves participation in psychotherapeutic intervention, both individual and group therapy. All of the men participate in a monthly "men's group" where support and confrontation are key elements for uncovering the factors associated with sexually offensive acting-out. The variety of "cognitive distortions" that have been used to perpetuate this offensive, victimizing behavior must be systematically broken down. Each individual must come to recognize that his behavior was indeed victimizing and hurtful to others, often with serious and lifelong consequences.

Additional sustaining factors for this behavior (power, anger, control) that have been identified by other sex offender treaters (Groth, 1979) must likewise be explored and addressed. Additionally, the group focuses on stress factors which seem to increase the risk for sexually aberrant acting- out (e.g., job problems, financial pressures, relationship frictions or failures, sense of low self-worth) as well as substance abuse (e.g., alcohol, illicit drugs) which reduces clear thinking, lowers inhibitions, and provides an opportunity for the cognitive distortions to become overwhelming. And finally, the group serves as a place where offenders can talk about their own sexual abuse. Approximately 50% of the men we have evaluated and treated were themselves victims of sexual abuse in childhood. Besides the group approach, individual psychotherapy plays a key role and is likewise scheduled on a monthly basis. This is the time to review one's progress in group as well as to address specific issues related to background, current lifestyle and relationships, and one's paraphiliac problem. Both individual and group psychotherapy should be continued at least as long as the pharmacological therapy.

PHARMACOLOGICAL ASPECTS OF THE TREATMENT PROGRAM

The initial weekly dose is 400 mg IM. Experience has shown that the men report much less tissue irritation with the 100 mg/cc of

DepoProvera; the 400 mg/cc dose is very irritating, although the volume is less. In fact, two 2cc injections are needed with the dilute form which the men prefer. This starting dose is maintained weekly as the patient is interviewed for changes in his mental processes. Our experience is that three-400 mg injections, one week apart, are necessary before the person notices a change in sexual thought patterns. Family members are asked for their observations. Their reports are very critical, especially in the head injured.

In this clinical situation, the family reports much less leering, better ability to maintain appropriate social distances, and less psychomotor agitation. "Calmness and less hyper" are consistent comments. Severe tiredness is usually the first reason for dose reduction, to 300 mg IM. Over a 30-day period, the serum testosterone level falls to preadolescent levels, e.g.,16 to 19 ng/dl in younger males, 70 to 90 ng/dl in older males. Three hundred mg IM weekly or every other week is an acceptable dose for most of the men. The typical patient receives DepoProvera for approximately two years before tapering further. One criticism is that we rely on self-report (as well as the obvious no rearrests) to judge efficacy. These men remain on therapy at personal and financial sacrifice, validating the efficacy of DepoProvera for the individual, as can be seen in the following case example.

A CASE HISTORY

B.H., a 37 year-old paroled reoffender, was ordered by the court to consider treatment for sex-offending behavior after he was rearrested for child molesting, only four months out of prison for a similar crime. He agreed to receive DepoProvera and after the screening began weekly injections; he has continued this medication over a five-year period. He lived at a halfway house, held various jobs, and began to form adult relationships. In individual psychotherapy he talked about his own victimization by a priest when he was a teenager. DepoProvera was slowly lowered over time. He developed an erectile problem as well as the loss of any ejaculate. Penile nocturnal tumescence completely disappeared. His masturbatory frequency dropped from several times a day to less than once a month.

In the first two years of treatment, B. pushed himself to establish some career goals. Using skills he had acquired in prison, he became a cook, employed in the halfway house. He formed some social contacts in his church. After two years he attempted to date and established some romantic, but not long-lasting, relationships. The DepoProvera was decreased to 300 mg weekly after two years. The testosterone remained between 30-40 ng/dl.

In the third year of treatment, B. was given more responsibility at the lodge, often admitting destitute women with young families. He spoke in therapy about the arousal problems he experienced in dealing with these needy children. So DepoProvera was not decreased and he was able to put up "red flags" in his environment. In the fourth year of treatment, he began to look for employment in the private sector, again as a cook, but with better benefits. He met a girl and was much more realistic about the viability of this relationship. The DepoProvera was maintained because he felt more secure with himself.

B. continued to be retested every six months with serum testosterone and general chemistry analyses, glucose tolerance tests, and gall bladder ultrasound studies. He was hospitalized on an emergency basis for acute abdominal pain, with the differential diagnosis of acute pancreatitis vs. food poisoning. The x-rays were felt to show duodenitis, which resolved rapidly and without specific therapy except 48 hours of nasogastric suction with intravenous rehydration.

By the end of the fifth year, he was receiving 200 mg of DepoProvera every other week, then every third week. He was then securely employed as a chef and had decided to live with the girlfriend. The decision was made to taper the DepoProvera to 100 mg IM every month for six months and then discontinue. He remained in group and individual psychotherapy, and he continued with his parole reporting as well. Currently, one year later, he remains in a monthly sex) offender group. He reports he continues to feel secure, with no paraphiliac thoughts of children. This will provide a very important self-policing factor.

TREATMENT OUTCOME

The previously described patient, at this point, represents a treatment success. He has accepted that treatment may never be completely over. Most patients experience a vacation from their sexual drive and are able to begin working on other issues in their lives. All patients who began DepoProvera took the medication at least six months. The typical patient received it more than two years. Money and Bennett (1981) reported that patients often reoffended while receiving and after stopping DepoProvera. In another report we have noted that seven of forty patients who started DepoProvera have reoffended while receiving the medication (Meyer, Cole, Emory, 1992). In one case, the dose had been inadvertently lowered and the protective effect of a low testosterone level was not in place. In the other six patients, no such factor could be found. However, all the reoffenses were to a lesser degree, albeit just as illegal and subject to all the consequences. The rapist being treated exposed himself; another compulsive exhibitionist inappropriately grabbed at an obviously very young girl; and a third patient, a fixated homosexual pedophile, developed close friendships with obviously sexually mature, but underage, 15- and 16-year-old males that he pressured to have sex with him. He had previously molested members of his cub scout troop. Of the 29 men who stopped DepoProvera prematurely, 35%, or 10, reoffended; 58% of a group, who refused DepoProvera in spite of their criminal history and admitted paraphilia, reoffended while still receiving therapy which was limited to individual and group psychotherapies (Meyer, Cole, and Emory, 1992). Medication specifically recommended to diminish sexual drive (e.g., Mellaril) was always offered and occasionally accepted. We are now offering Anafranil (clomipramine) as an alternative.

We have treated five closed-head-injury young men whose entire rehabilitation program was blocked (some with criminal charges to answer for) because of sexual behaviors. MPA was the treatment of last resort in all cases. Tegretol, Lithium, and major tranquilizers had been used, plus a variety of behavioral and cognitive therapies, all without success. All of them responded to MPA. However, this group had a particularly high reoffense rate when the MPA was reduced or stopped.

Only one patient ever denied any diminution of his sexual drive on DepoProvera. This was a 15-year-old rapist certified as an adult who received 800 mg weekly IM. His testosterone, initially 556 ng/dl, fell to 116 ng/dl, but he continued to be very sexual and exposed out the windows of a locked adolescent ward. This behavior persisted in spite of six months of intensive inpatient milieu, daily 15-20 minute individual sessions and twice weekly one-hour group

Table 2: Risk for Reoffense in Chemically Treated Sex Offenders

- *High initial plasma testosterone*
- *Regressed behavior type (Groth et al., 1982)*
- *Paraphilic behavior = exhibitionism*
- *Continued substance abuse*
- *Major head injury*

therapy. He was finally released, given probation, and reoffended. He is a severe anti-social personality, and, as such, the paraphilia had little chance of successful treatment.

In retrospect, almost universally all the patients have appreciated the diminished libido which gave them the opportunity to control their aggressive drives and to think about themselves without continuing further compulsive, illegal, harmful behaviors. By including DepoProvera in our treatment plan for sex offenders, we believe pharmacological security is in place, allowing the sex offender to discuss his aberrant behaviors and to learn ways to place obstacles in front of these behaviors. Many of these men had relied on sexual activity to deal with non-sexual problems: loneliness, isolation, low self-esteem, so the cognitive psychotherapy aspect of the program is also very critical. Table 2 lists five major risk factors for reoffending in spite of receiving ongoing DepoProvera therapy (see Meyer, Cole and Emory, 1992, for details).

But why, with evidence for change and control, did anyone continue to act out in a sexually offending way? The only explanation we have to offer is that there was a failure or a major lack of a "pair bond." This concept from Money and Bennett (1981) implies a strong, dedicated emotional commitment to another person with sexual, communal and financial ties. Therefore, it has seemed critical to the patient's support to establish pair bonds that have some chance of succeeding, and to offer a substitute bond (e.g., the men's group, Alcoholics Anonymous, the transference of the therapeutic relationship) until a more lasting ideal bond can be established.

PROFESSIONAL AND ETHICAL ISSUES

The treatment of sex offenders poses unique problems of ethics and professional conduct. In very few areas of medicine does society seem to demand accountability for outcome from the professionals. When an identified sex offender presents for treatment, usually after external coercion, how voluntary is his consent? If he feels accepting treatment is the only way to avoid going to prison, is he sincerely motivated or does he want to look good for the court? This clinical concern is usually seen in the preadjudication phase when the defense attorney is trying to mitigate for probation vs. prison. Wouldn't almost any man agree to any option to maintain his freedom? Courts will often give a probated sentence, with the order for treatment as well as supervision, that is the offender's choice as well as his punishment.

Because courts are increasingly sophisticated about medical intervention, judges have even been known to order a man to undergo chemical castration with anti-androgens, without any prior medical evaluation. It is our opinion that this is a vastly inappropriate decision, basically putting the court in the business of practicing medicine without a license. Unless we are to become total agents of the state, we must ethically insist that whatever therapy is to be undertaken, it be done with respect for the offender's right to choose. Some would say a convicted felon has no rights. Seymour Halleck (1981) voiced his concern. DepoProvera, already controversial in the public's mind, is not approved by the United States Food and Drug Administration for psychiatric medical conditions (Rosenfield, Maine, Rochat, Shelton, Hatcher, 1983).

It is for this reason that our patients must read and sign a three-page consent form that is reviewed annually by the UTMB Institutional Review Board. We also require that family members read and sign the form. A number of side effects that have been observed with DepoProvera are well-documented in the consent form. In the forty individuals previously discussed, four had gall stones, three had diabetes, and three had hypertension severe enough to require medication. Less troublesome side effects included excessive weight gain, malaise, migraine headaches, leg cramps, and gastrointestinal complaints (see Meyer, Cole and Emory, 1992, for details). We have been very careful to point out that in addition to the known side effects, long-term side effects may yet be discovered. There have been two reports of animal models developing tumors while receiving DepoProvera (Rosenfield et al. 1983). With 25 years' experience, we have not yet seen any similar problems in the human model.

Teratogenecity is another concern. We ask these men to avoid conception because of abnormal sperm/azoospermia and low testosterone (Meyer et al., 1985), but of two live children conceived by fathers on DepoProvera, one had a heart defect. Unfortunately, the controversy about DepoProvera being a contraceptive agent in women has added to the negative image.

Another area of professional and ethical concern is the therapist's responsibility to the community. By admitting this person to the general psychiatry unit, we are exposing staff and patients to further violent actions by a known felon. A very disorganized manic can be much harder to handle, but he doesn't have the history of criminal behavior. Also, admitting a sex offender does not endear one to hospital administrators who are rightly concerned about patient safety and adverse publicity. Given our current standards of conduct, mandatory child abuse reporting laws and the judicial precedents in Tarasoff of duty to warn/duty to protect, how can we take care of our patient without breaching confidentiality, filing applications for emergency detentions, "snitching" to their probation officer for poor attendance, or doing whatever paternal intervention is necessary?

Our sex offenders as a group have notoriously poor luck, exercise terrible judgment, and demonstrate destructive impulsivity. Therefore, we attempt to create as much of a safety network as possible in collaboration with probation, parole, Children's Protective Services, local Alcoholics Anonymous, other medical people, and patient's family and employer. We have come to appreciate the cooperation and interactions with other professionals. We don't want it to be adversarial, but these patients can't be treated in a professional vacuum. Another very sensitive area in working with sex offenders is one's interaction with colleagues, especially those who openly say that crucifixion is the treatment of choice. A defensive, isolative posture can develop as even family and friends recoil when hearing about your work. Medical endocrinologists aren't eager to work with you. Only the surgeons for whom we generated four cholecystectomies seem to be willing to discuss "Lester the Molester" with brief interest. Other psychiatrists and therapists may openly wonder what one could possibly obtain from this work. The Church of Scientology and National Organization of Women have together been very critical and vociferous of DepoProvera used to treat these patients. While everyone would agree that treatment over incarceration makes humane as well as fiscal sense, we must work to define the patients who can be helped, and in what setting, measured by what parameters, to find that middle-of-the-road between therapeutic nihilism and a discrediting crusader complex.

CONCLUSION

In conclusion, we have evaluated and recommended for treatment with high dose DepoProvera a select group of sex offenders. These men, because of their persistence in deviant, illegal, and harmful sexual activities, cause a great deal of physical and emotional pain to their victims as well as create a very disturbed, uncomfortable consciousness in the community. All persons, all of society, deserve and demand to be protected from the predatory results of these compulsive, reprehensible acts. And if these individuals sincerely want to change their lives, control their offending, and refocus themselves, DepoProvera can be a critically important therapy. Our experience suggests that DepoProvera may allow carefully selected men to participate in an outpatient program to deal with sexual offending behaviors. The program allows them to maintain their family relationships and vocational goals for a comprehensive treatment plan of rehabilitation and restitution.

REFERENCES

Berlin, F.S., & Coyle, G.S. (1981) Psychiatric clinics at the Johns Hopkins Hospital. *Johns Hopkins Medical Journal*, 149, 119-125.

Blumer, D. & Migeon, C. (1975) Hormone and hormonal agents in the treatment of aggression. *Journal of Nervous and Mental Disorders*, 160, 127-137.

Gagne, P. (1981) Treatment of sex offenders with Medroxyprogesterone acetate. *American Journal of Psychiatry*, 138, 644-646.

Gee, K.W. (1988) Steroid modulation of the GABA/benzodiazepine receptor-linked chloride ionophore. *Molecular Neurobiology*, 2, 291-317.

Groth, A.N., & Birnbaum, H.J. (1979) *Men Who Rape: The Psychology of the Offender*. New York: Plenum Press.

Groth, A.N., Hobson, W.F., & Gary, T.S. (1982) The child molester: Clinical observations. In: J. Conte and D.A. Shore (Eds.), *Social Work and Child Sexual Abuse*, pp. 129-144. New York: The Haworth Press, Inc.

Halleck, S.L. (1981) The ethics of antiandrogen therapy. *American Journal of Psychiatry,* 138, 642-643.

Heim, N., and Hursch, C.J. (1979) Castration for sex offenders: Treatment or punishment? A review and critique of recent European literature. *Archives of Sexual Behavior,* 8, 281-304.

Meyer, W.J. III, Cole, C.M., & Emory, L.E. (1992) DepoProvera treatment for sex-offending behavior: an evaluation of outcome. *Bulletin of the American Academy of Psychiatry & the Law,* in press.

Meyer, W.J. III, Walker, P.A., Emory, L.E., & Smith, E.R. (1985) Physical, metabolic, and hormonal effects on men of long-term therapy with medroxyprogesterone acetate. *Fertility and Sterility,* 43, 102-109.

Money, J. (1968) Discussion on hormonal inhibition of libido in male sex offenders. In: R. Michael (Ed.), *Endocrinology and Human Behavior*. London: Oxford University Press.Money, J. (1986) *Lovemaps*. New York: Irvington.

Money, J., & Bennett, R.G. (1981) Postadolescent paraphilic sex offenders: antiandrogen and counseling therapy follow-up. *International Journal of Mental Health,* 10, 122-133.

Rosenfield, A., Maine, D., Rochat, R., Shelton, J., & Hatcher, R.A. (1983) The Food and Drug Administration and medroxyprogesterone acetate. *Journal of the American Medical Association,* 249, 2922-2928.

Walker, P.A., & Meyer III, W.J. (1981) Medroxyprogesterone acetate treatment for paraphiliac sex offenders. In: Hayes, J.R., Roberts, T.K., Soloway K.S. (Eds.), *Violence and the Violent Individual.* New York: SP Medical & Scientific.

Walker, P.A., Meyer, W.J., Emory, L.E., & Rubin, A.L. (1984) Antiandrogenic treatment of the paraphilias. In: Stancer, et al. (Eds.), *Guidelines for the Use of Psychotropic Drugs*. New York: Spectrum.

AUTHORS' NOTES

L. E. Emory, M.D., is clinical assistant professor in the Department of Psychiatry and Behavioral Sciences, University of Texas Medical Branch and Rosenberg Clinic, Galveston.

C. M. Cole, Ph.D., is clinical assistant professor in the Department of Psychiatry and Behavioral Sciences, University of Texas Medical Branch and the Rosenberg Clinic, Galveston.

Walter J. Meyer, III, M.D., is a member of the faculty in the Department of Psychiatry and Behavioral Sciences, University of Texas Medical Branch, Galveston.

This project was partially supported by the Clinical Research Center Program grant RR73-UTMB. The authors would like to extend their gratitude to Ms. Nita Brannon for preparing the manuscript.

Address for correspondence: Walter J. Meyer, III, M.D., Department of Psychiatry and Behavioral Sciences, University of Texas Medical Branch, Galveston, TX 77550.

SEX OFFENDER TREATMENT: PSYCHOLOGICAL AND MEDICAL APPROACHES. Pp. 141-165.

☐ DECISION PROCESS ANALOGUE

Perceptions of Child Sexual Assault

The Effects of Victim and Offender Characteristics and Behaviour

Jeffrey Edwin Drugge

University of Toronto

ABSTRACT The effects of gender of victim and offender, age of victim, and initiator of interaction (victim or offender) on the general public's perceptions of, and judgments about, cases of child sexual assault, were investigated in two experiments conducted at the Ontario Science Centre, using a total of 282 adult volunteer subjects. In Experiment 1, subjects were presented with brief descriptions of a case of child sexual assault, and responded to a series of questions regarding the scenario. The gender of the victim and offender, and the identity of the initiating party, were manipulated in a $2 x 2 x 2$ fully-crossed design. In Experiment 2, subjects were administered a similar procedure, with the age of the victim and the identity of the initiating party manipulated. In both experiments, the manipulation of the identity of the initiating party was found to have the strongest and most consistent effects. Implications of these findings regarding reporting biases, and legal and clinical decision-making are discussed.

The sexual abuse of children by adults is a social problem which has, in recent years, prompted an increasing amount of public interest and legal initiative. Much of this current concern comes as a result of an emerging awareness, both public and academic, of the extent of the problem. Recent survey data (Finkelhor, 1979, 1984; Badgley, 1984) have indicated that as many as one in every five female and one in every ten male children will experience some form of sexual victimization by adults. In Canada, such strong public interest in the problem has prompted, in addition to substantial academic research, substantial change in the way the issue of child sexual abuse is dealt with by the legal system (Badgley, 1984). These factors in combination seem to have produced an increase in the rate of prosecution of cases of sexual abuse of children in Canada as well.

Such an increase in prosecution has, necessarily, resulted in an increase in the number of individuals sentenced for crimes of child sexual abuse. Although a considerable body of research in psychology, criminology and sociology has investigated variables related to the imposition of sentence, research on sentencing of offenders who have committed sexual abuse against children remains sparse. Although some portion of general sentencing research might be applied to the specific area of child sexual abuse, there are indications that generalization may not be valid. One such indication is that some studies have found that sex offenders in general (Walsh, 1984) and child sex offenders in particular (Champion, 1988; Deitz & Sissmann, 1984) receive harsher sentences than other felony offenders.

Sentencing research on adult sexual assault has a number of interesting effects, some of which may be important in the study of child sexual abuse. In his review of the then-current evidence, Pallone (1990, pp. 41-43) observed that

> . . . a generalized model of female sexuality, which holds in essence that women precipitate sexual encounters, supports notions like "contributory fault" and "negligence" both within the social climate and in the law and the formal operation of the criminal justice system. That model convincingly appears to influence how third-party observers assess the victim of sexual assault. A substantial body of research evidence of international dimensions has demonstrated a generalized tendency for *women* . . . to *display greater sympathy for, and to attribute less blame toward, the female victim,* and conversely for men to display less sympathy and to attribute more blame toward the victim . . . The "blame the victim" effect, with male-female gender differences between respondents, obtains whether the respondents [are] college and university undergraduates in the United States, or undergraduates in Canada, or non-student citizens in Britain, or India, or Sicily . . . or, more disturbingly, nursing or medical students in the United States . . . [or] jurors who have served in tape trials . . . and even among spouses whose partners have been victimized [and] behavioral science researchers . . . and, of course, the same effect is observed among offenders themselves, so that it might be concluded that *offenders and the general public equally enjoy "blame the victim" as a pastime* . . . This effect is especially strong [when] the victim

> failed to take appropriate precautions or had herself consumed alcohol prior to, or during, the interaction that led to the rape, had otherwise engaged in extramarital sexual behavior . . . [or when the scenario involves] an unattractive rape victim [who] resisted the rape by fighting her attacker . . . [Some researchers] conclude that "rape vulnerability" is the product of psychosocial incompetence *on the part of the victim*. Even more disturbingly, in an analysis of the decisions of British appellate courts in cases in which the penalty for incest was at issue, "where the daughter was not a virgin, the court all but held her responsible" . . . studies [of] prospective or actual jurors [have] found that lack of empathy for the victim influences jurors' ratings of defendant guilt and their recommended sentences, along with their attributions of responsibility for the crime . . . [there is] a belief common among rapists that their victims derive pleasure from being assaulted. To judge by the universality of responses to the "blame the victim" situation, that belief is by no means limited to those who perpetrate crimes of sexual violence.

Studies of the effect of *offender* characteristics in cases of sexual assault have been fewer in number, and have revealed less conclusive effects. A study by Bradmiller and Walters (1985), of sexual assault cases prosecuted in Ohio, obtained significant effects for the race of the offender (i.e., black offenders received more serious charges than white offenders); and for the relationship of the offender to the victim, (i.e., offenders related to their victims received less serious charges than offenders unrelated to their victims). From the perspective of child sexual abuse, it is significant that this study did not find the age of the victim to be a factor. This may mean that the mitigating effect of offender-victim relatedness was not due simply to more lenient attitudes towards marital rape; offenders who incestuously assaulted their own children received less serious charges than those who sexually assaulted the children of others.

A recent study by Esses and Webster (1988) found that sexual offenders were more likely to be seen by subjects as meeting the Canadian Criminal Code Dangerous Offender criteria if they were also judged to be unattractive. Other studies of sexual offender characteristics, however, have not found such clear relationships. Notably, Sealy and Wain (1980) found that in rape trial simulations, the defendant's "trustworthiness" as perceived by the jurors was not correlated with the the verdict, but that such a correlation did exist in simulated trials for nonsexual offenses.

A study by Yarmey (1985) combines many of these variables in a single, elegant experiment. Yarmey presented eight rape scenarios, containing two victim variables (demeanor/dress and resistance to the rapist) and one offender variable (demeanor/dress), to two mixed-sex groups of old and young subjects, at average ages of 58 and 20 years, respectively. Yarmey found main effects for age of subjects, such that younger subjects recommended longer sentences than did older subjects, and victim demeanor, such that rapists who attacked a demure victim were seen by subjects as deserving longer sentences than rapists who attacked a provocative victim. The age and sex of the subjects, and the demeanor of the victim, interacted to produce the following descending order pattern of subject recommendations of sentence length: the most severe sentences were recommended by young males in the demure victim condition, followed by young females, provocative victim; young females, demure victim; old females, demure victim; young males, provocative victim; old females, provocative victim; old males, demure victim ; and finally, old males in the provocative victim condition recommended the most lenient sentences. No effects were found for the variable of rapist demeanor.

As Yarmey's study indicates, victim characteristics, offender characteristics, and subject characteristics can interact in a complex fashion in investigations of attribution of blame and prescription of penalty in cases of the sexual assault of adults. But information about such variables in cases of the sexual assault of children by adults is sparse indeed. Only a handful of studies examine, even tangentially, the effects of victim, offender, and subject characteristics on sentencing recommendations for child sexual abuse cases. Results from the Bradmiller and Walters (1985) study indicate that the offender's relationship to the victim may have some mitigating effects on the seriousness of the charge, which may in turn lead to shorter sentences. A recent study by Stermac & Segal (1989) found that male subjects saw adults in child sexual abuse scenarios as significantly less responsible for the abuse than did female subjects. However, the authors make no attempt to tap sentencing recommendations directly. Some very recent, unpublished work by Hanson (1990) and Hanson & Slater (in preparation) also bears on this issue. Hanson (1990) found that approximately one- quarter of male and female subjects asked to generate a "good excuse" for the behaviour of an offender in a child sexual abuse scenario would generate a victim-blaming excuse, but that female subjects were more likely than males to generate victim-blaming accounts when asked to provide a "bad excuse." Hanson & Slater (in preparation) had a population of therapists and parole officers read and rate a series of motivational accounts of child molesters, and found that both groups were likely to be sympathetic to those accounts which emphasized external causes for the offenders behaviour, and that such accounts reduced the likelihood of a recommendation of incarceration.

A study of perceptions of non-sexual child abuse may be instructive. Dukes and Kean (1989) presented a series of vignettes of child neglect and of physical and psychological abuse to a large sample of subjects. Psychological abuse was seen as having relatively more serious consequences for older children, whereas neglect was seen as having more serious consequences for younger children. In vignettes in which psychological or physical abuse was presented as having been "precipitated" by something the child had done, the children were viewed as being less innocent than children in vignettes where the abuse occurred as a result of something beyond the child's control. Some effects were also found for the sex of the child. Male children were seen as being less innocent in vignettes of physical and psychological abuse, while female children were seen as being less innocent in cases of neglect. Age and sex effects were also found for the subjects. Female subjects saw more abuse in the vignettes than did male subjects, and older subjects saw more abuse than did younger subjects.

Perhaps the most comprehensive study in the area of adult perceptions of child sexual abuse is that of Finkelhor (1984). In an examination of the types of adult-child interactions defined by the general public as sexual abuse, Finkelhor examined nine variables in a vignette-study format: age of victim, age of perpetrator, relationship between victim and perpetrator, sex of victim, sex of perpetrator, type of sexual act, consent, consequence for the victim, and sex of the respondent (subject). While the design of the study — a factorial survey technique — made it impossible to assess higher-order interactions, many interesting main effects and lower- order interactions were observed: *Age of perpetrator:* Rated abusiveness of acts committed by those under the age of 20 declines rapidly with the age of the perpetrator. *Type of sexual act* described in the vignette was found to have a large effect on the abusiveness rating. Vignettes which described sexual intercourse were seen as most clearly abusive, descriptions of genital fondling of the victim less so, and depictions of genital fondling of the perpetrator less so again. Two of the act ratings were also affected by the sex of the respondent: females saw vignettes describing adults having sex in the presence of the victim as more clearly abusive than males did, while males saw vignettes in which the victim was repeatedly called a "whore" or a "faggot" as more clearly abusive than did females. *Conditions of consent* on the part of young children were not seen as mitigating the abusiveness of the interaction, while the consent of older children had a mitigating effect. *Age of victim* was curiously interpreted. Respondents saw vignettes involving very young or adolescent victims as less abusive than vignettes involving children between the ages 8 to 12. *Relationship between victim and perpetrator* was differentially inflected. Although respondents made few major differentiations in terms of abusiveness between different victim-perpetrator relationships, there were some sex differences; male respondents saw some relationships as more abusive than females did, and vice-versa. *Consequences for the victim* made very little difference in respondent's ratings of abusiveness.

Some inferences about sentencing recommendations for child sexual abuse might be drawn from these studies. One might hypothesize that the ratings of abusiveness derived from Finkelhor's (1984) vignette study translate in some straightforward fashion into sentence lengths. However, few studies have attempted to examine sentencing recommendations directly, using either such vignettes of child sexual abuse or other experimental designs.

The two studies described in this report thus represent an attempt to address an apparent gap in the literature relating to public perceptions of child sexual abuse. In order to assess the effects of victim, offender, situation, and subject characteristics on the length of sentencing recommendations, vignettes were constructed from the present author's clinical impressions, gained from experience in treating pedophiles at the Clarke Institute of Psychiatry. These vignettes were constructed so as not to reflect any one particular case. In order that all the interactions present in the studies might be assessed, the number of variables and variable levels were kept to a low level. The basic vignette, a description of a child- adult sexual interaction involving genital fondling, was altered, in the first study, in accordance with the following variables: (1) Sex of victim at levels female and male, (2) Sex of offender at levels female and male, and (3)

Initiating party at levels "victim initiates interaction" and "offender initiates interaction."

The third variable, initiating party, has been selected due to some current real-world interest in just this question. In a recent court case in Vancouver, British Columbia, a provincial judge sentenced an offender in a child sexual abuse case to eighteen months probation. The judge stated that in his opinion, the child, a three year old female, had been "sexually aggressive," and that he considered this to be a mitigating factor in the sentencing ("Judge finds," 1989). Despite a large-scale public outcry and a legal appeal, the sentence (eighteen months' probation), perceived by many to be overly lenient, has been upheld (Regina v. Leeson, British Columbia Court of Appeals, 1990).

Particular emphasis was placed in these studies on three variables: *Sex of victim, sex of offender,* and *initiating party.* Moreover, it was anticipated that interactive effects of several sorts might be observed.

EXPERIMENT 1

Overview

Subjects were presented with a short written scenario describing a sexual assault on a child and were requested to answer a series of questions regarding the assault, including a judgment of appropriate punishment for the offender, and a series of questions designed to tap the subjects' attitudes about the crime, the offender and the victim. The offender's gender, the victim's gender, and the initiator (child or adult) of the interaction that led to the assault were manipulated in a between-subjects design.

Subjects and Design

Subjects were 164 adult volunteers (87 females, 77 males) recruited at the Ontario Science Centre in Toronto, Canada. Previous research concerning legal issues (c.f. Doob & Roberts, 1983; Gebotys, Roberts, & Das Gupta, 1988) has not found the attitudes of this subject population to differ in important ways from those of a larger survey population. The subjects ranged in age from 18 to 64 years, with a mean age of 30.35 years. They were randomly assigned to one of eight conditions in a 2 *x* 2 *x* 2 completely randomized factorial design, with 19 to 23 subjects in each condition.

Materials

Subjects were presented with a booklet containing the necessary materials for completion of the experiment. The booklet consisted of a short description of the study, a consent form, a short passage describing a sexual assault upon a child (the scenario), and a series of questions relating to the scenario. Subjects were informed as to the nature of the material they would be asked to read, and that they would be asked to make a sentencing judgment based on the information available in the scenario.

Independent (scenario) variables. Due to the sensitive nature of the topic under discussion, and the conditions under which subjects were being recruited, the eight scenarios used in the study were designed so as to keep possibly offensive details and terminology to a minimum. Each of the scenarios gave a description, labelled as a "case summary," of an interaction between a (male or female) adult and a (male or female) child. The adult and child were described as being "next door neighbors." Manipulation of the variable "initiator of interaction" was achieved in the following way. In the adult-initiated conditions, the adult approached the child near the adult's home, invited the child inside, placed the child on his/her lap, and asked the child to play a "game" consisting of mutual genital fondling. In the child-initiated conditions, the child approached the adult near the adult's home, asked to be invited inside, sat on the adult's lap, and asked the adult to play the "game" mentioned above. All the information in the scenarios was described as being "according to police reports," rather than from any particular individual's testimony. Subjects were asked to imagine that they were "a judge passing sentence in the trial of an adult accused of sexually molesting a child." Subjects were also instructed that the defendant in the case had pled guilty to the charges, so that guilt or innocence was not an issue in the decision.

Dependent variables. After reading the scenario, subjects were asked to respond to a series of questions. The first of these was a "sentencing decision" in which subjects were asked to choose the sentencing option that they felt was most appropriate in this case.

Seven possible options were presented, in order of severity, ranging from probation to a prison term of at least five years. Subjects were also asked, in a separate item, if they felt that the offender should receive some form of psychological treatment in addition to the sentencing option chosen.

Following these two items was a series of questions, anchored to seven point rating scales, designed to tap subjects' perceptions of the offense (in terms of seriousness, likelihood of the act, and harm to the victim), the offender (in terms of likelihood of recidivism, extent of psychological disturbance, possible benefit from treatment, and responsibility for actions), and the victim (in terms of responsibility for actions). The final three questions in the booklet concerned demographic information (age, sex, parental status) about the subjects.

After completing the questionnaire, subjects were instructed to return the booklet to the experimenter, whereupon they were thanked for their participation, and provided with a written debriefing form.

Results

Due to the sheer number of analyses performed on the questionnaire data in this study, it was decided in the interests of brevity and clarity to report only those F-statistics which have associated p-values of .06 or less, a total of 18 reported analyses. Significant findings for this study are represented in tabular form in Tables 1 and 2; short descriptions of those findings follow .

- *Sentencing decision.* What length of sentence should this offender receive? An ANOVA of subjects' responses to this item revealed a significant main effect of Initiator (child or adult), $F(1,156) = 13.54$, $p = .01$, such that subjects recommended harsher sentences for offenders in scenarios in which the adult initiated the interaction than in scenarios in which the child initiated the interaction.
- *Attitudes about the offense, offender, and victim.* How likely is this scenario? An ANOVA of subjects' responses to this item revealed three main effects. The first of these was a significant main effect of Initiator, $F(1,155) = 12.06, p = .01$, so that child- initiated scenarios were rated by subjects as being far less likely to occur than were adult-initiated scenarios. The second significant main effect was that of Child Gender, $F(1,155) = 3.96, p = .05$, so that scenarios involving female children were seen as more likely to

happen than were those involving male children. Finally, there was a significant main effect of Adult Gender, $F(1,155) = 5.28, p = .05$, indicating that scenarios involving female adults were seen as being more likely to occur than were those involving male adults.

- *How harmful is this offense?* A significant two- way interaction (see Figure 1) between Adult Gender and Initiator, $F(1,156) = 8.29, p = .05$, was evident for this item, suggesting that scenarios involving male adults were seen as more harmful to the child in the adult-initiated conditions than in the child-initiated conditions, while no changes in subjects' ratings of harmfulness were evident across initiation conditions in scenarios involving female adults.
- *How likely is this offender to reoffend?* An ANOVA of subjects' responses to this item revealed a significant main effect of Initiator, $F(1,156) = 22.92$, $p = .01$, indicating that subjects saw adults in adult-initiated scenarios as far more likely to reoffend than adults in child-initiated scenarios.
- *How psychologically disturbed is this offender?* An ANOVA of subjects' responses to this item revealed a significant main effect of Initiator, $F(1,156) = 11.33, p = .01$, such that offenders in child-initiated scenarios were rated by subjects as being much less disturbed than offenders in adult-initiated scenarios. A significant two-way interaction (see Figure 2) between Adult Gender and Child Gender, $F(1,156) = 7.06, p = .01$,was also evident, such that offenders involved in heterosexual acts were rated by subjects as being less disturbed than adults involved in homosexual acts.
- *How much could this offender benefit from treatment?* An ANOVA of subjects' responses to this item revealed a significant main effect of Adult Gender, $F(1,155) = 6.11, p = .05$, so that female offenders were seen by subjects as being more likely to benefit from treatment than male offenders.
- *How responsible is this offender for his/her actions?* An ANOVA of subjects' responses to this item revealed a significant three-way interaction between Adult Gender, Child Gender, and Initiator, $F(1,156) = 5.18, p = .05$. While this interaction is best explained through graphical depiction (see Figures 3, 3.1), it can be encapsulated as follows: in adult-initiated scenarios, male offenders are seen by subjects as bearing more responsibility when the child involved is female than when the child is male. For female offenders in adult-initiated scenarios, the opposite relationship obtains; they are seen as bearing more responsibility when the child involved is male. In child-initiated conditions, these relationships are completely reversed. Male adults are seen as bearing more responsibility when the child involved is male, and female offenders are seen as bearing more responsibility when the child involved is female.

◻ *Table 1: Study 1 — Significant results — Scenario variables*

Questionnaire item	Scenario variable[s]	F	p
Sentencing decision	Initiator	13.54	.01
Likelihood	Initiator	12.06	.01
	Child gender	3.96	.05
	Adult gender	5.29	.05
Harmfulness	Adult gender by initiator	5.03	.05
Recidivism	Initiator	22.92	.01
Disturbance	Initiator	11.33	.01
	Adult by child gender	7.06	.01
Benefit	Adult gender	6.11	.05
Adult responsibility	Three-way interaction	5.18	.05
Child responsibility	Initiator	49.71	.01
	Adult gender by child gender	7.87	.01

- *How responsible is this child for his/her actions?* An ANOVA of subjects' responses to this item revealed a significant main effect of Initiator, $F(1,156) = 49.71, p = .01$, indicating that children were seen by subjects as bearing far more responsibility for their actions in the scenario when the interaction was initiated by the child than when the interaction was initiated by the adult. A significant two-way interaction (see Figure 4) between Adult Gender and Child Gender, $F(1,156) = 7.87, p = .01$, was also evident, such that ratings of child responsibility did not differ widely between male and female children when the adult offender in the scenario was male, but became widely divergent in female-offender conditions, such that male children were seen as bearing a much greater amount of responsibility than female children, when the adult involved was a female.

Subject Variables

- *Sex of subject effects.* Analyses of variance revealed significant main effects of respondent gender for two items on the questionnaire. These were (1) Psychological disturbance of offender, $F(1,156) = 7.45, p = .01$, such that female subjects saw offenders as being more psychologically disturbed than did male subjects, and (2) Possible benefit of treatment for offender, $F(1,155) = 5.42, p = .05$, indicating that female subjects saw offenders as being more likely to benefit from treatment than did male subjects.
- *Age of subject effects.* Analyses of variance comparing the responses of subjects who were older or younger than the mean age of 30.35 years revealed significant main effects for age of respondent for two items: (1) Sentencing decision, $F(1,156) = 4.97, p = .05$, such that older subjects recommended more lenient sentences than did younger subjects; and (2) Likelihood of scenario, $F(1,155) = 9.69, p = .01$, such that older subjects saw the scenarios in the study, on the whole, as less likely to occur than did younger subjects.
- *Parental status of subject.* Analyses of variance revealed significant main effects of parental status for one item, Likelihood of scenario, $F(1,155) = 4.12, p = .01$, indicating that subjects who had at least one child saw the scenarios in the study to be more likely, on the whole, than did subjects who were childless.
- *Interactions between subject variables.* Analysis of variance revealed a significant two-way interaction, between the subject variables Sex and Age, for one item, Seriousness of offense, $F(1,157) = 5.57, p = .05$, suggesting that younger male subjects saw the crimes in the scenarios as more serious than did older male subjects, but younger females saw the crimes as less serious than did older females.

Discussion

This study provided clear evidence that subjects' sentencing recommendations are more lenient for offenders in scenarios where the child initiated the interaction. But no significant relationships were

Figure 1: Harmfulness of Offense

GENDER OF SUBJECT BY INITIATOR

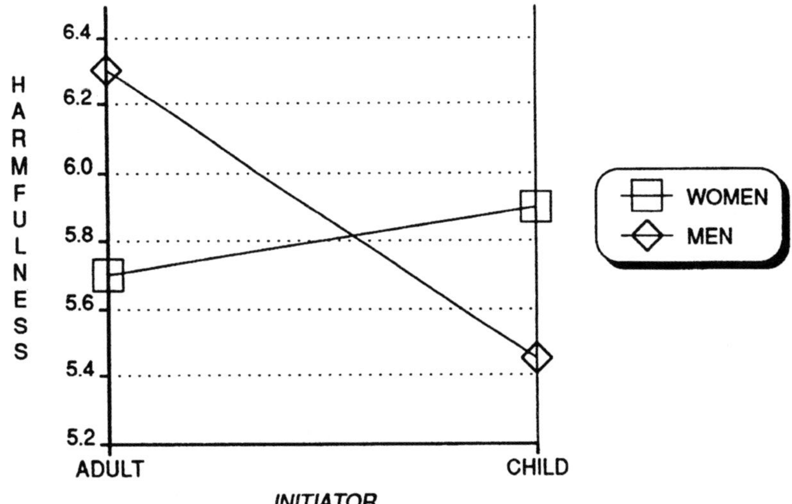

Figure 2: How Disturbed Is Offender?

GENDER OF SUBJECT BY GENDER OF CHILD

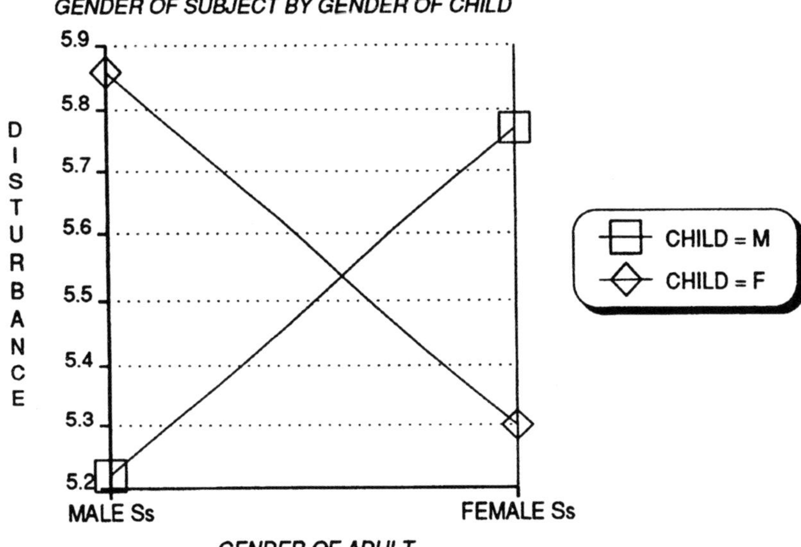

Figure 3: Responsibility of Offender

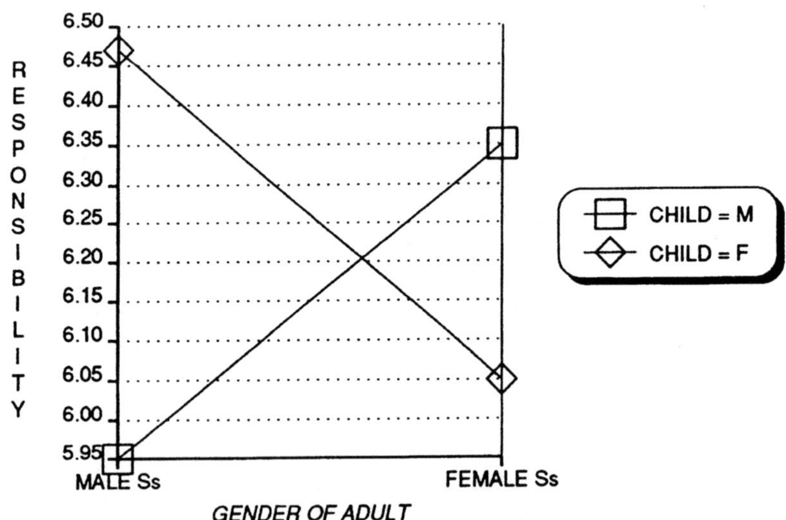

Figure 4: Responsibility of Child

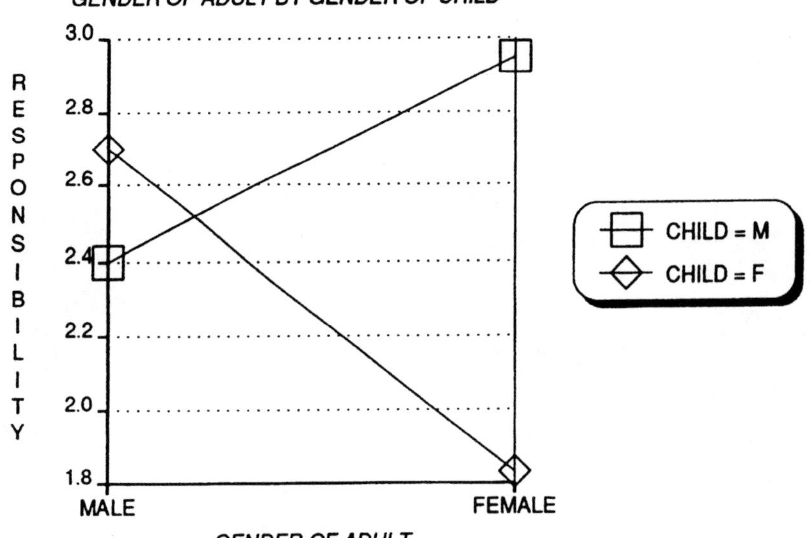

□ *Table 2: Study 1 — Significant results — Subject variables*

Subject variable	Questionnaire item[s]	F	p
Subject gender	Disturbance	7.45	.01
	Benefit	5.42	.05
Subject age	Sentencing decision	4.97	.05
	Likelihood	9.69	.01
Parental status	Likelihood	4.12	.01
Gender by age	Seriousness	5.57	.05

observed between sentencing recommendation and gender of the offender, gender of the victim, or when the scenario combined female adults and female children, or the gender or age of the respondent.

An examination of the pattern of results for the subsidiary questionnaire items indicates the strength of the Initiator manipulation. The variable manifests strong, significant main effects throughout the data. Effects of Child and Adult Gender are conspicuous, for the most part, by their absence, manifesting main effects for only a handful of items. It seems clear that, while Gender variables can have some effects on subjects' perceptions of an incident of child sexual assault, these effects are not as wide-ranging or as powerful as those of the variable Initiator, and do not, in any case, seem to affect subjects' actual sentencing behavior. Similarly, while demographic characteristics of the subjects would seem to be diagnostic of some of their attitudes about the scenario, such attitudes seem to have little effect upon sentencing recommendations.

EXPERIMENT 2

The results of Study 1 indicated that subjects' sentencing behavior, and attitudes about the crime, sentence, offender, and victim could be influenced substantially in a vignette study of this type, by manipulating the initiator of the interaction, i.e., making the initiator the adult or the child. In particular, subjects were seen to be greatly influenced by this variable in their judgments of the amount of responsibility that could be accredited to the child in the scenario.

The strength of the manipulation led the present author to speculate that the manipulation manifested its effects through causing subjects to view children who initiated sexual interactions with adults as being more like adults, and more subject to adult codes of sexual behavior, than children who did not initiate such acts. Thus it seemed likely that, if the age of the child involved were manipulated, subjects might see older children as more subject to adult codes of sexual behavior than younger children, and that this would especially be the case in scenarios where the child initiated the interaction.

In order to test this assumption, as well as to replicate the Initiator effects from the first study, a second study was performed, in which the age of the child in the scenarios was set at levels four, eight, and twelve years of age.

Overview

Subjects were presented with a short written scenario describing a sexual assault on a child and were requested to answer a series of questions regarding the assault, including a judgment of appropriate punishment for the offender, and a series of questions designed to tap the subjects' attitudes about the crime, the offender and the victim. The victim's age and the initiator (child or adult) of the interaction that led to the assault were manipulated in a between-subjects design.

Subjects and Design

Subjects were 118 adult volunteers (72 females, 46 males) recruited at the Ontario Science Centre in Toronto, Canada. The subjects ranged in age from 18 to 66 years, with a mean age of 29.50

years. They were randomly assigned to one of six conditions in a 2 *x* 3 completely randomized factorial design, with 19 to 20 subjects in each condition.

Materials

Subjects were presented with a booklet similar to the one used in Study 1, and given identical instructions. The only changes to the materials or procedures involved in the study were in minor changes to the written scenario, the deletion of some questionnaire items, modification of one item, and the addition of one new item (see below).

Independent (scenario) variables. In order to keep the number of conditions in the study to a minimum, the variables "gender of adult" and "gender of child" were dropped. In all scenarios in this study, the adult was identified as a male, and the child as a female. It was felt that gender- neutral scenarios, while offering the possibility of removing gender effects as a confound, would lack in external validity to too great a degree. Although the scenarios in the study suffer from a potential lack of generalizability to other victim and offender gender combinations, they do at least represent what seems to be the most common combination of these two variables in the real world (cf. Finkelhor, 1979). Manipulation of the variable "initiator of interaction" was achieved in the same fashion as in the first study. Manipulation of the variable "age of victim" was achieved by describing the victim as being either four, eight, or twelve years of age.

Dependent variables. Subjects were asked to respond to a series of questions, the bulk of which were identical to the items in Study 1. The item which asked subjects to make a yes/no decision regarding the desirability of treatment for the offender was modified to a seven-point rating scale in which subjects were asked to indicate how important they felt it was that the offender in this case receive treatment, as the original dichotomous wording of the question had failed to distinguish between conditions. In the section of the questions devoted to subjects' perceptions of the offense, a new item was added which asked subjects to indicate, on a seven-point rating scale, how morally wrong they felt the act in question was.

Table 3: Study 2 — Significant results — Scenario variables

Questionnaire item	Scenario variable[s]	F	p
Sentencing decision	Initiator	7.32	.01
Moral wrongness	Initiator	6.50	.05
Likelihood	Initiator	8.75	.01
Recidivism	Initiator	12.98	.01
Disturbance	Initiator	12.55	.01
Treatment	Initiator	8.76	.01
Child responsibility	Initiator	47.92	.01

After completing the questionnaire, subjects were instructed to return the booklet to the experimenter, whereupon they were thanked for their participation, and provided with a written debriefing form.

Results

Similarily to Study 1, F-statistics for analyses performed on questionnaire items in Study 2 are only reported below if the associated *p*-value is .06 or less. In addition, three-way interactions among subject variables were disregarded due to the extremely unbalanced nature of the cells in the analyses. The 14 effects which meet these criteria are represented in tabular form in Tables 3 and 4. Short descriptions of these findings are given below.

- *Sentencing decision*. What length of sentence should this offender receive? An ANOVA of subjects' responses to this item revealed a significant main effect of Initiator, $F(1,112) = 7.32$, $p = .01$, such that subjects recommended harsher sentences for offenders in scenarios where the adult initiated the interaction than in scenarios where the child initiated the interaction.

- *Attitudes about the offense, offender, and victim.* How likely is this scenario? An ANOVA of subjects' responses to this item revealed a significant main effect of Initiator, $F(1,110) = 8.75, p = .01$, such that scenarios in which the child initiated the interaction were seen by subjects to be less likely to occur than were scenarios in which the adult initiated the interaction.

- *How harmful is this offense?* An ANOVA of subjects' responses to this item revealed a significant main effect of Initiator, $F(1,112) = 5.79, p = .05$, such that subjects rated scenarios in which the child initiated the interaction as being slightly less harmful to the child involved than were scenarios in which the adult initiated the interaction.

- *How morally wrong is this act?* An ANOVA of subjects' responses to this item revealed a significant main effect of Initiator, $F(1,112) = 6.50, p = .05$, such that subjects rated sexual acts between an adult and a child as less morally wrong in child- initiated scenarios than in adult initiated scenarios.

- *How likely is this offender to reoffend?* An ANOVA of subjects' responses to this item revealed a significant main effect of Initiator, $F(1,112) = 12.98$, $p = .01$, such that subjects saw offenders in scenarios where the child initiated the interaction as less likely to reoffend than offenders in scenarios where the adult initiated the interaction.

- *How psychologically disturbed is this offender?* An ANOVA of subjects' responses to this item revealed a significant main effect of Initiator, $F(1,112) = 12.55, p = .01$, such that offenders in scenarios where the child initiated the interaction were seen by subjects as being less psychologically disturbed than offenders in scenarios where the adult initiated the interaction.

- *How important is treatment for this offender?* An ANOVA of subjects' responses to this item revealed a significant main effect of Initiator, $F(1,112) = 8.76, p = .01$, such that treatment of the offender was seen by subjects as being more important in scenarios where the adult initiated the interaction than in scenarios where the child initiated the interaction. How responsible is this child for his/her actions? An ANOVA of subjects' responses to this item revealed a significant main effect of Initiator, $F(1,112) = 47.92, p = .01$, such that subjects saw children in child-initiated scenarios as being much more responsible for their actions than children in adult-initiated scenarios.

□ *Table 2: Study 2 — Significant results — Subject variables*

Subject variable	Questionnaire item[s]	F	p
Subject gender	Sentencing decision	12.66	.01
	Seriousness	4.93	.05
	Harmfulness	14.23	.01
Parental status	Seriousness	3.77	.05
Gender by parental status	Harmfulness	7.45	.01
	Benefit	4.05	.05

Subject Variables

- *Sex of subject effects.* Analyses of variance revealed significant main effects for respondent gender for three questionnaire items. These items were: (1) *Sentencing decision,* F(1,110) = 12.66, p = .01, such that male subjects recommended more lenient sentences than did female subjects. (2) *Seriousness of offense,* F(1,110) = 4.93, p .05, such that male subjects saw the offenses in the scenarios, on the whole, to be less serious than did female subjects. (3) *Harmfulness of the offense,* F(1,110) = 14.23, p = .01, such that female subjects rated the acts in the scenarios as more potentially harmful to the child involved, than did male subjects.
- *Parental status of subject.* Analyses of variance revealed no significant main effects for this variable. However, a nearly significant effect for parental status of subject was evident for the item Seriousness of Offense, F(1,110) = 3.77, p = .06, suggesting that subjects who were parents saw the offenses in the scenarios, on the whole, as slightly more serious than did subjects who were not parents.
- *Interactions between sex of subject and subject's parental status.* Analyses of variance revealed two significant two-way interactions for the subject variables Sex and Parental status: (1) Harmfulness of act, F(1,110) = 7.45, p = .01, such that female subjects with children rated the acts described in the scenarios as slightly more harmful than did childless females, but males

with children rated the acts as slightly less harmful than did childless males; and (2) Possible benefit of treatment for offender, $F(1,110) = 4.05, p = .05$, such that female subjects with children saw offenders as being more likely to benefit from treatment than did childless female subjects, while male subjects with children saw the offender as being less likely to benefit from treatment than did childless male subjects.

Discussion

The Initiator manipulation proved once again to be very powerful. Initiator effects were replicated, at comparable levels of strength, for all of the items in which they were present in the first study. But no strong effects were observed for the age of the child involved in the scenario (although a weak effect in subjects' ratings of the likelihood of the scenarios was observed). One of the new items added to the questionnaire, regarding subjects' perceptions of the moral wrongness of the act, showed strong Initiator effects.

The modified item, regarding the importance of treatment for the offender in the scenario, showed strong Initiator effects, in contrast to the null finding for this item in the first study, when it was presented as a dichotomous choice rather than as a rating on a seven-point scale. It seems from these two results that, while members of the the general public regard treatment as important for all sexual offenders, they do make some distinctions based upon their perceptions of the offenders' role in the interaction, i.e.,whether or not the offender was "provoked" by some actions on the part of the child.

Subject effects in this study were also of some interest. In contrast to the first study, sex of subject effects were present in several items, most notably the sentencing decision, so that male subjects recommended considerably more lenient sentences than did female subjects, and viewed the scenarios more leniently in general. This pattern of results seems problematic unless the fact that the present study provides a replication of only two of the cells of the first experiment, those with the male-adult female-child gender combinations, is taken into consideration. It then seems possible that female subjects react more strongly to this specific combination of victim and offender than do male subjects, but that such reactions "wash out" in a fully crossed design, i.e., Study 1. While it is not feasible (due to low *n*) to test this hypothesis directly, by looking for a four-way interaction in the first study, it is interesting to note that the study from which interest in the sex-of-subjects effect was derived (Stermac & Segal, 1989) used only vignettes with male-adult/female-child combinations.

GENERAL DISCUSSION

These two studies examined the effects of offender, victim, scenario, and subject characteristics on subjects' perceptions of vignettes depicting child sexual assault. The variable which exhibited the most consistent, strongest effects, over a variety of questions designed to tap subjects' attitudes and perceptions, was the variable, Initiator of the Interaction. It seems clear from these studies that when members of the general public are presented with information which depicts children as having initiated a sexual interaction with an adult, this information has measurable effects on the ways in which this interaction, and these interactants, are perceived. Thus, these results indicate that findings from research concerning the effects of adult victim behavior in a sexual assault scenario (e.g., Jones and Aronson, 1973) can in some sense be extended into the area of child sexual abuse. That is, children, like adults, can be seen to be "asking for it" if their behavior is not sufficiently demure.

Many other predictions suggested by previous research were not supported by the data gathered in these two experiments. The studies do not show strong effects for the genders of the interactants, as suggested by Finkelhor (1984), or for the perceivers (subjects) as suggested by Stermac and Segal (1989), except in certain cases. Predictions following from Yarmey's (1985) research on subject age and attitudes about sexual assault were also not supported by the data. This failure to replicate, while perhaps indicative of some difference between public attitudes about the sexual assault of adults versus that of children, may also be due to differences in sampling, as Yarmey's subject populations varied more widely in age than did the subject population in either of the two studies discussed here.

The pattern of results found in these two experiments leads the present author to surmise that, in real-life cases of child sexual assault, those cases in which evidence is introduced suggesting that the child did something to invite or initiate the assault will be viewed more leniently by the general public (i.e., any adult who has knowledge of the assault), than other, adult- initiated cases. Furthermore, if recent research by Doob and Roberts (1983), which demonstrated that subjects operating with similar amounts of information as actual judges about a crime make similar sentencing decisions, can be extended to this area of legal decision making, it might be anticipated that judges within the legal system would react similarly to the general public, to information of this kind. The recent case in British Columbia, mentioned above, provides one real-world example of this phenomenon in action. It can also be expected that other decision-makers, whether inside the legal system or not, might be similarly affected by such information. It seems evident that the sexual abuse of children is recognized by the general public to be a crime, and a particularily heinous one. It is not so clear, as the above studies indicate, that the legal principle of consent not being an issue where children are concerned, has the effect of reducing the mitigating effects of children's consent to a sexual interaction with an adult. Although such interactions are recognized by the public as crimes, and deserving of some form of punishment, they are viewed with a more lenient eye.

It is interesting to note that, in the studies above, information about the initiator of the act did not appreciably alter subjects' perceptions of the responsibility borne by the offender. Rather, it was subjects' perceptions of the responsibility of the child that were strongly affected by this manipulation. Given the emphasis the legal system places on children's inability to be held responsible for, or consent to, their behavior with or without the presence of an adult, such perceptions seem particularily hypocritical. In the present author's opinion, these findings suggest that legal and mental health professionals, as well as members of the general public, should look with greater concern towards the administration of justice in cases of child sexual assault.

REFERENCES

"Aggressive" Tot ruling upheld in B.C. sex case, Toronto Star, January 14, 1990.

Badgley, R.F. Sexual Offences against children: A report to the committee on sexual offences against children and youth. Ottawa, Minister of Supply and Services, 1984.

Bradmiller, L.L. and Walters, W.S. Seriousness of Sexual Assault Charges: Influencing factors. Criminal Justice and Behaviour, 1985, 12(4), 463-484.

Champion, D.J. Child Sexual Abusers and Sentencing Severity. Federal Probation, 1988, 52(1), 53-57.

Deitz, S.R. and Sissman, P.L. Investigating Jury bias in a child molestation case. Behavioral Sciences and the Law, 1984, 2(4), 423- 434.

Dukes, R.L. and Kean, R.B. An experimental study of gender and situation in the perception and reportage of child abuse. Child Abuse and Neglect, 1989, 13(3) 351-360.

Esses, V.M. and Webster, C.D. Physical Attractiveness, Dangerousness, and the Canadian Criminal Code. Journal of Applied Social Psychology, 1988, 18(12) 1017-1031.

Feldman-Summers, S. and Lindner, K. Perceptions of Victims and Defendants in Sexual Assault Cases. Criminal Justice and Behavior, 1976, 3(2) 135-150.

Finkelhor, David. Child Sexual Abuse: New Theory and Research. New York, The Free Press, 1984.

Finkelhor, David. Sexually Victimized Children. New York, The Free Press, 1979.

Gebotys, Roberts, and Das Gupta. News media use and public perceptions of crime seriousness. Canadian Journal of Criminology, 1988, 30, 3-16.

Hanson, R.K. Victim blaming as an excuse for child molesting. Presentation at the Canadian Psychological Association Convention, Ottawa, June 2, 1990.

Hanson, R.K. and Slater, S. Reactions to motivational accounts of child molesters. Manuscript in preparation.

Judge finds assault victim, 3, was "sexually aggressive." Vancouver Sun, November 24, 1989.

Lafree, G.D.; Reskin, B.F.; and Visher, C.A. Juror's responses to victims behavior and legal issues in sexual assault trials. Social Problems, 1985, 32(4), 389-407.

Landy, D. and Aronson, E. The influence of the character of the criminal and his victim on the decisions of simulated jurors. Journal of Experimental and Social Psychology, 1969, 5, 141-152.

Myers, M.A. and Lafree, G.D. Sexual Assault and its prosecution: A comparison with other crimes. Journal of Criminal Law and Criminology, 1982, 73(3) 1282-1305.

Pallone, N.J. *Rehabilitating Criminal Sexual Psychopaths: Legislative Mandates, Clinical Quandaries.* New Brunswick, NJ: Transaction Books, 1990.

Regina v. Leeson, British Columbia Court of Appeals, 1990.

Sealy, A.P. and Wain, C.M. Person Perception and Juror's Decisions. British Journal of Social and Clinical Psychology, 1980, 19, 7- 16.

Stermac, L.E. and Segal, Z.V. Adult Sexual Contact With Children: An Examination of Cognitive Factors. Behavior Therapy, 1989, 20, 20-28.

Walsh, A. Differential sentencing patterns among felony sex offenders and non-sex offenders. Journal of Criminal Law and Criminology, 1984, 75(2), 443-458.

Walsh, A. Gender Based Differences: A study of Probation Officer's attitudes about, and recommendations for, felony sexual assault cases. Criminology, an Interdisciplinary Journal, 1984, 22(3) 371-387.

What the Judge said to the convicted child molester. Vancouver Sun, December 1, 1989.

Yarmey, D.A. Attitudes and Sentencing For Sexual Assault as a Function of Age and Sex of Subjects. Canadian Journal on Aging, 1985, 4(1), 20-28.

AUTHOR'S NOTE

Jeffrey Edwin Drugge is at the Department of Psychology, University of Toronto, Toronto, Ontario, CANADA M5S 1A1. *Address correspondence* to the author.

SEX OFFENDER TREATMENT: PSYCHOLOGICAL AND MEDICAL APPROACHES. Pp. 167-189.

The Remodeling Process

A Grounded Theory Study of Perceptions of Treatment among Adult Male Incest Offenders

Rochelle A. Scheela
Bemidji State University

ABSTRACT This grounded theory study explored incest offender perceptions of treatment in order to generate an explanatory theory of the sexual abuse treatment process. The research question was, "What is the process adult male incest offenders experience as they progress through treatment?" Symbolic Interactionism was the sensitizing framework for this study (Blumer, 1969). Methodology included 20 audio-taped interviews, direct observations of 65 group therapy sessions, and record analysis. The subjects were a theoretical sampling of 20 adult male incest offenders currently in, graduates of, or drop-outs from, a community sexual abuse treatment program. Constant comparative analysis was utilized to collect and analyze the data concurrently (Glaser & Strauss, 1967). Offenders indicate there is a *remodeling* process that occurs as they face discovery of their abuse and go through treatment. This dynamic, nonlinear, and often simultaneous remodeling process involves the offenders' worlds *falling apart*, the offenders *taking on* the project of remodeling themselves, *tearing out* the damaged parts, *rebuilding* themselves, their relationships, and their environments, *doing the upkeep* to maintain the remodeling that has been accomplished and, eventually *moving on* to new remodeling projects. Knowledge of this remodeling process enables therapists to tailor treatment more specifically to individual offender needs. Also, using remodeling as a metaphor offers a concrete, visual way to discuss the treatment process and expectations with the offenders.

Incest has been documented throughout history; however, it has been recognized as a major societal issue in this country only since the late 1970s (Finkelhor, 1986a, b). Consequently, research in the field of incest is relatively new and underdeveloped (Araji & Finkelhor, 1986). The majority of incest literature focuses on the victim, and the literature that does focus on the incest offender is conceptually and methodologically diverse and flawed (Finkelhor, Hotaling & Yllo, 1988). Broad generalizations are based on small, biased research samples, and research methods and designs are so diverse that comparison is difficult (Peters, Wyatt & Finkelhor, 1986). A majority of the studies are not replicated.

There are no definitive data available on the actual number of offenders, although the majority of reported offenders are known to be male (Ballard, Blair, Devereaux, Valentine, Horton & Johnson, 1990; Roundy & Horton, 1990). A significant number of researchers are concluding that there is no profile of incest offenders; they are a complex, heterogeneous group with no classic characteristics who look like everyone else (Ballard et al., 1990; Bolton & Bolton, 1990; Bolton, Morris & MacEachron, 1989; Conte, 1990; Horton, Johnson, Roundy & Williams, 1990; Langevin, Handy, Russon & Day, 1985; Salter, 1988). Most of the offender research has been based on institutionalized offenders, an unrepresentative fraction of all offenders (Finkelhor, 1986a; Russell, 1986), and little of the literature has investigated the offender's personal perspective.

There is little agreement in the offender literature as to the etiology of incest (Araji & Finkelhor, 1986). It is apparent from the literature that there is no simplistic explanation for this problem; rather, a complex pattern of variables must be considered (Finkelhor, 1986a). There also is no singular proven treatment approach for alleviating sexual abuse. The numerous treatment approaches for incest offenders and their families suggested in the literature stem directly from the participants involved, the treatment modalities employed, and/or the issues to be addressed. Participants sometimes include just the offenders, and sometimes parts of or the whole family. The treatment modalities differ depending on whether they offer individual therapy, group therapy, support groups, couples counseling, family therapy, or a combination of all the different modalities. The treatment focus is behavioral in some programs, cognitive in others, physical in some, and eclectic in others. In a recent article, Marshall, Jones, Ward, Johnston, and Barbaree (1991) describe treatment approaches as physical, and/or psychological. Treatment issues center around past trauma, personality dysfunctions, abuse dynamics, and future prevention.

Kelly (1982) reviewed the treatment literature and concluded that there were many problems such as publication and response bias, and lack of control techniques, valid assessment tools, and follow-up. MacFarlane (1983) reports that there is a lack of available evaluation data on the efficacy of treatment programs and validity of different treatment methods. Marshall et al. (1991) conducted a review of treatment effectiveness literature and concluded that comprehensive cognitive/behavioral programs are most likely to be effective for child molesters, exhibitionists, and incest offenders, and that anti-androgen adjunctive therapy is useful for offenders with excessively high sexual activity rates.

Treatment effectiveness is often measured in terms of recidivism, but Finkelhor (1986b) reports that there is minimal research on recidivism and what there is, is flawed. Incest offenders are not distinguished from other sex offenders, the research is not longitudinal, sexual reoffenses are not differentiated from other types of reoffenses, and most subjects have been incarcerated offenders who are more likely to reoffend. However, a significant number of studies document that incest offenders tend to have lower recidivism rates than other sex offenders (Finkelhor, 1986a; Frisbie & Dondis, 1965; Lang, Pugh & Langevin, 1988; Simkins, Ward, Bowman, Rinck & DeSouza, 1990), that treated offenders recidivate less than untreated offenders (Berner, 1989; Freeman-Longo & Wall, 1986; Meyer & Romero, 1980; Owen & Steele, 1991; Simkins, Ward, Bowman & Rinck, 1990), and that first time offenders recidivate less (10-21%) than repeat offenders (33-71%) (Marshall et al., 1991). One study investigated the benefits versus the costs of offender treatment in terms of reoffense risk, and found that it is cost effective for society to treat offenders (Prentky & Burgess, 1990).

Many theoretical frameworks and approaches have been posited to explain incest, but the majority focus on the victim or family. Theoretical/conceptual frameworks that specifically address the offenders are less common, and none focus on the treatment process offenders experience while in treatment. The sexual addiction model (Carnes, 1983, 1989, 1990) is based on the Alcoholics Anonymous program and involves four components: (a) a faulty belief system, (b) impaired thinking, (c) the addiction cycle, and (d) unmanageability. The model is well developed and tested for alcoholics; and Carnes (1989) is in the process of extensively testing it with sex offenders. However, according to the literature, only about 4% of incest offenders are sexual addicts (Finkelhor, 1986a), thus, it is questionable if the model will fit with this particular type of sex offender. The model focuses on the etiology and addictiveness of the abuse, not the treatment process.

A chain of discovery and offender identification model has been suggested which addresses the stages of offender identification, the offender's awareness phases of the abuse, and the systems involved in the abuse, discovery, and intervention (Ballard, Williams, Horton & Johnson, 1990). The descriptive study that served as the basis of this model is "The Incest Perpetrator Project" which included in-depth interviews with 374 incest offenders involved in Parents United, in maximum security prisons, mental health facilities, and private agencies treating incest offenders. This model has not been tested outside this study, and it addresses the actual phases of abuse for the offenders, not the time after disclosure and during treatment.

Finkelhor (1986a) recommends a multifactor theory which includes the following four factors: (a) emotional congruence, where the adult finds sex with a child emotionally gratifying and congruent, (b) sexual arousal, where the adult is sexually aroused by a child, (c) blockage, where the adult is frustrated in efforts to obtain sexual and emotional gratification from more socially approved sources, and (d) disinhibition, where an adult is not deterred by incest taboos. Simkins, Ward, Bowman, Rinck, and DeSouza (1990) studied 122 child molesters to examine the utility of Finkelhor's multifactor theory (among other things) as a predictor of treatment outcomes. Family of origin, and behavior deficit were positively correlated to treatment gains while rejection by adult peers was inversely related. However, the researchers found that treatment attendance and therapists' ratings of attitudes and behavior during treatment accounted for considerably more variance than Finkelhor's factors. More research is needed before this theory is considered well established and tested. It, too, addresses the etiology of the abuse, not the disclosure and treatment phases.

A socialization process model has been proposed to explain how offenders "groom" their victims. The incest offenders use trust, favoritism, alienation, secrecy, boundary violations, and evaluation to socialize their daughters into the abuse, thus not requiring violence (Christiansen & Blake, 1990). This model is supported by a series of research studies begun in 1986 with both offenders and victims (Christiansen & Blake, 1990). But again, as with some of the other frameworks mentioned above, this model has not been tested by other research studies, and it addresses the etiology and process of abuse, not the issues that deal with the offender in treatment.

Pithers, Kashima, Cumming, and Beal (1988), based on literature and experience, have developed a relapse prevention treatment program for sex offenders which uses a variety of modalities designed to strengthen self-control. Offenders learn how to identify problematic situations, analyze decisions that set up situations enabling reoffending, and develop internal as well as external strategies to prevent, avoid or minimize these situations (Pithers, 1990). The model is being used successfully in many treatment programs, but it does not address the treatment process itself.

Trepper and Barrett (1989) have written a book on the systemic treatment of incest families. Their Vulnerability to Incest Model proposes that there are socio-environmental, family of origin, family, and individual factors as well as precipitating events and coping mechanisms that come into play for incest to occur. Their model suggests that treatment must be focused at multiple system levels, and treatment of the whole family is essential. Although this approach appears to accurately reflect the reality of incestuous situations, at this point in time it is based on clinical experience, not research. Formal research is underway.

It is evident from the literature that there is no one accepted and tested framework for incest offender research, and much of what is suggested needs further study and testing. Futhermore, none of the frameworks deal specifically with the process offenders experience in treatment. Conte (1990) says, "it appears that many of the currently accepted concepts about incestuous offenders should be viewed quite cautiously as untested theories" (p. 23). According to Finkelhor (1986b) "the most important component to a successful research design is a conceptual framework to guide the design. Conceptual frameworks give coherence to the work, answer many questions, and provide a basis for interpreting results" (pp. 213-214).

One can conclude from a review of the literature that the incest research is plagued with problems and controversies, and there is no well developed theoretical/conceptual framework upon which to base a study of the process offenders experience in treatment. There is also a dearth of information from the offenders' perspective. Since the incest offender is the abuser of the child and prevention cannot occur until offending ceases, it is vitally important to gain an understanding of this key figure. Therefore, this study explored incest offender perceptions of treatment in order to gain a better understanding of the offenders, and to generate an explanatory theory of the sexual abuse treatment process. The research question was: "What is the process adult male incest offenders experience as they progress through treatment? Symbolic Interactionism was the sensitizing framework" (Blumer, 1969).

METHOD

Design

The design of this study was grounded theory, a qualitative research method developed by sociologists Glaser and Strauss (1967) ". . . that uses a systematic set of procedures to develop an inductively derived grounded theory about a phenomenon" (Strauss & Corbin, 1990, p. 24). The theory is grounded in reality, and the antecedent conditions, contexts, intervening conditions, action/interaction strategies, and consequences are identified and analyzed for all data (Strauss & Corbin, 1990). Grounded theory methodology allows researchers "to discover what is going on, rather than assuming what should be going on" (Glaser, 1978, p. 159).

Subjects

In a grounded theory study, the subjects are called informants and are selected through theoretical sampling, "a process of data collection for generating theory whereby the analyst jointly collects, codes, and analyses his data and decides what data to collect next and where to find them, in order to develop his theory as it emerges" (Glaser, 1978, p. 36). Thus, the sample size was based on the need to collect adequate data to examine categories and their relationships, and to assure that maximum variation in the categories existed (Chenitz &

Swanson, 1986). The informants for this study were a theoretical sample of 20 adult male incest offenders involved voluntarily or by court mandate in the Sexual Abuse Treatment Program (SAT) at a mental health center in northern Minnesota, where the researcher works part-time as a therapist. SAT is a two year multifaceted outpatient treatment program involving individual, group, family, and marital counseling for the offenders, and their families if they plan to reunite. Participation in the study was voluntary, and, to insure maximum variation, involved offenders at any point in the two year SAT program, dropouts, those ejected from the program, and SAT graduates.

Twenty-six offenders were invited and twenty agreed to participate in the study, for a response rate of 77%. The informants ranged in age from 26 to 66, with a mean age of 42.65. Educational levels ranged from 6 to 17 years, with a mean of 12.7 years. Ninety percent of the informants were Caucasian with the other 10% part or full-blooded Native American. The median annual income was $17,500, with a range of less than $10,000 to $50,000. Twelve (60%) of the offenders were skilled or unskilled laborers, 1 (5%) was a student, 3 (15%) were prisoners, 1 (5%) was retired, 1 (5%) was unemployed, 1 (5%) was self-employed, and 1 (5%) was a professional. The men listed varied religious preferences; however, the majority were Christians. Nine (45%) informants were married, 6 (30%) were separated, 4 (20%) were divorced, and one (5%) never married. Eleven (55%) had no prior criminal record, 4 (20%) had misdemeanor records, and only 5 (25%) had previous felony records. These data support researchers' reports of the absence of a distinct demographic sex offender profile. However, a majority of the offenders had been abused as children; 15 (75%) physically, 14 (70%) sexually, and all 20 (100%) emotionally. The offenders' victims were female in 17 (85%) cases, male in 2 (10%) cases, and both sexes in 1 case (5%). The abuse included fondling (95%), masturbation (5%), oral (40%), anal (5%), and vaginal (55%) penetration.

Data Collection

Data collection involved in-depth interviews averaging two hours in length, direct observations during group therapy, and record analysis. Eighteen interviews were tape recorded and transcribed verbatim. Two offenders refused to be tape recorded, and in those cases, extensive notes were taken. A written consent form was signed with the stipulation that a participant could withdraw at anytime. Risk to the offenders was considered low as they were already in or had access to treatment, and therapists were available 24 hours a day free of charge if problems surfaced. Confidentiality was maintained at all times by use of a coding system so that the identity of the offenders and responses were known only to the researcher. However, the offenders were reminded prior to the interview that admission of new sexual offenses must, by law, be reported to the law enforcement and social services authorities. Direct observations were made during 65 group therapy sessions and focused on the offenders' behaviors, conversations, and interactions. Record analysis involved an in-depth analysis of the informants' court documents, sexual history, evaluation and test results, treatment assignments, and the charting of individual and group therapy sessions for demographic data and for data that supported or contradicted the themes and patterns that emerged through constant comparative analysis of the interviews and observations. Record analysis also identified variation, filled information gaps, and provided additional details and explanations.

Controls in the Research Procedure

A grounded theory study, by its very nature, creates many threats to reliability and validity (Chenitz & Swanson, 1986; Goodwin & Goodwin, 1984; Guba & Lincoln, 1981; Sandelowski, 1986; Stern, 1985). However, controls were included in the study to minimize or eliminate these threats such as assessing the meaning and importance of events which occurred during the study period; using multiple sources of data (observation, records, and interviews); using biographical and demographic information to clearly describe characteristics of the informants; using interviews, field notes, and comparative analysis to examine the extent of bias and determine ways to correct it; analyzing the data for contrasting cases; addressing results of the researcher's presence through careful, detailed description and analysis of the situation; obtaining validation of the study results from the informants, treatment resource people, and methodology experts; and establishing a decision trail ("describing and justifying what was actually done and why," according to Sandelowski, 1986, p. 34).

Analysis

The data to be analyzed were collected from the transcribed taped interviews, interview notes, observed interactions in therapy sessions, field notes taken in the observed group sessions, and informants' treatment records. Constant comparative analysis (Glaser & Strauss, 1967; Strauss & Corbin, 1990) was used to collect and analyze the data concurrently. Constant comparative analysis requires that once an interview or an observation is completed, the researcher must analyze and code the data before going on to the next interview or observation, because the emerging data determine who is to be interviewed next, what questions will be asked, and what should be observed. As new data are collected, they must be analyzed, coded and compared with all the other data already collected before moving on to new data sources. The constant comparative process involves the steps of data collection, concept formation (coding and categorizing data), concept development (reducing categories to core variables, and selective sampling of relevant literature and data), and concept modification and integration (development of an integrated theoretical framework) (Chenitz & Swanson, 1986; Glaser, 1978). Validation of the analysis and interpretation of the data was obtained from the informants, the co-therapist of the offenders' group, two clinical psychologists involved with offenders in the SAT program, the SAT director, the SAT women's group, and three well known grounded theory methodology experts (personal communications, 1991, from Corbin, Strauss, and Stern).

RESULTS

The Remodeling Process

The adult male incest offenders indicate there is a *remodeling process* that occurs as they face discovery of their abuse and go through treatment. One of the offenders suggested this idea of remodeling in his interview:

> I think [treatment has] been great. I think that it has been miserable and hard at times, but I think the overall picture of it, it's great. It's like building a house, there's lots of sweat, but one day when you set down at that kitchen table, you know, it's all worth it! [Then I asked him, "So , you're building a new you?"] Well, at least remodeling it good.

Subsequently, the other informants agreed remodeling is an accurate description of the treatment process. The remodeling process involves the offenders' world *falling apart*, the offenders *taking on* the project of remodeling themselves, *tearing out* the damaged parts, *rebuilding* themselves and their relationships and their environments, *doing the upkeep* to maintain the remodeling that has been accomplished and, for some, eventually *moving on* to new remodeling projects. Although this remodeling process is dynamic, nonlinear, and often simultaneous, for clarity, the components are addressed separately below. Direct quotes from the offenders are presented for substantiation and illumination, and are cited verbatim to preserve the flavor and reality of the statements. However, words have been added in brackets when clarification is necessary. To insure confidentiality, no names, aliases, or initials are used.

Falling Apart

Once the abuse is reported and can no longer be hidden or ignored, the offenders describe their world falling apart emotionally and physically. "The whole world has changed. It changes everything." The offenders describe intense physical reactions such as anorexia, insomnia, nausea and vomiting, weight loss, uncontrollable crying, and chest pain. Some require medication. One offender said, " . . . for the first week you can do nothin' but cry and cry and cry and not eat, and if you ate, you vomited." For some offenders these symptoms are life-threatening.

The offenders also talk about falling apart emotionally. "I was a nervous wreck! It was just a whole bunch of mixed up feelings." Falling apart emotionally involves the offenders experiencing the feelings of shock and disbelief at what has happened and confusion regarding what will happen to them and their families. One offender said, "[I] felt like I was in a fog, a state of shock, like I was hanging by a thread, . . . it was like a nightmare." Another said, "I'd rather of been dead. The offenders express fear of incarceration, the unknown, and of losing everything, but feel helplessness to do anything to help themselves. They feel intense guilt and shame because of the public humiliation they experience and because of the "horrible deed" they have done:

> I was everything I despised in a human, a degenerate, a sexual deviant. I was all those things that I personally just abhorred and would not touch with a foot-long pole, and yet I was that person. . . . And there's a look she had in her eyes that I can't describe. . . . I don't want to ever see that look again [since] that's a look where you can only feel, and I don't have the vocabulary or the where with all to be able to describe the pure anxiety that she had, the bewilderment that . . . this man that she had trusted had completely violated her trust. . . . I worried about the shame that I had brought down on their heads through no fault of theirs just because they cared for me, and the only thing I could do was to end it all.

One said that when he told his wife, she asked him how he could do such a thing and her look "reached in and tore my heart right out." The offenders describe feelings of self-pity but also anger towards themselves, those that reported the abuse, the victim or family, "the system," or even God.

Paradoxically, in the midst of physically and emotionally falling apart, offenders talk about experiencing relief because the abuse is finally out in the open and they will receive help for their problems. One offender said, "I think I always knew I was going to get caught. . . . [I felt] relief, sounds stupid. . . . It was like a big weight lifted off my shoulders. I just didn't have to live a secret anymore." Another offender said, "I felt a tremendous relief when I got caught. Thank God it's over, now I can get help. I can be like me again."

Taking On the Remodeling

The taking on process involves the offenders taking on the responsibility for the abuse, for working in treatment, and for doing the remodeling. One offender said:

> I think that the hardest part . . . is the person to get to the point where he's ready to say "heh, I want help. I want to deal with it. I want to understand my life. I want to understand why I made the decisions I made. . . . Quit denying and blaming.

This is usually done cautiously and a bit at a time:

> After awhile I found I got more used to the group, . . . started talking a little bit. . . . I took a couple of steps but then I'd step back . . . like testing the

> water a little bit, then I stick my foot in and um that don't feel too bad, maybe I'll stick both in. Well, that don't feel too bad, yet. Well, a little bit farther, it got kind of cold, so I jumped back out.

As they open up and participate more, most offenders also report enjoying the treatment group, even though it requires painful and difficult work, and report missing the group when there is a holiday or day off. " . . . I got to the point where I actually wanted to come to the programs instead of stayin' away." Another said, " . . . for me, at first, like one night a week wasn't enough. I needed more time — God, when is it going to be here? . . . It definitely was a life-line." A few offenders never reach the decision to take on the remodeling project or do so only minimally. They decide to keep the old structure, and this decision radically hinders treatment progress.

Tearing Out

As the offenders take on the responsibility of the abuse and the remodeling project, they become involved in the tearing out process. An offender identified the process of tearing out when he was discussing the remodeling process, "Yeah, I feel like that pretty much; tearing out the old stuff and remodeling and putting better things in. . . . It feels terrible at times . . . *ja,* tearin' it out!" The term "tearing out" fits well because it can be an extremely painful process. "I wanted answers so badly, because if I can come up with the reason why I abused, I can twist and wrench it out — tear it out!" Tearing out involves the processes of assessing the damage, searching for the connecting pieces, and sorting out what is good and should stay and what is damaged or rotten and must be removed.

Assessing the damage. Assessing the damage involves the offenders evaluating areas of their lives from childhood to the present in terms of themselves and their relationships, and trying to identify factors that played a part in their becoming incest offenders. It involves examining how they tried to bury the guilt by minimizing, rationalizing, and blaming. "You stop wanting to complain so much about the other person, and you want to look at yourself." Assessing the damage also involves facing the damage done to others. One offender said:

> As I think back, I see many things in my life that my abuse has changed. I had become a tyrant. I demanded perfection in my wife and children. I could

> not stand to see in them the same faults I saw in myself. The effects I had on my family are they lost faith in their dad/husband. . . . They could no longer trust me to not explode violently or sexually against them. My children became angry with me and with themselves because of their mixed emotions. They hated what I was doing but wanted to love and respect me. Their grades in school diminished from A's and B's to D's and F's. My . . . son was placed in a boy's counseling center . . . for over a year. All my family . . . went through intensive psychotherapy because of my abuse.

Searching for connections. As assessing the damage continues, the offenders start searching for connections. The offenders start to see patterns and connections in terms of life and the abuse, and face the fact that they are abusers and have done terrible things. The offenders are able to relate what they are learning to their own lives. It all starts making sense, and that helps the offenders face the reality of the abuse. One offender said that the "games" started "probably with backrubs and . . . it just progressed from there."

Sorting out. As the offenders assess the damage and make connections regarding what has happened and the reasons why, they begin sorting out what stays in their lives and what must be removed. They begin accepting themselves as abusers, realizing that there is no cure, seeing themselves realistically (the good as well as the bad qualities), and forgiving themselves and others. One reported:

> I guess I just shut doors on it. You know, all of these years of shuttin' doors in all these different rooms and now, the way I look at it, . . . what I'm doin' now is re-opening 'em, goin' in 'em , seein' what's in there, and deal with it, takin' what's good and what's not, and sortin' it out type thing. . . . It's like a thorough housecleaning. You take all the bad stuff and you get rid of it, and you . . . replace it with good stuff.

Oftentimes there is intense remorse and pain amidst the tearing out process:

> You want to understand it, you don't want that hurt ever again no place. But at the same time you're feelin' that hurt, probably what makes it even worse is you're really not the one feeling the hurt. It's your victim that's feeling the hurt. So you're carrying a double burden, a hurt that your victim didn't deserve, plus your own hurt for realizing what the hurt is.

Along with the pain, however, most of the offenders report also experiencing relief once they have faced the damage done to themselves and others:

> It was like a piano dropped off my back and, you know. I feel like a new man and ready to jump for joy . . . Before it was so dark and gloomy . . . And after I admitted it, the piano fell off my back and all of a sudden, bright sun light!

For most offenders, it takes a while in treatment to get to assessing the damage, searching for connections, and sorting out what is to be removed and what remains. However, some offenders move very quickly into these processes, especially if they have waited a long time for treatment, feel a tremendous need to find the answers, see treatment as an opportunity, and/or have had prior counseling or group experience. The tearing out process is neither smooth nor simple, and usually involves assessing the damage, searching for connections, and sorting out some issues, which stimulate the need to take on a new part of the remodeling process, begin assessing the damage, searching for connections, and sorting out other areas.

Rebuilding

Along with falling apart, taking on, and tearing out, the remodeling process also involves rebuilding.

> There's a thing we went through this last Sunday in church where the potter takes the clay, and . . . it's got a defect. So, what he does, he breaks it all down and rebuilds it to a blemishless pottery piece. And that's kinda like this, you know. We get down to rock bottom and . . . rebuild. It's a long process . . . . but it's a rebuilding.

Rebuilding involves offenders making changes to put their lives back together. The offenders have the same foundations of their lives (history, memories, experiences, I.Q., personality, the abuse), but have torn out some of the problem areas. They are not totally different people, but they are becoming dramatically remodeled. As the offenders regain a sense of control over their lives, they begin making changes in themselves, their relationships, find better ways to deal with things, and generally take charge of their lives. Many talk about the "new me" versus the "old me" or the "old way" versus the "new way." They see themselves as changed for the better: One offender said, "I'm feeling good about myself, because I'm in treatment and doing something about my problems." Another reported, "I went from being a drug addict, an alcoholic, um, an abuser, um, to being, happy with myself, my family . . . I couldn't ask for anything more."

Although many offenders reported improved relationships with their families, not all the changes in relationships are perceived as positive. One offender said that he feels less close to his wife and children now. "I think I really have a little less contact with the kids,

. . . probably not as close. It probably is to kind of avoid getting into anything that might . . . resemble . . . what had happened before." Sometimes the present relationships don't last and new relationships are needed. This can occur when the family or significant others terminate the relationship, or when the offender decides changes are necessary. Some offenders have never had real relationships, and making changes involve actively establishing relationships for the first time.

Doing the Upkeep

As the offenders make changes in their lives, they begin to see remodeling as a life-long process. They are never cured, so they make plans to identify and get their needs met in healthy ways, and protect themselves from reoffending. They need to maintain the changes they have made. This is doing the upkeep. An offender who graduated from our treatment program but later reoffended, referred to this process when interviewed in jail:

> Well, yeah, it's just like an old house that's going to fall down. You could go in there and put different things into it in order to get it up to standards again, you know. . . . Same thing for the abuse program, . . . you remodel yourself, take out the bad things, put in new things as much as you can. But like I say, you should have to really go along with the program all the time. More like upkeep on the house . . . if you don't keep it up, why, it's gonna fall apart again.

All the offenders talk often about doing the upkeep. One offender said, "I don't think the sexual stuff ever goes away. You just better learn how to handle it. I don't think you're ever cured and probably the day I think I am, I'll probably get in trouble." This life-long upkeep isn't just in terms of the offenders protecting themselves from reoffending either. It also involves the offenders protecting themselves from society's unwillingness to forgive and forget. Not everyone in society reacts negatively to the offenders, but there is a pervasive attitude of "lock them up and throw away the key!" One offender described it this way:

> It scares the hell out of me . . . if [someone] would say "he tried something with me," I haven't got a leg to stand on . . . That's what keeps me very very observant . . . I am very much on guard. This is something I have to live with for the rest of my life.

Moving On

Moving on involves offenders moving on to new issues and processes in treatment when other issues are resolved (as already discussed), and, near the end of treatment, separating from the group. Sometimes offenders grieve the loss of the treatment group, yet most excitedly reach out to others and focus on life after treatment. They talk about their lives outside of treatment and the use of supports in the community. They are moving on.

The Remodeling Model

The processes involved in remodeling occur in a nonlinear, somewhat unpredictable, and sometimes simultaneous fashion. For instance, an offender could be *rebuilding* in one area of his life, while *tearing out* in another area, and *taking on* yet a third issue all at the same time. One offender that is currently in treatment is in the *tearing out*, *rebuilding*, and *doing the upkeep* processes for his own victimization as a child and his marital and parenting issues, yet is dealing with the *falling apart* and *taking on* processes for some new charges of sexual abuse that have just surfaced.

Although the remodeling process is nonlinear, various of its components may be more prominent at different times in the two year treatment process. The *falling apart*, *taking on*, and *tearing out* processes tend to be most prominent during the beginning and middle part of treatment, while *rebuilding* and *doing the upkeep* dominate the latter part of treatment. *Moving on* tends to predominate at the end of treatment and afterwards. However, these processes can occur at any time and in any order throughout treatment, and the offenders identified many factors that helped or hindered the remodeling process including support from family and other important people in their lives, the way "the system" and the treatment team treated them, the group process, and the offenders' own attitudes and behaviors. Figure 1 depicts the complexity, nonlinearity, and interrelationships of the remodeling process.

DISCUSSION

The remodeling process is based on data that emerged from a grounded theory research study of 20 adult male incest offenders in an outpatient treatment program. The results of this study suggest that there is a process that incest offenders experience as they progress through treatment, and that the order and sequence of this process are unique to each offender. Knowledge of this remodeling process has implications for practice and research.

First, there is a great need to provide counseling and support for the offenders and their families experiencing the *falling apart* process but are not yet in treatment. For many it is a life-threatening crisis, and no organized resources exist to combat this problem. Further research needs to be conducted to identify the best approaches to provide such services without compromising the legal process that is often underway. Another implication is that offenders who have graduated from treatment indicate they need to touch base with the treatment program from time to time, because the abuse "is not something we can talk with just anyone about." Resources are needed for graduates to continue *doing the upkeep* and *moving on.*

An implication for therapists is that the remodeling process can be used as a metaphor to explain the treatment process to offenders. It stems from their own words and experiences, and provides a concrete, visual image of treatment. By explaining the whole remodeling process and the falling apart, taking on, tearing out, rebuilding, doing the upkeep, and moving on processes within the remodeling, the offenders get a better idea of what will happen in treatment and what is expected of them. Using the metaphor can also clarify for them how much flexibility there is, and that it is their responsibility to determine how the remodeling will be done; they are the carpenters and their work is customized. Different rooms can be worked on, different projects can be going on simultaneously, and offenders will have different rates of completion.

The remodeling metaphor can be used to illustrate the variations in progress, and examine why some offenders are not doing as well as others in treatment. Some offenders just try to do a make-shift repair job, while others do a complete remodeling. Some remodel only certain rooms, others gut the whole inside and rebuild it all. Some actually totally tear down some rooms and rebuild. Some patch

FIGURE 1

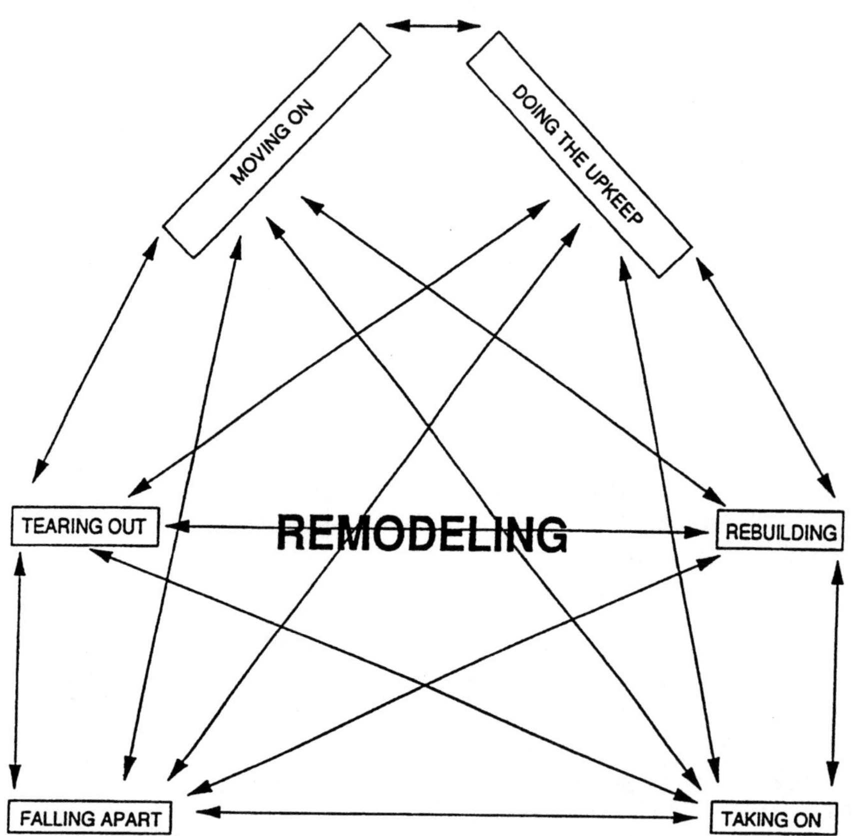
MOVING ON
DOING THE UPKEEP
TEARING OUT
REMODELING
REBUILDING
FALLING APART
TAKING ON

the leaks or cover the cracks or slap a quick coat of paint on over the damaged parts, and don't really remodel at all. Some build walls or fences around their houses, and don't let anyone in. They do not accept the help offered, and don't want any part of remodeling. The metaphor can be used to reassure offenders that experiencing the falling apart, taking on, or tearing out processes more than once in treatment is not a sign of failure, but just part of the remodeling process. They may totally remodel one or more rooms, but find other rooms or closets that need to be remodeled as well. The remodeling metaphor can also be used to address the possibility of recidivism. The remodeled structure will be a combination of the old and new, but in a new arrangement with problem parts removed. However, the foundation and some of the framework will always be there (memories, personality disorders, intelligence, the abuse). The foundation is strengthened and fortified, but not totally removed or re-done. The offender is not cured and must guard against reoffending.

Another implication of this research is that the remodeling framework is useful for therapists in terms of understanding the process offenders are experiencing, as well as providing interventions congruent with the process or processes each offender is engaging in at any one time. Identifying and understanding the various processes involved in remodeling assist therapists in using the most appropriate strategies for each process. Much flexibility is needed to meet the needs of the offenders as they experience the different parts of the remodeling process. There is no one right way and no one right time. However, therapists must confront those offenders who are not doing any remodeling, and in those cases, must provide direction and structure.

The remodeling process is based on data that emerged from a grounded theory study of 20 adult male incest offenders in one outpatient treatment program, and thus cannot be generalized to other populations. However, extending this research to more offenders in the same treatment program would increase the sample size and thus enhance the credibility of the findings, as would a longitudinal study of these offenders. Other sexual offender treatment programs need to be studied as do other types of sex offenders to determine if the remodeling process can be generalized to other treatment programs and offenders. For instance, will the remodeling process fit rapists, obscene phone callers, and extrafamilial sex offenders? Experimental studies using this framework versus other frameworks are needed. Experts in the field suggest that the remodeling process may also relate to other types of people in treatment such as family members of sex offenders that are also in treatment, batterers, chemically dependent people, or those in the process of major life changes. Further research needs to be conducted to determine if the remodeling process relates to them as they experience treatment and change.

SUMMARY

The adult male incest offenders in this study indicate there is a dynamic, nonlinear, often simultaneous *remodeling process* that occurs as they go through treatment. This remodeling process involves the offenders' world *falling apart*, the offenders *taking on* the remodeling project, *tearing out* the damaged parts, *rebuilding* themselves and their relationships, *doing the upkeep* to maintain the remodeling, and *moving on* to other remodeling projects. Some offenders achieve much more in this remodeling process than others. However, all of the offenders report feeling treatment is (or was) an excellent experience, and that they have learned a great deal that will affect the rest of their lives. One offender said, "The treatment program gives the tools to live a hell of a life!" Knowledge of this remodeling process enables therapists to tailor treatment to individual offender needs, and use it as a concrete, visual metaphor to discuss the treatment process and expectations. Further research is needed to test this explanatory theory of the treatment process and determine its generalizability to other populations.

REFERENCES

Araji, S., & Finkelhor, D. (1986). Abusers: A review of the research. In D. Finkelhor, S. Araji, A. Browne, S.D. Peters, G.E. & Wyatt, G.E. (Eds.), *A sourcebook on child sexual abuse* (89-118). Beverly Hills: Sage.

Ballard, D.T., Blair, G.D., Devereaux, S., Valentine, L.K., Horton, A.L., & Johnson, B.L. (1990). A comparative profile of the incest perpetrator: Background characteristics, abuse history, and use of social skills. In A.L. Horton, B.L. Johnson, L.M. Roundy, & D. Williams (Eds.), *The incest perpetrator: A family member no one wants to treat* (pp. 43-64). Newbury Park: Sage.

Ballard, D.T., Williams, D., Horton, A., & Johnson, B.L. (1990). Offender identification and current use of community resources. In A.L. Horton *et al.*, *op. cit.*, (pp. 150-163).

Berner, W. (1989, May 21-23). *Voluntary and involuntary treatment of sex offenders.* Paper presented at the First International Conference on the Treatment of Sex Offenders, Minneapolis, MN.

Blumer, H. (1969). *Symbolic interactionism: Perspective and method.* Englewood Cliffs, NJ: Prentice-Hall.

Bolton, S.R., & Bolton, F.G. (1990). Meeting the challenge: Legal dilemmas and considerations in working with the perpetrator. In A.L. Horton *et al.*, *op. cit.*, (pp. 29-39).

Bolton, F.G., Morris, L.A., & MacEachron, A.E. (1989). *Males at risk: The other side of child sexual abuse.* Newbury Park: Sage.

Carnes, P.J. (1990). Sexual addiction. In A.L. Horton *et al.*, *op. cit.*, (pp. 126-143).

Carnes, P. (1989). *Contrary to love: Helping the sexual addict.* Minneapolis, MN: CompCare Publishers.

Carnes, P. (1983). *Out of the shadows: Understanding sexual addiction.* Minneapolis, MN: Compcare Publishers.

Chenitz, W.C., Swanson, J.M. (1986). *From practice to grounded theory: Qualitative research in nursing.* Menlo Park: Addison-Wesley.

Christiansen, J.R., & Blake, R.H. (1990). The grooming process in father-daughter incest. In A.L. Horton *et al.*, *op. cit.*, (pp. 88-98).

Conte, J.R. (1990). The incest offender: An overview and introduction. In A.L. Horton *et al.*, *op. cit.*, (pp. 19-28).

Conte, J. R. (1985). Clinical dimensions of adult sexual abuse of children. *Behavioral Sciences, 3* (4), 341-354.

Finkelhor, D. (1986a). Abusers: Special topics. In D. Finkelhor *et al.*, *op cit.* (pp. 119-142).

Finkelhor, D. (1986b). Prevention: A review of programs and research. In D. Finkelhor *et al.*, *op cit.* (pp. 224-254).

Finkelhor, D., Hotaling, G., & Yllo, K. (1988). *Stopping family violence: Research priorities for the coming decade.* Newbury Park: Sage.

Freeman-Longo, R., & Wall, R. (1986, March). Changing a lifetime of sexual crime. *Psychology Today*, pp. 58-64.

Frisbie, L. V., & Dondis, E. H. (1965). *Recidivism among treated sex offenders.* Research Monograph No. 5 State of California Department of Mental Hygiene.

Glaser, B. G. (1978). *Advances in the methodology of grounded theory: Theoretical sensitivity.* Mill Valley, CA: Sociology Press.

Glaser, B. G., & Strauss, A.L. (1967). *The discovery of grounded theory: Strategies for qualitative research.* Chicago: Aldine.

Goodwin, L. D., & Goodwin, W. L. (1984). Are validity and reliability "relevant" in qualitative evaluation research? *Evaluation & The Health Professions*, *7* (4), 413-426.

Guba, E. G., Lincoln, Y. S. (1981). *Effective evaluation.* San Francisco: Jossey-Bass.

Horton, A.L., Johnson, B. L., Roundy, L. M. , & Williams, D. (1990). *The incest perpetrator: A family member no one wants to treat.*

Kelly, R. J. (1982). Behavioral reorientation of pedophiliacs: Can it be done? *Clinical Psychology Review, 2* (2), 387-408.

Lang, R. A., Pugh, G. M., & Langevin, R. (1988). Treatment of incest and pedophilic offenders: A pilot study. *Behavioral Sciences & the Law, 6*(2), 239-255.

Langevin, R., Handy, L., Russon, A. E., & Day, D. (1985). Are incestuous fathers pedophilic, aggressive, and alcoholic? In R. Langevin (Ed.), *Erotic Preference* (pp. 161-179). Hillsdale, NJ: Erlbaum.

MacFarlane, K. (1983). Program considerations in the treatment of incest offenders. In J. G. Greer & I. R. Stuart (Eds.), *The sexual aggressor: Current perspectives on treatment* (pp. 62-79). New York: Van Nostrand Reinhold.

Marshall, W. L., Jones, R., Ward, T., Johnston, P., & Barbaree, H. E. (1991). Treatment outcome with sex offenders. *Clinical Psychology Review, 11*, 465-485.

Meyer, L. C., & Romero, J. (1980). *A ten year follow- up of sex offender recidivism.* Philadelphia: Joseph J. Peters Institute.

Owen, G., & Steele, N., (1991). Incest offenders after treatment. In M.Q. Patton (Ed.), *Family sexual abuse* (pp. 178- 198). Newbury Park: Sage.

Peters, S.D., Wyatt, G.E., & Finkelhor, D. (1986). Prevalence. In D. Finkelhor, S. Araji, A. Browne, S.D. Peters, & G.E. Wyatt (Eds.), *A sourcebook on child sexual abuse* (pp. 15-59). Beverly Hills: Sage.

Pithers, W.D. (1990). Relapse prevention with sexual aggressors: A method for maintaining therapeutic gain and enhancing external supervision. In W.L. Marshall, D.R. Laws, & H.E. Barbaree (Eds.), *Handbook of sexual assault: Issues, theories, and treatment of the offender* (pp. 343-361). New York: Plenum..

Pithers, W.D., Kashima, K.M., Cumming, G.F., & Beal, L.S. (1988). Relapse prevention: A method of enhancing maintenance of change in sex offenders. In A.C. Salter (Ed.), *Treating child sex offenders and victims: A practical guide* (pp. 131-170). Newbury Park: Sage.

Prentky, R., & Burgess, A.W. (1990). Rehabilitation of child molesters: A cost-benefit analysis. *American Journal of Orthopsychiatry, 60*(1), 108-117.

Quinsey, V.L., & Marshall, W.L. (1983). Procedures for reducing inappropriate sexual arousal: An evaluation review. In J. G. Greer & I. R. Stuart (Eds.), *The sexual aggressor: Current perspectives on treatment* (pp. 267-289). New York: Van Nostrand Reinhold.

Roundy, L. M., & Horton, A.L. (1990). Professional and treatment issues for clinicians who intervene with incest perpetrators. In A.L. Horton *et al., op. cit.*, (pp. 164-189).

Russell, D. E. H. (1986). *The secret trauma: Incest in the lives of girls and women.* New York: Basic.

Salter, A. C. (1988). *Treating child sex offenders and victims: A practical guide.* Newbury Park: Sage.

Sandelowski, M. (1986). The problem of rigor in qualitative research. *Advances in Nursing Science, 8*(3), 27-37.

Simkins, L., Ward, W., Bowman, S., & Rinck, C. (1990). Characteristics predictive of child sex abusers' response to treatment: An exploratory study. *Journal of Psychology & Human Sexuality, 3* (1), 19-55.

Simkins, L., Ward, W., Bowman, S., Rinck, C., & De Souza, E. (1990). Predicting treatment outcome for child sexual abusers. *Annals of Sex Research, 3*, 21-57.

Stern, P. N. (1985). Using grounded theory method in nursing research. In M. M. Leininger (Ed.), *Qualitative research methods in nursing* (pp.149-160). Orlando: Grune & Stratton.

Strauss, A., & Corbin, J. (1990). *Basics of qualitative research: Grounded theory procedures and techniques.* Newbury Park: Sage.

Trepper, T.S., & Barrett, M.J. (1989). *Systemic treatment of incest: A therapeutic handbook.* New York: Brunner/Mazel.

AUTHOR'S NOTE

Rochelle A. Scheela, PhD, RN, is Associate Professor of Nursing at Bemidji State University and a therapist for sex offenders at Upper Mississippi Mental Health Center.

Address for Correspondence: Dr. Rochelle Scheela, Bemidji State University, Department of Nursing, 1500 Birchmont Drive NE, Bemidji, MN 56601.

SEX OFFENDER TREATMENT: PSYCHOLOGICAL AND MEDICAL APPROACHES. Pp. 191-203.

☐ CLINICAL PROCESSES

Outpatient Treatment for Adolescents with Sexually Inappropriate Behavior

Program Description and Six-Month Follow-up

Tom Mazur
Children's Hospital of Buffalo

P.M. Michael
Children's Hospital of Buffalo

ABSTRACT This paper describes an adolescent program for the management of sexually inappropriate behavior, a family-based, 16-week group intervention protocol. Also described are the ten individuals (ages 13-17) who completed this program. Outcome data generated from follow-up at six months post-treatment are presented.

By taking detailed sexual histories, Abel and Rouleau (1990) determined that 53.6% of 561 adult male sex offenders reported the onset of at least one deviant sexual interest prior to age 18. A 1987 FBI report indicates that males under the age of 19 are responsible for 19% of forcible rapes and 18% of other sexual offenses, excluding prostitution. This information confirms an earlier report (Groth et al., 1982) that many adults reported committing their first sexual offense as a teenager.

In an attempt to address adolescent sexual crimes, and hopefully reduce potential adult sexual offending, professionals have created adolescent treatment programs. The National Task Force on Juvenile

Sexual Offending in its 1988 report states that the number of programs mushroomed from approximately 20 in 1982 to over 500 in 1988! Most of these programs are composed of multiple components such as individual, group, and family therapy. Within and across each of these components certain factors (anger, low self-esteem, family communication) which are believed to be contributing to sexual misconduct are addressed. Steen and Monnette (1989) provide an example of such a multicomponent program for the treatment of adolescent sex offenders in the community. There is a treatment program (Becker, Kaplan & Kavoussi, 1988) which utilizes a specialized cognitive-behavioral approach in addition to the other components mentioned by Steen and Monnette. These behavioral techniques (satiation therapy and covert sensitization) are aimed at reducing deviant sexual arousal, which is believed to be present in adolescent sex offenders.

The purpose of this report is to describe a 16-week outpatient treatment program utilizing a family communication approach (Hayes, 1987) on the topics of sexuality education and relapse prevention (Pithers, 1990). The role of parents in promoting positive and responsible sexual behavior and in inhibiting sexual misconduct was employed by having them involved from the very beginning of treatment, teaching them what was to be taught to their children and having them comment on it, and finally having them become the teachers of their children by participating in group therapy sessions with their children. Ten children and their parents successfully completed the 16 weeks, and data on the first six-month follow-up are provided.

METHOD

Subjects

Ten subjects ranging in age between 13 and 17, and their parents, completed the 16-week treatment program. All had average or above full- scale IQ's. Seven were referred by mental health professionals (e.g., psychologists, social workers), and three were self-referred meaning that their parents, having heard about our program, requested evaluation and treatment. Four were court mandated to our program.

Table 1 outlines the sexual misconduct of the ten juveniles. No one denied the allegations. Four (40%) were living in single parent homes (three mothers, one father). Four (40%) were living in intact families. One teenager was living with his aunt and uncle and one was living with his mother and step-father. Based upon Hollingshead and Redlich's two factor index of socioeconomic status (1958), all five categories were represented. Two of the ten reported a prior history of being sexually abused by an older individual.

Procedure

At the initial session each juvenile and their parent(s) were given a complete description of the evaluation, 16-week program, its design and rationale. At the close of this session, each family was handed a written consent to participate, signed by both parent and child. They were instructed to bring the signed consent with them to their next visit which would commence the evaluation phase of the program. All program participants were treated in accordance with the ethical standards (Principle 9) of the APA.

The evaluation phase consisted of sessions in which the parents and children were seen separately. Parents completed a battery of questionnaires designed to provide information on (1) their child's behavior in various domains, (2) their family functioning, and (3) their own individual attitudes toward a variety of sexual behaviors. A semi- structured interview was also administered to obtain additional information regarding (1) the sexual offenses committed, (2) their response to learning that the behavior had occurred, (3) sexual information provided to their child at home and in school, (4) their child's pattern of socialization (including their child's relations to other family members), (5) their child's academic performance, (6) their child's employment history, and (7) the nature of their child's free-time activities.

In addition to responding to semi-structured interviews, the adolescents also completed questionnaires paralleling those administered to their parents.

Following assessment, the 16-week treatment phase began. These families returned for follow-up at six months post-treatment to repeat

Table 1: Reasons for Referral

Subject 1	Age = 13; sex = M; race = C
Location[s]	Bus stop
Victim[s]	F; ages unknown
Behavior/Frequency/Force	Exposure, touching breasts of victim; multiple; no coercion
Subject 2	Age = 13; sex = M; race = C
Location[s]	Home
Victim[s]	F; sibling, cousin; ages = 3, 6
Behavior/Frequency/Force	Vaginal penetration; multiple; no coercion
Subject 3	Age = 13; sex = M; race = C
Location[s]	Home
Victim[s]	M, F; neighbor, sibling; ages = 6, 12
Behavior/Frequency/Force	Anal penetration; single occurrence; no coercion
Subject 4	Age = 14; sex = F; race = C
Location[s]	Baby-sitting
Victim[s]	M, M; cousins; ages = 3, 7
Behavior/Frequency/Force	Simulated intercourse; multiple; no coercion
Subject 5	Age = 14; sex = M; race = C
Location[s]	Baby-sitting
Victim[s]	F; neighbor; age = 3
Behavior/Frequency/Force	Fondling vagina; single occurrence; physical coercion [restrained by hand]
Subject 6	Age = 14; sex = M; race = B
Location[s]	Home
Victim[s]	F, F, F; cousins, niece; ages = 7, 4, 3
Behavior/Frequency/Force	Fondling vagina, anal penetration with penis; single occurrence; physical coercion [restrained by hand]
Subject 7	Age = 14; sex = M; race = C
Location[s]	Home
Victim[s]	F; sibling; age = 7
Behavior/Frequency/Force	Fondling vagina; multiple; no coercion
Subject 8	Age = 15; sex = M; race = C
Location[s]	Home
Victim[s]	F; sibling; age = 14
Behavior/Frequency/Force	Vaginal intercourse; single occurrence; verbal coercion [threats of parental punishment]
Subject 9	Age = 16; sex = M; race = C
Location[s]	Home
Victim[s]	M, M, M, M; young children; ages = 5, 5, 6, 6
Behavior/Frequency/Force	Fondling penis; multiple; nocoercion
Subject 10	Age = 17; sex = M; race = C
Location[s]	Home
Victim[s]	M, M; cousin, sibling; ages = 9, 12
Behavior/Frequency/Force	Oral, anal penetration; multiple; no coercion

Table 2: Time Schedule and Topic Distribution

Phase	Duration in Weeks	N Parents' Meetings	N Adolescents' Meetings	N Joint Meetings
1: Orientation	2	1	2	
2: Human sexuality interaction education	8	4	7	1
3: Relapse prevention	4	1	4	
4: Transition to follow-up	2			2
Total	16	6	13	3

selected questionnaires not reported herein and to report on the degree to which treatment goals were achieved and maintained. Each teenager was interviewed separately from his parents. Both were interviewed in the presence of both therapists. When there were two parents, they were interviewed together.

PROGRAM DESCRIPTION

Table 2 outlines our 16-week adolescent program which is divided into four phases, with parents and adolescents participating in all phases. All meetings lasted 1 1/2 hours. The adolescents were divided into two groups: one group consisted of three 13 year olds, and the other consisted of seven 14-to-17 year olds.

Phase I: Orientation

Parents During this phase parents were told what information would be given to their children and shown the visual aids to be used. They were also informed that their meetings were strategically placed so that they were not only informed of what their children would be learning, but also able to comment on any feedback from their children. At this first meeting parents were shown an excerpt of *Lucas* (Seltzer, 1986), the first video to be shown to their children during the orientation phase, and were given an explanation of why this film was selected to begin the program.

The film does not show explicit sexual behavior, but it does illustrate aspects of psychosexual and psychosocial development, or lack thereof, through the eyes of a teenage boy. The movie also provides a nonthreatening starting point to begin discussing the fact that sexual behavior (e.g., thoughts, feelings, actions) is influenced by many factors.

Adolescents During week 1 the adolescents viewed the first half of *Lucas*, followed by discussion. The meeting concluded with a written homework assignment. The goal of this assignment was to make them aware of life around them and to differentiate external events from thoughts and feelings.

Week 2 opened with a discussion of the homework task followed by the second half of *Lucas*. A second homework assignment was given. They answered the question: Why would a counseling program dealing with sexually inappropriate behavior begin with a film containing no inappropriate sexual behavior?

Phase II: Human Sexuality Interaction Education

Parents During this eight-week period parents were introduced to the materials used to teach their children the facts of what constitutes healthy human sexual interaction. They were shown slides depicting (1) genital growth in utero, (2) genital growth from infancy through puberty to adulthood, (3) female and male sexual anatomy, internal and external, (4) vaginal birth, (5) various sexual behaviors including heterosexual, homosexual, and oral, as well as different sexual positions, (6) various forms of contraception and their uses, and (7) the different types of venereal disease.

They also viewed excerpts of the videos to be shown to their children. In order of presentation these films are : (1) *What's Happening to Me?* (Mayle, 1986), a short animated video covering the basic elements of pubertal development, (2) *The Miracle of Life* (Erikson and Lotmen, 1986), a 60-minute documentary of conception and birth, (3) *Physiological Responses of the Sexually Stimulated Female in the Laboratory* (Wagner, 1973), a 16-minute film created by Dr. Gorm Wagner of Copenhagen documenting physiological changes of a female while masturbating in a laboratory setting, (4) *Physiological Responses of the Sexually Stimulated Male in the Laboratory* (Wagner, 1973), a 16-minute film by Dr. Wagner similar to #3 but depicting male sexual response, and (5) *Sexual Intercourse* (Bergstrom-Walan, 1971), a 16-minute film from the Swedish Institute for Sexual Research showing physiologic changes during heterosexual intercourse and a range of emotional factors related to the experience. Videos depicting explicit sexual behavior (#3,4,5) were selected by the parents after viewing a number of such visual materials.

Also during Phase II, there were discussions about the use of the visual material and what was known and not known about the effects of viewing such films. Theories of psychosexual differentiation and development were also discussed. Parents were invited to discuss their own childhood sex education, aided by the task of listing (1) three questions about the biologic aspects of sex and (2) three questions about sexual feelings and thoughts they would have liked their parents to have discussed with them before they became sexually active.

Weaved into the various discussions were brief reports on their children's comments about their sessions. Parents gave their responses.

Adolescents The homework assignment from week 2 was discussed. A series of sexual education sessions were held using the visual materials seen and approved by their parents. Like their parents, they were asked to write three questions about sexuality they wanted discussed.

Discussions during this phase ranged across every conceivable aspect of sexuality, usually prompted by the particular visual material used. These discussions became a mix of the factual material presented and personal revelations. Through this format the adolescents began to share and trust each other with personal and often unspoken material.

Joint Session As preparation for this session parents were given an exercise to carry out with their children at home. Each parent was to give their child 15 minutes of uninterrupted attention while the child responded to one or two nonsexual questions we gave the parents. During the joint session this same technique was employed, but this time there was no question, but a statement that implied that sexual development and behavior, if repressed, may have serious negative outcome. Each parent was to listen to their child discuss this statement without interrupting. Then the child was to listen to their parent. Afterward each family reported their discussion to the group and a general discussion followed.

The goals of this session were to (1) strengthen family communication skills around sexual issues, and (2) provide a controlled setting where both parent and child could become aware that they could learn from one another.

Phase III: Relapse Prevention

Parents The purpose of the only parent meeting in this phase was to explain the concept of relapse prevention. The parents were informed that their child, with the help of the group and of the therapists, would create their own personalized prevention plan. At the next joint meeting their child would share this plan with their parents.

Adolescents Based upon information from every available source, detailed accounts of their sexually inappropriate behavior were written in document form and given to the teenagers. They in turn extracted features from these accounts that were perceived as signals of potential risk for recurrence of their sexually inappropriate behavior. Using those signals each adolescent developed a specific plan of action for dealing with each signal should it appear in their everyday life. Assistance was given to the adolescents via group therapy and individual attention by the therapists.

Phase IV: Transition to Follow-Up

Joint Meeting At these two meetings each child privately presented his "relapse prevention plan" to his parent(s). Parents were encouraged to ask questions of their child regarding the components of the prevention plan and to help improve it by offering suggestions. Signatures of both parent and child at the bottom of the plan were intended to signify that both would cooperate in implementing the strategy.

Included in this phase were two guest presentations. One presentation was made by an adult female victim of incest over many years. A second presentation was made by an adult male victim/perpetrator who spoke not only of the impact of his behavior on his life, but how at his present age of 50 years he continues to implement a "relapse prevention plan" of his own making. Adolescent attendance for the 16 weeks ranged from 82% (4 adolescents) to 100% (4 adolescents) with a mean of 92%. Parental attendance ranged from 50% (2 families) to 100%, with a mean of 78%.

RESULTS

Relapse/Opportunity for Relapse/Use of Relapse Prevention Plan

Table 3 shows that no adolescents reported relapse of the sexual behavior that brought them into the program and that their parents, to their knowledge, reported the same.

The absence of relapse without the opportunity to do so does not provide the ability to assess the goal of decreasing the chances of recurrences. Therefore, each person was asked about such opportunities. Table 3 indicates that eight adolescents and nine parents reported that there were opportunities to relapse. Two teenagers reported no such opportunity. These two individuals said they had no contact with the children they molested and that they did not even "hang around" younger children. One parent confirmed his son's report.

No teenager reported utilizing their individually created relapse prevention plan. The most often heard reason was "I didn't need to." One boy, age 17, said "The desire wasn't there. It was just a fluke thing back then." Another boy when asked why he had not used the plan said, "Because now I know what I did was wrong." All parents said that they had not discussed the plan.

Table 3: Status at Six-Month Follow-up

	Adolescent's Report	Parent(s)' Report
Inappropriate Sex Behavior		
Relapse	0	0
Opportunity for relapse = Yes	8	0
Opportunity for relapse = No	2	1
Use of relapse prevention plan = Yes	0	0
Use of relapse prevention plan = No	10	10
Initiated Appropriate Sex Behavior	2	2

Appropriate Sexual Behavior

Two individuals noted on Table 3 reported sexual behavior that was initiated between the termination of treatment and the six-month follow- up. One teenager, age 17, initiated age-appropriate consenting heterosexual intercourse. A condom was always used. The second boy, age 15, reported a new sexual behavior, masturbating for the first time in the privacy of his bedroom.

None of the remaining eight teenagers reported any new sexual behaviors and no one at follow-up was engaging in unsafe sexual practices.

DISCUSSION

There were two objectives of this program. The first goal was to decrease the probability that sexually inappropriate behavior would reoccur. The second goal was to educate the adolescents and their parents about what was sexually appropriate and responsible. The hope was that when the adolescents initiated their sexual lives it would be age appropriate, mutually consenting, and safe. Follow-up data suggest that the two goals were achieved. However, this conclusion is made with caution for there are obvious limitations. First, the number of participants is small. Second, and most important, the follow-up is only six months post-treatment and based solely on verbal reports. Despite this limitation of verbal reporting, we do feel somewhat confident because the adolescent verbal reports are corroborated by their parents. While obviously not foolproof, it does provide a measure different from the youngsters' self-reports alone. A third limitation is the fact that a number of families were self-referred and were selected because they were willing to participate in this program. Owing to these limitations follow-up of these adolescents and their families will continue yearly through high school.

The diagnosis of a specific paraphilia could not be made. No adolescent reported the essential feature of this class of sexual disorder; namely, a recurrent intense sexual urge and sexual arousing fantasies that are not part of normative arousal patterns. This might explain why these adolescents during follow-up reported not using the relapse prevention plans. Not having these recurrent urges and fantasy patterns meant they did not have an established cycle of inappropriate behavior. This interpretation is made with caution because the intervention was possibly made before a paraphilia and a subsequent sexual offense cycle was established. It also might be that these adolescents were denying or minimizing their sexual urges and fantasies, characteristics often ascribed to individuals with paraphilias. It is characteristic of adults with paraphilias that they do not regard themselves as ill or in need of mental health services. The adolescents were not thought to be denying because they admitted to their sexually inappropriate behavior and in some cases even reported inappropriate behaviors not heretofore disclosed.

Assuming paraphilias were not yet established, what factors might be involved in establishing such a disorder or continuing to maintain sexually inappropriate behavior that is not paraphiliac in nature? While more research and clinical investigation are needed to answer this question, some clues perhaps can be found in the fact that both parents and adolescents at follow-up asked for further help. The help they asked for was not specifically targeted for sexually inappropriate behavior or even for more sexual education. Two boys said that their families still needed help in learning how to communicate in a positive but firm manner. Two other boys were better able to define their issues in terms of the family: one 16-year-old boy said, "I think my mother and I need to work more on trusting one another." The other boy wished that his relationship with his alcoholic father was better. A parent voiced concern over her son's continued social isolation, and a 16-year-old boy requested help in managing his anger.

The phrase "adolescent sex offender" tells us very little about the nature of this behavior and does not further our understanding of the complex factors involved. Only systematic investigation will move us beyond "clinical impression and opinion" (Davis and Leitenburg, 1987).

REFERENCES

Abel, G.G. and Rouleau, J.L. (1990). The nature and extent of sexual assault. In W.L. Marshall, D.R. Laws, and H.E. Barbaree (Editors), *Handbook of Sexual Assault: Issues, Theories, and Treatment of the Offender*. New York, Plenum, pp. 9-21.

Becker, J.V., Kaplan, M.S., and Kavoussi, R. (1988). Measuring the effectiveness of treatment for the aggressive adolescent sexual offender. In R.A. Prentky and V.L. Quinsey (Editors), *Human Sexual Aggression: Current Perspectives. Annals of the New York Academy of Science* 528:215-222.

Bergstrom-Walan, M. (Director) (1971). *Sexual Intercourse* (VHS). Huntington Station, New York, Focus International, 14 Oregon Drive 11746-2627.

Davis, G.E., and Leitenberg, H. (1987). Adolescent sex offenders. *Psychological Bulletin* 101:417-427.

Erikson, B.G., and Lotmen, C.O. (Directors) (1986). *The Miracle of Life* (VHS). New York, New York, Crown Video, 225 Park Avenue South, 10003.

Federal Bureau of Investigation (1987). *Uniform Crime Reports*. Washington, D.C., Department of Justice.

Groth, N.A., Longo, P.E., and McFaden, J.B. (1982). Undetected recidivism among rapists and child molesters. *Crime and Delinquency* 128:450-458.

Hayes, C.D. (Editor) (1987). *Risking the Future: Adolescent Sexuality, Pregnancy and Childbearing*. Washington, D.C., National Academy Press.

Hollingshead, A.B., and Redlich, F.C. (1958). *Social Class and Mental Illness*. New York, Wiley.

Mayle, P. (Director) (1986). *What's Happening to Me?* (VHS). Los Angeles, New World Video, LCA.

National Adolescent Perpetrator Network. Preliminary Report from the National Task Force of Juvenile Sexual Offending (1988). *Juvenile and Family Court Journal*, pp. 5-67.

Pithers, W.D. (1990). Relapse prevention with sexual aggressors: a method for maintaining therapeutic gain and enhancing external supervision. In W.L. Marshall, D.R. Laws, and H.E. Barbaree (Editors), *Handbook of Sexual Assault: Issues, Theories and Treatment of the Offenders*. New York, Plenum, pp. 343-361.

Seltzer, D. (Director) (1986). *Lucas* (VHS). Livonia, Michigan, CBC/Fox Video.
Steen, C., and Monnette, B. (1989). *Treating the Adolescent Sex Offender in the Community*. Springfield: Charles C. Thomas.
Wagner, G. (Director) (1973). *Physiological Responses of the Sexually Stimulated Female in the Laboratory* (VHS). San Francisco, Multi Media.
Wagner, G. (Director) (1973). *Physiological Responses of the Sexually Stimulated Male in the Laboratory* (VHS). San Francisco, Multi Media.

AUTHORS' NOTES

T. Mazur, PsyD, and P.M. Michael are with the Psychoendocrinology Unit, Division of Child and Adolescent Psychiatry. Children's Hospital of Buffalo.

This work was supported by grants from the Children's Justice and Assistance Act, New York Department of Social Services (#C003573), the Buffalo Foundation, and the Josephine Goodyear Committee of the Children's Hospital of Buffalo. The authors gratefully acknowledge Susan Rubino for her assistance in manuscript preparation.

Address for correspondence: Tom Mazur, PsyD, Director, Psychoendocrinology, Division of Child and Adolescent Psychiatry, Children's Hospital of Buffalo, 219 Bryant Street, Buffalo, NY 14222.

SEX OFFENDER TREATMENT: PSYCHOLOGICAL AND MEDICAL APPROACHES. Pp. 205-216.

□ CLINICAL PROCESSES

Developing Insight in Incestuous Fathers

Ronald E. Zuskin
University of Maryland

ABSTRACT Given the portrait of incest fathers, the clinician's role in promoting their development of insight is a formidable task. In this paper the concept of insight is explored and preconditions for the development of insight are suggested. A framework which promotes insight in incest fathers developed for use in the Baltimore County Sexual Abuse Treatment Program is detailed, as are suggestions for applying the framework in offender treatment. Insight is possible in incest fathers. It can promote mastery of stressors which, in the past, led to incestuous behavior, generate psychological growth in the offender, and prevent relapse.

Fathers who commit incest present significant obstacles to the clinician attempting to help them develop insight. Descriptions in the literature paint a bleak portrait of their intrapsychic awareness and interpersonal skills. Perhaps the most thorough portrait of the incest father is drawn by Taylor (1986). He sees these men having problems with abandonment, loss of self esteem, insecurity, and inadequacy. They are immature and prone to use escapist modes of stress management. They are reactive to problems and stressors, have a fear of authority which leads them to be avoidant and/or compliant with authority figures, and gain compensatory power through control. Incest offenders have a sense of powerlessness, devaluation, and isolation, which leaves them with a marked lack of empathy. They are narcissistic, and emotionally unaware, which leads them to be "alexithymic"—that is, unable to experience or express age-appropriate emotions. Incest fathers are inept at communicating feelings and inadequate at solving problems. They have a variety of sexual problems. In addition, incest fathers suffer from a variety of anger dysfunctions. Many of these men have experienced childhood sexual victimization themselves and have all the problems of untreated victimization. These descriptions have been observed by other authors (Finkelhor, 1987; Groth, 1981; Ingersoll & Patton, 1990; Rosenfeld, 1979; and Summit & Kryso, 1978). Additionally, Weiss (1984) notes that child molestors may have disturbed thought processes.

INSIGHT

Authors and clinicians in a wide variety of disciplines operating from varied theoretical frameworks have touted the value of insight to the therapeutic process (David, 1990; Langs, 1976, 1976, 1979; Pennebaker, 1990; Reid & Finesinger, 1952; Richfield, 1954; Yalom, 1975, 1980; Zilboorg, 1952). The value of insight for most authors is in its utility in the change process (Freedman, Kaplan, & Sadock, 1972; Langs, 1976, 1979; Reid & Finesinger, 1952; Yalom, 1975, 1980). The changes resulting from insight include adaptation, empowerment, forgiveness, guilt reduction, enhanced problem-solving, reduction of tension, the release of psychic energy, increased self-knowledge, symptom relief, better understanding, and strengthened will. Although most authors hold that change results from insight, there are those who believe that insight can occur without change (David, 1990; Reid & Finesinger, 1952; Richfield, 1954), or that insight occurs following change (Freedman et al., 1972; Selvini, 1988), that change can occur without insight (Watzlawick, Beavin, & Jackson, 1967; Yalom, 1975), or that insight may serve to resist change (Hatcher, 1973; Silverberg, 1955). However, Yalom's (1975) research with encounter groups revealed that in patients' reports at the end of therapy the eight items they deemed as most helpful were all related to insight.

Some authors complain that clinicians and theoreticians are not clear about the nature of insight (Reid & Finesinger, 1952; Zilboorg, 1952). This may be due to the fact that, as Yalom (1975) points out, insight defies precise description because it is not a unitary concept. In its broadest clinical sense, he sees "insight" as a "sighting inwards."

Several authors have reviewed the historical development of the concept of insight (David, 1990; Hatcher, 1973; Richfield, 1954). A brief review of the literature, however, reveals that "insight" can mean many things to many people. Authors have freely defined a potpourri of types of insight. These include "authentic" (Kernberg, 1975); "curative" (Richfield, 1954; Zilboorg, 1952); "descriptive" (Richfield, 1954); "dynamic" (Reid & Finesinger, 1952); "early" (David, 1990; Heinrichs, Cohen, & Carpenter, 1985); "emotional" (Hatcher, 1973; Reid & Finesinger, 1952; Talbott, Hales, & Yadofsky, 1988; Zilboorg, 1952); "generic" (Reid & Finesinger, 1952); "gestalt" (David, 1990); "intellectual" (Cambell, 1981; Reid & Finesinger, 1952; Zilboorg, 1952); "neutral" (Reid & Finesinger, 1952); "ostensive" (Richfield, 1954); "partial" (David, 1990; Zilboorg, 1952); "preliminary" (Richfield, 1954); "pseudo" (David, 1990; Reid & Finesinger, 1952; Richfield, 1954); "psychoanalytic" (David, 1990; Hatcher, 1973); "psychological" (Richfield, 1954); "psychiatric emotional" vs. "psychoanalytic emotional" (Zilboorg, 1952); "reality-oriented" (Hatcher, 1973); "retrospective" (David, 1990); "unconscious" (Zilboorg, 1952); and "verbal" insight (Richfield, 1954). There are also insight into illness (David, 1990; Heinrichs et al., 1985; Zilboorg, 1952); insight into another's illness (David, 1990); and insight through transference (Zilboorg, 1952). Making the picture even more complex are authors who describe dimensions, levels, or degrees of insight (David, 1990; Yalom, 1975).

In part the confusion about insight derives from its very complexity. Further confusion grows out of the fact that authors speak of insight both as a process and the product of that process. Yalom (1975) states that what is important is that insight occurs, and that it is more important to attend to how it occurs than to what it contains.

Richfield's work grows out of the thought of Lord Bertrand Russell, who suggests two types of knowledge. The first is knowledge by description, or knowledge "about." This transcends the limits of private experience and is knowledge that something is true. A second type of knowledge is knowledge by acquaintance, or knowledge "of." This occurs when knowledge is obtained without logical dependence upon any inferential process or other knowledge of facts.

This knowledge is directly attained through experience and includes a cognitive component which reflects one's awareness of one's experience. The former produces descriptive insights — those which provide the subject with truths about himself by making use of his capacity to comprehend words employed in interventions. The latter produces ostensive insights — those which incorporate the actual, conscious experience of their referents, and are obtained through direct experience. Insight, then, can occur through learning and through experience. Insight derived from experience requires self-observation, as described in detail by Hatcher (1973). Ostensive insights grow out of experiential and reflective self-observation, and must precede descriptive insights for change to occur. As Richfield (1954) states, "first to know, then to face and handle."

Insight, then, is a process through which knowledge is gained as a result of experience and learning. The content of the knowledge may be information about oneself, about one's relatedness to others, and or about the context within and around which the self and its relatedness to others is organized.

In addition to the capacity for self-observation there are other preconditions required for the development of insight. Sound ego functioning, in general, is required, especially consciousness, reality testing, integrative functioning, controlled ego regression, direct experience with fresh material, control over discharge of affects, and tolerance of unpleasant affect (Hatcher, 1973). Cognitive abilities such as perceiving, identifying, and remembering are necessary (Reid & Finesinger, 1952), as are judgements, description, and evaluation, especially in the context of the framework of a set of principles or knowledge (Richfield, 1954). In addition, the relationship between therapist and client requires a compliant and cooperative client viewing a therapist as competent, warm, helpful, and safe. The therapist must teach self-observation, self-reporting, and intervene verbally and non-verbally to stimulate insight that will be emotionally reinforced and dynamically effective (Reid & Finesinger, 1952).

The population of incest fathers in treatment presents significant clinical challenges to the therapist attempting to help these offenders develop insight. A recent study shows the urgency of this for incest fathers. Yalom's (1975) research results show that "those subjects who obtained insight and were able to organize their experience in some coherent pattern had a positive outcome."

A FRAMEWORK FOR DEVELOPING INSIGHT

The framework presented here has been used by the Baltimore County Sexual Abuse Treatment Program in group and individual treatment modalities. We treat incest fathers who admitted their abusiveness, demonstrated remorse, and accepted some responsibility for abuse following disclosure. Fathers who do not meet this criteria are referred to other community resources for therapy, while case management may continue within the SATP. The framework presented in this paper is shared with the offender and used by the father and the clinician to help organize the mass of clinical material presented by the offender in order to promote the development of insight.

The framework consists of five factors which must be elucidated, explored, and integrated by the offender during therapy: predisposing factors, precipitating factors, instigating factors, abuse factors, and instrumental factors.

Predisposing Factors

Predisposing factors, or "stage setters," are factors which render a person susceptible to the sexual abuse of children. These factors occur well in advance of abusive behavior and include events in a person's early life history, his characteristic and adapted responses to those events, as well as to thematically similar recurring events. They also refer in general to basic elements of the offender's personality. Predisposing life history events include childhood sexual abuse (see numerous citings in Faller, 1989), physical or emotional abuse in childhood, early experiences in any relationship involving extreme abuses of power and control, early losses or abandonment, and early involvement in impulsive, compulsive and/or self-destructive behaviors. Predisposing characteristic adaptions include self-isolation, withdrawal from or provocation of authority figures, abuse of power in relationships, and poor problem-solving skills. Predisposing personality elements may consist of the habitual use of primitive defenses, the use of others to perform self object functions, alexithymia, avoidance, concrete thinking, and the use of interactional defenses (see Langs, 1976, 1979).

Precipitating Factors

Precipitating factors, or "stressors," refer to reality and psychological events which overwhelm the coping ability of a person susceptible to child sexual abuse. This creates regressive adaptive attempts, a search for more primitive coping mechanisms, and a high risk for sexually abusive behavior. Other authors have discussed the effects of stress and precipitating events on offenders (Groth, 1981; Ingersoll, 1990; Trepper, 1986). These factors may occur well in advance of or very near the onset of abusive behavior. If abuse becomes an ongoing pattern these factors will present with regularity and may escalate in terms of frequency and intensity during the ongoing perpetration. Precipitating factors include identifiable environmental or psychological stressors which increase tension, stress and anxiety, promote regressed functioning, decrease impulse control, and precipitate sexualized acting out. Such environmental factors may be marital discord, sexual dissatisfaction, events reflecting loss or abandonment themes, involvement as a subordinate in relationships, financial difficulties, and problems in the extended family. Precipitating psychological states and events include modified relationships with self objects, abandonment panic, a sense of inner death, disintegration, or void, anger and rage, and an increased reliance on primitive defenses.

Instigating Factors

Instigating factors, or "triggers," are reality or psychological events or processes which incite a regressed person susceptible to child sexual abuse into incestuous action. These events or processes precede the abuse with relative immediacy. They tend to be highly idiosyncratic. For some offenders abusive behavior is experienced as a compelling explosion of abusive feelings and behaviors. Others experience a sequential building up of impulses (the trigger sequence). The instigating factors which occur before abuse is patterned may be quite different from those which evolve after the pattern is set. Attention should be given to exploring both.

For some offenders physical proximity to or contact with a child may incite abuse. Mood factors such as the time of day, music, or lighting may trigger abuse. Some incest fathers report obsessive and compulsive fantasies about the abuse, coupled with masturbation. Many offenders report a high degree of non-sexual arousal and excitation in anticipation of successful imminent taboo violation.

Many incest fathers use perceptual distortions or rationalizations to justify the incest. Frequently reported perceptual distortions include "I could tell she wanted me to"; "She came on to me"; and "She enjoyed it." Rationalizations frequently reported include "I wanted to teach her about sex"; "I wanted her to know what to expect from boys her own age"; and "I didn't want her to have hang-ups when she got older." Some offenders use drugs or alcohol, seeking an intoxicated state before abusing. This disinhibition increases the effectiveness of whatever form of justification the father utilizes.

Early in the patterning of abuse these justifications tend to occur outside the awareness of the offender. As incest becomes more patterned and predictable, fathers report becoming more aware of their justifications and may use rationalizations consciously and strategically to overcome their ambivalence about abuse. Fathers who are conscious of their justifications report that they experience this as "giving themselves permission to abuse." Whether the father uses justification unconsciously or strategically, the clinician should search for and identify such distortions and rationalizations, as they generally mark the beginning of the trigger sequence.

Abuse Factors

Abuse factors refer to the details of the abuse itself. Details related to the strategic planning of abuse, the location, the father's thoughts, feelings and sensations during abuse episodes, what he looked at, and the reactions of the victim should be explored. The physical description of the victim should be elicited, including the presence or absence of secondary sexual characteristics. Details about how the episode ended should be explored in depth.

Instrumental Factors

Instrumental factors, or "rewards" refer to reality and psychological effects which occur during or after incest and which serve to reinforce the likelihood of the recurrence of abusive behavior. These factors are "instrumental" in the behaviorist sense — abusive behaviors are shaped and maintained by their consequences for the offender or by their effects on the environment. Experiences of power and control, of sexual gratification, and of existential reaffirmation may occur during the abuse. Enhanced self-esteem, tension reduction, and improved capacity to approach peers — even the spouse — may result from the abuse. The stabilization of family relationships may be enhanced by the abuse. Additionally, careful attention must be given to the instrumental advantages which accrue to what offenders report as "negative" consequences of the abuse. Many fathers experience guilt and shame almost immediately following incest. They may ferociously punish themselves. For some offenders these experiences represent anxiety about being caught. Their self-punishment can be interpreted as an attempt to scare themselves out of further abuse. In other offenders, however, self- punishment following incest is part of a "Blame-Guilt-Shame-Punishment-Absolution Cycle." This is also a reenactment of childhood punishment when harsh parental punishment or physical abuse may have expiated their experience of guilt, promoted denial, and absolved them of responsibility. In many ways this reaffirms the offender's sense of "bad self." The internal replaying of this cycle collectively reinforces the likelihood of the recurrence of abuse by absolving the father of responsibility, aiding in denial and the illusion of regained control over his behavior, and, by his failure to confront his abusiveness, generate stress which overwhelm his coping mechanisms in a circular and predictable manner.

APPLICATION OF THE FRAMEWORK

This framework is shared with fathers in treatment. It provides a cognitive tool for both offender and clinician in organizing material, identifying problem areas, strategizing interventions, and assessing the father's development of insight.

Since so many incest offenders are ill-equipped to begin the process, exercises have been developed which strengthen the preconditions for insight. Exercises which help the father learn to identify and express feelings, to empathize with the victim and with other group members in therapy, to observe one's behaviors, and to learn of one's effects on others pave the way for the development of insight.

In beginning therapy most adult offenders find it less threatening to explore predisposing factors. For many fathers, who are not psychologically-minded, this is the first opportunity to connect current behavior with past experience. The clinician must be cautious that the offender does not use this knowledge as a justification for the abuse. Exploration of "stage setters" can help the father understand his susceptibility to the sexual abuse of children and can permit his distant ownership of the decision to abuse.

The exploration of precipitating factors permits the offender to identify his specific stressors and his poorly adapted coping strategies which led to the gradual regression of his functioning. Many offenders wish to account for their abusiveness on the basis of stressors alone. This should be confronted as the wish to blame others for the abuse, and as denial of responsibility.

For most offenders, instigating factors are the most difficult to identify. Acknowledgement of triggers brings responsibility for the abuse to rest squarely on the offender's shoulders. This eradicates lingering denial and confronts the offender with his own planning and manipulation of others. The father can own his depersonification of the victim as the final step necessary to instigate abuse. In wrestling with instigating factors fathers may experience depression and the return of disintegrating anxiety which was warded off with onset of the abuse itself.

Exploring abuse factors in intimate detail can be extremely difficult for incest fathers. Many are very concrete thinkers for whom words are not experienced as abstractions, but serve to reinvoke the events being described. Exercises directing the offender to "make a movie" of the abuse can be helpful in structuring his recounting of details. The "movie camera" can move from the point of view of the offender's eyes, to the eyes of the victim, to a place on the wall overlooking the abuse. The movie should continue until the father and the victim are alone again, and should describe the behaviors of each at that point. This technique is helpful in providing the offender some experiential distance from his report. Many offenders describe dissociative experiences of self- distraction during abuse. Others never look at the victim's face, or they blank it out or imagine someone else's face. Recounting of abuse incidents can invoke powerful feelings of guilt and shame. These can generate intense self-punitive and self-destructive reactions in the offender. The clinician must be attuned to such possibilities by striving to remain empathic during the retelling of events which may be stressful to hear. Such negative experiences can be reintegrated by the offender and can lead towards self-forgiveness if they are dealt with directly and with immediacy.

Exploration of instrumental factors can promote growth and mastery in the offender by helping to identify the needs which were being met through child sexual abuse. The incest father can be taught communication skills, problem-solving strategies, and the development of appropriate alternatives for meeting his needs.

Constant reference to this framework during the course of treatment averaging more than two years provides the incest father and the clinician with a shared language and perspective on clinical material. Incest fathers develop an evolving capacity for insight into their own abusive patterns which promotes mastery, growth, and change.

Twenty-six offenders have been treated in our program since the inception of this framework, over three years ago. There have been no known instances of recidivism. Several offenders terminated from therapy have used their capacity for insight to return to treatment when recognizing their renewed experience of debilitating stressors or the onset of trigger sequences.

SUMMARY

Given the portrait of incest fathers, the clinician's role in promoting insight in these offenders is a formidable task. Their characteristics mitigate against the complex requirements of developing insight. The use of a shared cognitive framework in organizing clinical material assists the offender and the clinician. For incest fathers, the development of insight is possible and has implications for aiding the offender's understanding of abusive behavior, for mastering the stressors which generated abusiveness, and for helping to prevent relapse.

REFERENCES

Campbell, R. J. (1981). *Psychiatric dictionary.* New York: Oxford.

David, A. S. (1990). Insight and psychosis. *British Journal of Pschology, 156,* 798-808.

Faller, K. C. Why sexual abuse? An exploration of the intergenerational hypothesis. *Child Abuse and Neglect: The International Journal, 13* (4), 543-548.

Finkelhor, D. The sexual abuse of children: Current research reviewed. *Psychiatric Annals, 17*(4), 233-241.

Freedman, A. M., Kaplan, H. I., & Sadock, B. J. (1972). *Modern synopsis of comprehensive textbook of psychiatry.* Baltimore: Williams and Wilkins.

Groth, A. N. (1982). The incest offender. In S. M. Sgroi (Ed.), *Handbook of clinical intervention in child sexual abuse* (pp. 215-239). Lexington, MA: D. C. Heath.

Hatcher, R. L. (1973). Insight and self-observation. *Journal of the American Psychoanalytic Association, 21*(2), 377-348.

Heinrichs, D. W., Cohen, B. P., & Carpenter, W. T., Jr. (1985). Early insight and the management of schizophrenic decompensation. *Journal of Nervous and Mental Disease,* 173(3), 133-138.

Ingersoll, S. L., & Patton, S. O. (1990). *Treating perpetrators of sexual abuse.* Lexington, MA: Lexington.

Kernberg, O. F. (1975). *Borderline conditions and pathological narcissism.* New York: Jason Aronson.

Langs, R. (1976). *The bipersonal field.* New York: Jason Aronson.

Langs, R. (1976). *Therapeutic interaction: Vol. 2. A critical overview and synthesis.* New York: Jason Aronson.

Langs, R. (1979). *The supervisory experience.* New York: Jason Aronson.

Pennebaker, J. W. *Opening up: The healing power of confiding in others.* New York: Morrow.

Reid, J. R. & Finesinger, J. E. (1952). The role of insight in psychotherapy. *The American Journal of Psychiatry, 108,* 726-734.

Richfield, J. (1954). An analysis of the concept of insight. *The Psychoanalytic Quarterly, 23,* 309-408.

Rosenfeld, A. A. (1979). Endogamic incest and the victim- perpetrator model. *The American Journal of the Disabled Child, 133,* 406-410.

Selvini, M. (Ed.). (1988). *The work of Mara Selvini Palazzoli* (A. J. Pomerans, Trans.). Northvale, NJ: Jason Aronson.

Silverberg, W. V. (1955). Acting out versus insight: A problem in psychoanalytic technique. *Psychiatric Quarterly,* 24, 527-544.

Summit, R. & Kryso, J. (1978). Sexual abuse of children: A clinical spectrum. *American Journal of Orthopsychiatry,* 48(2), 237-251.

Talbott, J. A., Hales, R. E., & Yadofsky, S. C. (Eds.). (1988). *The American Psychiatric Press textbook of psychiatry.* Washington, DC: American Psychiatric Press.

Taylor, J. W. (1986). Social casework and the multi-modal treatment of incest. *Social Casework: The Journal of Contemporary Social Work*, 10-86, 451-459.

Trepper, T. S., & Barrett, M. J. (Eds.). (1986). *Treating incest: A multiple systems perspective*. New York: The Haworth Press, Inc.

Watzlawick, P., Beaven, J. H., & Jackson, D. D. (1967). *Pragmatics of human communication: A study of interactional patterns, pathologies, and paradoxes*. New York: W. W. Norton.

Weiss, Michael J. (1984, November). Child molesting: What must be done to protect our children. *Ladies' Home Journal*, pp. 114-117, 198-202.

Yalom, I. D. (1975). *The theory and practice of group psychotherapy* (2nd ed.). New York: Basic Books.

Yalom, I. D. (1980). *Existential psychotherapy*. New York: Basic Books.

Zilboorg, G. (1952). *The emotional problem and the therapeutic role of insight*. The Psychoanalytic Quarterly, 21, 1-24.

AUTHOR'S NOTE

Ronald E. Zuskin, LICSW, is an instructor in the School of Social Work at the University of Maryland at Baltimore. The concepts presented here were developed and applied during his service as a member of the Baltimore County Department of Social Services' Sexual Abuse Treatment Program.

Address for Correspondence: Ronald E. Zuskin, University of Maryland at Baltimore, School of Social Work, 525 W. Redwood Street, Baltimore, MD, 21201-1777.

SEX OFFENDER TREATMENT: PSYCHOLOGICAL AND MEDICAL APPROACHES. Pp. 217-223.

☐ CLINICAL PROCESSES

What Happens to Therapists Who Work with Sex Offenders?

Toni Farrenkopf
Farrenkopf & Associates, Portland, OR

ABSTRACT Following pilot interviews, 24 experienced therapists working with sex offenders were surveyed regarding the personal impact of this work. Clients' criminality is often the target for change, and therapists become socializing agents. Client traits of irresponsibility, lack of change motivation and self centeredness affect the therapy process. The majority of therapists reported a shift in their perspective, becoming discouraged about client change. Half of the therapists experienced emotional hardening, rising anger and confrontation. Over one-third suffered frustration with the correctional system or society. One third, female therapists in particular, reported increased suspiciousness and vulnerability. Several adjustment phases were reported. Upon initial exposure to this work, many therapists experienced "shock," bewilderment and vulnerability. A period of professional "mission" followed, including hopes for effectiveness, non-judgmental work ethics and empathy for clients. Next, a surfacing of repressed emotions was reported, including "anger" and cynicism, often leading to "erosion," a sense of disenchantment. One quarter of the study sample experienced burnout. An alternative to burnout is *adaptation*: a lowering of expectations, objective detachment, acceptance of the human dark side. Other coping strategies include work diversification and increased support systems.

Counseling and attempting to affect change in others impacts the practitioner (Maslach, 1982; Farber, 1983). Such stress may be severe if working with sex offenders. Gene Abel (1983, pp. 283-250) states that "one cannot ignore the very personal impact of working day in and day out with rapists, and potential rapists. The recounting and exploring of the details of such violent fantasies and atrocious acts in effect serve to surround the therapist in an emotional world of violence on top of violence. If the work force to prevent sexual violence is to be effective with its difficult task, we must be aware of the high 'burn-out' of personnel and provide staff training and staff development that can maintain that work force." So what makes criminals such a challenging client population?

Because many of these clients pose a threat of harming others, most criminal clients are mandated for therapy by some social agency. Most are not voluntarily clients. Criminal behavior is often the target for change, a prospect that has been repeatedly questioned (Clackley, 1964; Suedfeld and Landon, 1975). Thus, the therapist is thrust into the role of a socialization agent, representing authority, directing, setting limits, expecting change. In comparison to voluntary clients, therapists report more stress from working with mandated clients (Steenson, 1987).

Sex offender traits and behaviors that affect the therapy process often include self centeredness, lack of empathy, manipulation, minimization or externalization of personal responsibility, and lack of internal change motivation, while at the same time resisting external influence (Strasburger, 1986). Some criminal population values, especially in prison, may be counter to therapy values, such as openness, honesty and trust. Scott (1989, p. 225) posits that psychotherapy with criminals "is the most demanding task in the entire arena of mental health."

METHOD

Following pilot interviews with 17 prison therapists, a structured questionnaire survey was presented to 35 Oregon mental health therapists known to work with criminal clients and sex offenders. Twenty-four responded, representing a 69% return rate. The survey topics included: personal impact of working with sex offenders, perceived phases of impact, differences between male/female therapists, personal coping strategies and the respondents' demographics.

The therapists were between ages 30 and 60 (Mean = 48), having between 10 and 30 years of experience (Mean = 17) with criminal offenders. Twenty (83%) were male, four (17%) female. Seventeen

(71%) held doctoral degrees in psychology, with seven (29%) holding master's degrees. Twenty-two (92%) respondents worked in private practice, thirteen (54%) of the total sample had experience working for public agencies.

RESULTS

Impact

Over half (54%) of the surveyed therapists reported a shift in their perspective, with diminished hopes and expectations in working with sex offenders. Their outlook became more cynical and objective, less liberal or "naive." They described having fewer illusions as a result of seeing the human dark side and becoming more pessimistic about the prospect of client change.

Almost half (42%) of the survey respondents disclosed a hardening or dulling of emotions. With rising anger and frustration, they became more confrontational and less tolerant of others' behavior. Therapists experienced this emotional distancing not only with their clients, but also within their own social circles. Some therapists reported a loss of humor; more than one disclosed they never made love on the day they consulted in the prisons. On the other side of the coin, some 17% reported increased sensitivity toward others, more empathy for human suffering, acting sexually more considerate of their partners.

Over one-third (38%) suffered frustration with the correctional system or with society. Therapists were disillusioned with the inconsistent justice system, complaining of punitive correctional staff attitudes and a pronounced lack of support or services. Some respondents were discouraged by society's "too little too late" reactive approach, and the lack of preventative programs.

Almost one-third (29%) felt they were more hypervigilant and suspicious of others and more protective of their own or their family's personal safety. Some therapists saw potential abusers everywhere. Female therapists in particular reported more fearfulness, even nightmares.

A feeling of generalized high stress, exhaustion, depression, or "burnout" was reported by 25% of respondents, at times leading to the termination of sex offender work. After interviewing offenders, one therapist reported a feeling that was "like after serious physical trauma." Multiple sources of stress were listed: (a) client's criminal personality; (b) an inadequate rehabilitative system; and (c) non-supportive responses from friends and colleagues, a "lack of allies" (Groth, 1984). In contrast, 17% of our survey expressed only minimal or short lived emotional impact from working with sex offenders.

Gender Differences

Female therapists working with predominantly male offenders were particularly prone to feeling increased vulnerability or threat of abuse, more paranoia and vigilance in their daily lives. Some experienced constant concern over their children encountering abusive situations, including in their own homes. Working with sex offenders may re-sensitize female therapists to their own past victimization experiences by men and may heighten their negative attitudes toward males in general. Along the same lines, some male therapists were aware of an increased "collective guilt" over male abusive behavior. Survey respondents observed that few female therapists work with offenders and that they tend to spend a shorter time doing so.

Phases of Impact

Most therapists observed an evolving progression in their reactions to this type of work. Phase One, "Shock" is the first and immediate reaction to encountering sex offenders on such a close-up, personal level. Feelings of fear and vulnerability are most evident at this stage. Some respondents were overwhelmed by the prevalence of abuse threat in society.

Phase Two, "Mission" characterizes the therapist's adaptation, the desire to help clients and a professional zeal for treatment effectiveness. Some referred to client empathy and non-judgmental work ethics with terms like "bleeding heart" or "naive." At this stage therapists exercise emotional repression and desensitization with regard to the client's sex offenses. Based on survey responses, this phase may vary from about one to five years.

Repressed emotions, feelings of "Anger," a confrontive attitude and intolerance of criminal thinking errors surface during Phase Three (Yochelson & Samenow, 1976). Client denial and victim stance, abusiveness and inevitable re-offense incidents are disheartening to therapists' professional idealism. The therapist becomes less allied with the offender client and identifies more with the victim and society at large. With little room for any "benefit of the doubt," client guilt may be assumed and client self reports devalued. Jerome Miller (1991) proposed that professionals working with sex offenders are too easily assuming the role of behavioral modifier in the service of law enforcement. Most therapists in this study reported a phase progression including Phases Two and Three.

Phase Four A, "Erosion," is an amplified extension of Phase Three, where anger and intolerance mount to a sense of resentment. Thoughts of treatment futility, feelings of exhaustion and depression were mentioned. One quarter of the survey sample reported "burn-out," one-fifth stopped working with sex offenders altogether. One therapist summarized her phase progression like this: "First 'Save the world,' then 'Save a few,' then 'Save yourself.'" Another psychologist expressed his feelings in poetry: "Tired and dejected / angry and abused / hopes dimmed / ideals soiled / time and again / and now my eyes too / look cold and hateful . . ."

As an alternative to "Erosion," therapists may regain their work motivation and therapeutic compassion in Phase Four B, "*Adaptation*," by adopting a more detached attitude, lowering their expectations, philosophically tolerating the human dark side. The phase progression discussed here does, indeed, resemble the trauma/grief cycle including shock, fear, repression, anger, depression and finally acceptance/recovery (Frederick, 1986).

Coping Strategies

For maintaining personal mental health and avoiding burnout, the therapists suggested several coping methods. More than half (58%) advocated diversifying one's work areas, decreasing or stopping work with sex offenders. Many respondents (38%) expressed the lack of support systems in working with this taxing client population. They proposed increased support from supervision, training, peer groups, case staffings and more financial support for programs.

"Attitude adjustment" was seen as a prominent survival technique by 25% of the survey respondents. This would mean a realistic detachment from client outcome or client change, a process called "detached concern" by Maslach (1982). Farber's (1983) strategies for stress management also reflected the suggestions of the present study: 1. peer involvement; 2. spouse support; 3. diversifying; 4. setting realistic goals and not expecting too much.

SUMMARY

Therapists working with sex offenders experience considerable stress due to clients' criminal personality traits and their offenses, the involuntary nature of treatment, questionable prognosis and recidivism, shortcomings of the judicial and rehabilitation system and a shortfall of support.

This study showed that therapists' reactions include heightened vulnerability and vigilance, especially in females. Impact from this work appears to progress from a period of professional zeal and client empathy to emotional hardening and decreased hope for effectiveness. Some workers experience burnout with this client population. For adaptation, therapists advocate a diversified case load, as well as a less expectant, more detached attitude. Increased institutional and social support resources are called for.

REFERENCES

Abel, G. (1983) Preventing Men from Becoming Rapists. In Albee, Gordon S., and Leitenberg, H. (Eds.) *Promoting Sexual Responsibility and Preventing Sexual Problems*. Hanover, NH: University Press of New England, (pp. 238-250).

Clackley, H. (1964) *The Mask of Sanity*. St. Louis: Mosby.

Farber, B. (1983) *Stress and Burnout in the Human Service Professions*. New York: Pergamon.

Frederick, C. (1986) Psychic Trauma in Victims of Crime and Terrorism. In VandenBos, G. and Bryant, B. (Eds.) *Cataclysms, Crises and Catastrophes*. Washington D.C.: American Psychological Association, (pp. 55-128).

Groth, N. (1984) Sexual Assault: Rape, Incest and Child Molestation. Training Seminar. Beaverton, Oregon.

Maslach, C. (1982) *Burnout — The Cost of Caring*. Englewood Cliffs: Prentice-Hall.

Miller, J. (1991) Mitigating Professional Arrogance in Treating Sex Offenders. Paper presented at the 2nd International Conference on the Treatment of Sex Offenders. Minneapolis, University of Minnesota, Sept., 24.

Scott, E. (1989) Is there a Criminal Mind? *International Journal of Offender Therapy and Comparative Criminology*, Vol. 33, No. 3, December, (pp. 215-226).

Steenson, N. (1987) A Comparison of the Stresses Generated for Mental Health Practitioners Working with Mandated and Voluntary Clients in Agency Settings and in Private Practice. Doctoral dissertation. Forest Grove, Oregon: Pacific University.

Strasburger, L. (1986) The Treatment of Antisocial Syndromes: Therapist's Feelings. In Reid, W. (Ed.) *Unmasking the Psychopath*. New York: W. W. Norton, (pp. 191-206).

Suedfeld, P. and Landon, P. (1975) Approaches to Treatment. In Hare, R. and Schalling, D. (Eds.) *Psychopathic Behavior: Approaches to Research*. New York: Wiley.

Yochelson, S. and Samenow, S. (1976) *The Criminal Personality*. New York: J. Aronson.

AUTHOR'S NOTE

Please address correspondence to Toni Farrenkopf, PhD, & Associates, 2256 NW Pettygrove, Portland, OR 97210.

SEX OFFENDER TREATMENT: PSYCHOLOGICAL AND MEDICAL APPROACHES. Pp. 225-233.

False Accusations of Nosocomial Sexual Abuse

The Hand Bitten by the Dog It Feeds May Be Your Own

John Money
Johns-Hopkins University

ABSTRACT *Nosocomial* signifies that which pertains to or originates in a clinic or hospital. A practitioner performing, for example, a routine physical examination may be falsely accused of nosocomial sexual abuse, as in a case in which a pediatrician was accused also of causing emotional trauma by not having first obtained a mother's signed consent to perform a physical examination on her encopretic son. The criminal justice system of adversarialism is incompatible with the biomedical system of prevention. It is responsible for having established a sexual-abuse industry the practitioners of which have a vested interest in maintaining the status quo of sexual criminalization. They themselves are at risk of being falsely accused of sexual abuse.

The term *nosocomial* means pertaining to or originating in a clinic or hospital. Etymologically, it derives from the Greek, *nosokomeion*, from *nosos*, disease, + *komeion*, to take care of. Thus, a nosocomial illness is one that is attributable to being hospitalized as, for example, when a bacterial infection spreads contagiously among hospitalized patients.

Sexual abuse, per se, does not qualify as nosocomial abuse simply because it happens to have occurred within the confines of a hospital or clinic. The term, nosocomial sexual abuse, signifies that a routine hospital procedure, for example, getting undressed, exposing the naked genitalia, and undergoing a physical examination of the genitalia, is misconstrued as sexual abuse. It is easy for children to make such an error, and to falsely accuse the doctor of sexual abuse. This is precisely what happened in a case that came to trial in Boston in 1991. The defendant in the case was a Harvard pediatrician who had examined the plaintiff, aged twenty, in 1991, several times between the ages of seven and thirteen for a complaint of persistent encopresis.

My involvement in the case was contingent on the fact that I had formulated and first used the concept of nosocomial abuse in the only two known papers on the subject in the medical literature. One paper bears the title: "Nosocomial stress and abuse exemplified in a case of male hermaphroditism from infancy through adulthood: coping strategies and prevention" (Money and Lamacz, 1986). The purpose of this paper was to put on record a case of male hermaphroditism in which multiple admissions for genital surgical repair in boyhood "were experienced and assimilated in the boy's own mind as nosocomial abuse."

The title of the second of the two papers is: "Genital examination and exposure experienced as nosocomial sexual abuse in childhood" (Money and Lamacz, 1987). The purpose of this paper was to sound "an alert" insofar as, "in a society permeated with sexual taboo, some children do, indeed, subjectively experience the physical examination or the procedure of medical photography of the genitalia not only as an invasion of privacy, but also as an equivalent of sexual assault. Children with a sexual syndrome often have been strongly indoctrinated at home to keep their condition undisclosed. The more they have assimilated the moral precepts of modesty, the more are they likely to be traumatized by being genitally exposed and genitally palpated by not one but many examining physicians and their trainees."

ON TRIAL: A CASE OF FALSE ACCUSATION

The following résumé of the case on trial in Boston is drawn from data in the public record. These data do not, therefore, require informed consent in order to be reproduced.

As a boy of thirteen, the plaintiff was on the threshold of puberty, and also on the threshold of being an offspring of divorce, with no chance of regaining his father as he had wanted to do during years of parental separation and disrupted family life. In a deposition made at age twenty, he said he was also "disappointed" with his doctor whom he had admired and looked up to since age seven as the one who would rid him of encopresis. But the problem of soiling himself was still haunting him.

"It occurred to me," he said, "that I had always felt uncomfortable about the [physical] examinations, and they had really been a burden on me. It was pretty much that I'd had all I could take . . . There was, I believe, a documentary on TV on the topic of sexual abuse in which they talked a lot about feelings I had, the feelings of uneasiness about an adult touching me, and the feeling that I should come out and tell somebody . . . It kind of was like a key piece to a puzzle that I had been keeping in my closet for a long time." He did not speak about it until, three or four months later, his scheduled return visit to the pediatrician was due. In the car en route to the hospital, he became so upset that his mother drove him back home, and he did not return to his pediatrician ever again.

A few months later, the mother consulted an attorney. A year later, two months before her son's fifteenth birthday, she wrote a letter of complaint to the president of the hospital. Her complaint was that when the doctor would examine the boy's testicles his penis would be touched by or be located very close to the doctor's cheek. "I have done some research," she wrote, "and no one has been able to explain the need for testicular examinations for a child suffering from encompresis (sic)."

AT ISSUE: INFORMED CONSENT

By the time that the case came to trial five and a half years later, the complaint of physical contact had been dropped. The pediatrician had in fact been doing a routine physical examination and, in addition, applying a stethoscope to the lower abdominal wall, listening for bowel sounds. The new charge was that the pediatrician had performed physical examinations of the boy's genitalia without first obtaining the mother's signed informed consent. In addition, it was charged that the boy was still suffering from nosocomial sexual abuse, newly and erroneously defined as being synonymous with posttraumatic stress syndrome, secondary to having been emotionally traumatized by the earlier genital examinations.

The trial ended with the court ruling in favor of the pediatrician. One deciding factor was that he had at each visit been doing a routine physical examination with no evidence of personal sexual or erotic involvement of the type that might signify, for example, pedophilia. A second deciding factor was that, insofar as the physical examinations of the genitals may have been emotionally stressful, the magnitude of emotional stress could not be partialled out from that attributable to an incontrovertibly turbulent family life. Nor could it be partialled out from the emotional stress of growing up as a victim of encopresis itself.

The outcome of this trial has significance not only for pediatricians, but also for all health-care practitioners. On the one hand, it has set a precedent in case law to the effect that a child's misconstruing of routine clinical or hospital procedures as nosocomial sexual abuse may not be legally construed as prima facie evidence of actual criminal sexual abuse. On the other hand, it has not settled the issue of alleged emotional trauma or mental suffering secondary to the child's misconstruing of routine clinical and hospital procedures as nosocomial sexual abuse.

In the present litigious climate of false accusations of sexual child abuse, health-care practitioners are at risk of being charged with malpractice not because of performing routine procedures, but because of emotional stress generated by the misperception and misconstruing of these procedures as nosocomial sexual abuse. Thus it may become legally prudent, if not legally mandated, to require every patient to give signed informed consent for every nosocomial procedure, or component part of a procedure, that may be construed by the patient as emotionally stressful, irrespective of the technical impossibility of measuring degrees of stress. In pediatric practice in the United States, the parent or guardian would be legally responsible on behalf of the child up to age eighteen. It is quite possible that the cost and time of explaining and obtaining informed consent would exceed that of actual services consented to.

It is regrettably true, today, that American zeal to protect children from sexual abuse has become overextended so that, contrary to the provisions of the Constitution, to be charged with sexual abuse is tantamount to being considered guilty until proven innocent. Thus, irrespective of the frivolity or gravity of the charge, the very fact of having been accused of nosocomial sexual abuse is an everlasting stigma, not to mention legal expense. Even a verdict of not guilty does not obliterate the charge from the practitioner's professional biography, nor from various official forms, documents, and questionnaires he must fill in, throughout the remainder of his career.

The outcome of a false charge of nosocomial sexual abuse is no better for the patient than for the practitioner. In the present instance, for example, the plaintiff will carry for the rest of his life the psychopathological aftermath of having been held for seven years as a virtual hostage to the promise of potentially great wealth, provided he upheld the untenable and unsubstantiated role of victim of sexual child abuse. Seven years of his life have been lived in a state of indoctrinated delusion.

ADVERSARIALISM VERSUS PREVENTION

The tragedy of his life is not only personal, but also the tragedy of the wrong-headedness of the entire social and legal system for the protection of children against sexual child abuse. It was the child-protection system that produced the television program of which the plaintiff saw just enough to pick up the message that prudishly avoided sexual explicitness and hid behind the evasions, still in vogue, of good touch and bad touch. It allowed him to jump to the wrong conclusion that his own discomfort was attributable not, as it should have been, to undressing for the physical examination and thereby exposing his soiled underwear, but, on the contrary, was attributable to being touched in the course of the examining the genital, perineal and rectal area for skin lesions secondary to fecal discharge. The television program also told him to report bad touch to a parent or someone in authority. Thus, a system designed to rescue a victim had had, instead, the converse outcome of creating a victim.

In effect, the boy became entrapped in the system, a victim of his own erroneous formulation and false accusation of sexual abuse.

The botching of his case was not a fortuitous event, but one that the system is doomed to proliferate, for there is a canker at its core, namely, incompatibility between the adversarial principle of the law and the preventive principle of biomedical science. Preventing the spread of a disease is not achieved by criminalizing, prosecuting and punishing people who have it and who may transmit it. In the case of AIDS, for example, the epidemic would not have been halted if, after the virus (HIV) was discovered, being HIV positive had been criminalized, and if the criminal justice system had been legislatively mandated to be exclusively responsible for control of the disease by apprehending, prosecuting, and punishing all suspected as well as overt carriers.

In the history of AIDS, before its viral origin had been pinned down, there were some Christian televangelists who preached that AIDS was a vengeful God's punishment of male homosexuals for a Biblically condemned sexual lifestyle, which alone was held to be responsible for the transmission of the disease. This is the logic of courtroom adversaries, the prosecution and the defense. Although it has been replaced by biomedical logic in the case of AIDS, adversarial logic is persistently reiterated in the case of sexual abuse and related paraphilic sexual offenses.

The paraphilias have a long history of being under the jurisdiction of the adversarial system of the courts and prisons. The position of the judicial system rests on the postulate that a paraphilia is not a disease, but a preferred form of sexual behavior that is voluntarily chosen and, having been decreed illegal, is subject to prosecution and punishment. Centuries of prosecution and punishment have not, however, had any recognizable effect in preventing the occurrence of paraphilic behavior in each new generation of the population at large, nor its recurrence in an individual paraphile.

CRIMINALIZATION: A CASE OF FAILURE

The adversarial system for the treatment of paraphilia by means of prosecution and punishment must be pronounced an abject failure. It is a failure that sometimes has horrendously tragic consequences. One such consequence occurred recently in Baltimore, as indicated in the following letter to the editor of the Baltimore Sun (Baltimore Sun, Letters to the Editor, "Sexological Ills," 4/12/91, p.8A).

Regarding the sadistic, lust-murder of Rodney James Champy, Jr., it may be correct to say (*The Sun*, Wednesday, March 20th, page 1) that the "murder suspect's probation was botched" by the state Division of Parole and Probation. It is far more to the point, however, to say that the entire system of imprisonment and probation for sex offenders is a botched up system. It is impossible to cure a disease by treating it with imprisonment and probation. Sexual sadism, including lust-murder (its Greek name is erotophonophilia) is a sexological disease. It is classified, along with pedophilia, as one of forty-odd paraphilias. Many patients afflicted with these diseases seek early treatment before their disease reaches its pathological peak. In Maryland, however, it is not feasible for a pedophile to seek treatment voluntarily, for Maryland's mandatory reporting law dictates that the doctor take an undercover police role and, instead of treating a pedophile, report him to the criminal justice system. Rodney's suspected murderer, Stephone Jonathan Williams, lived within walking distance of the Johns Hopkins clinic for the treatment of sexual disorders. He did not refer himself to the clinic which he might have done had there been a guarantee that the clinic would not be obliged to act as informant, and would not be required by law to refer him to the sexual abuse authorities. So his disease went unchecked and unheeded by the criminal justice system until, for Rodney, it was tragically too late. For the future protection of themselves and their children, the citizens of Maryland need a more rational biomedical and scientific approach to the sexological diseases of sex offenders. The annual cost of incarcerating sex offenders is staggering. A wise citizenry would demand that their tax money be more effectively spent on the maintenance of sexological treatment clinics, and the advancement of sexological research.

Rodney was seven years old, and in the second grade. His mother had gone to work and he was at home alone, preparing to go to school. He opened the door for Stephone Williams because he knew him; he was the man who had helped his mother move furniture into their new apartment. Six months earlier, Williams had been released on probation from prison, after having served two of the ten years to which he had been sentenced for sexually abusing his former girlfriend's daughters, aged four and seven.

In the foregoing two cases, there were four chief victims. In the first case, the pediatric patient was a victim of his own encopresis and pathological family life. He was a victim also of the television program in which the untested dogmas of the sexual child-abuse industry were aired without precaution, and without warning that they are hazardous to one's mental health if misapplied in a false accusation. The pediatrician was also the victim of these dogmas, misapplied in a false accusation of child sexual abuse. In the second case, the seven year old boy was the victim of a deadly disease, paraphilic lust-murder. The murderer himself was a victim also of this same disease for which he will be either executed or life-imprisoned.

SEXUAL-ABUSE INDUSTRY

For the reader of this paper, the object lesson of the two cases is that a new nonadversarial paradigm is needed for dealing with the phenomenon of sexual child abuse. Currently, however, the forces of conservative antisexualism, not sexual reform, dominate public and professional policy. The majority of those whose career is in sexual child abuse have a vested interest in maintaining the status quo, for they are hired and paid by some branch of the adversarial system. Like military healthcare practitioners, they owe their first allegiance to the system that employs them, not to the individuals under their care. Their very vocabulary is adversarial, as when a person is characterized not as a patient or client but as a perpetrator, a victim, or a survivor of abuse. Even the legal terms, accused and plaintiff are disregarded.

Healthcare practitioners within the sexual-abuse industry are not themselves immune to becoming victims of the failure of their own system. As much as anyone else, if not more so, they are at risk for false accusations of sexually abusing their own clients or patients — or of emotionally abusing them under the guise of treatment. These risks account for the subtitle of this paper: "The hand bitten by the dog it feeds may be your own." It is in everyone's own self-interest not to endorse the adversarial system, even by default, but to promote a preventive system.

One of the first maneuvers will be to saturate the media, nationwide, with explicit information about sexological health and pathology. It will be aimed at children and teenagers as well as adults. It will tell them what to do if they suffer a sexological disorder, and where to find help. It will be honest about the law of mandatory reporting so that the citizenry may bring pressure to bear on legislators to restore the right of confidentiality in the doctor-patient relationship for those who seek treatment early. In this way, it will become possible for either the actual practice or the false accusation of sexual child abuse to be aborted before it occurs.

REFERENCES

Money, J., and Lamacz, M. Genital examination and exposure experienced as nosocomial sexual abuse in childhood. *Journal of Nervous and Mental Disease*, 175(12):713-721, 1987.

Money, J., and Lamacz, M. Nosocomial stress and abuse exemplified in a case of male hermaphroditism from infancy through adulthood: Coping strategies and prevention. *International Journal of Family Psychiatry*, 7:71-105, 1986.

Money, J., and Kendall, J. Letters to the Editor. Sexological ills. *Baltimore Sun*, 4/12/91, p.8A.

AUTHOR'S NOTE

John Money, PhD, is Professor Emeritus of Medical Psychology and Pediatrics at The Johns Hopkins School of Medicine, Baltimore.

Address for correspondence: John Money, PhD, The Johns Hopkins School of Medicine, 1235 E. Monument Street, Suite LL20, Baltimore, MD 21202.